POLITICIANS, BUREAUCRATS, AND THE CONSULTANT

POLITICIANS, BUREAUCRATS, AND THE CONSULTANT

A Critique of Urban
Problem Solving

GARRY D. BREWER

Basic Books, Inc., Publishers

NEW YORK

Library of Congress Catalog Card Number: 73-80729
SBN 465-05948-1
Manufactured in the United States of America
Designed by Vincent Torre
73 74 75 76   10 9 8 7 6 5 4 3 2 1

To

HAROLD D. LASSWELL

Teacher, Colleague, Friend

with

Respect and Affection

for

Many Hard Lessons Well Taught

CONTENTS

PART I

THE APPRAISAL FUNCTION

Preface   xi

Introduction   3

1. An Overview of the Task   11

2. Views of the World   15

    The Reflective Mode   16
    The Explanatory Mode   17
    The Manipulative Mode   18
    Emphasis and Tension   20

3. Theoretical Appraisal   23

    "The Question is . . ."   23
    Concepts: Elements, Structure, Behavior   24
    Selectivity   25
    Theories Represented by Computer Programs   28
    Expository Procedures   30

4. Technical Appraisal   34

    Translating Theory: Formalization   34
    Further Specification   38
    Assumptions   40
    Running the Model—Gross Fits   42
    Tuning the Model—Sensitivity Testing   44
    Criteria   47

5. Ethical Appraisal   48

    The Value of Context—The Context of Values   48
    Convergence: Manipulation, Projection   49
    Problems Impeding Ethical Integration   51
    Responsibilities of Ethical Appraisal   52
    Integrating a Perspective   53

6. Pragmatic Appraisal   54

    Data Manipulation Applications   55
    Measurement Applications   55
    Theoretical Applications   56
    Educational Applications   57
    Policy-Making Applications   58
    Synopsis   62

CONTENTS

PART II

COMPLEXITY, SIMULATION, AND THE
SOCIAL PROCESS

Introduction   67

7. On Size and Organized Complexity: Some Theoretical Considerations   70

    Human Limitations 70
    Organized Complexity 71
    Decomposability 73
    Images, Totems, and Utopias 76
    Orientation, Purpose, and Simplicity 77
    Dimensions 78
    Summary 82

8. On Size and Organized Complexity: Some Operational Considerations   83

    Introduction 83
    Fragmented Problem-Solving 83
    Misperception of the Difficulty of the Task 86
    "What's the Question?"—"What's an Answer?" 89
    The Context of Research Is as Important as the Research Itself 90

9. Disentangling the Problem-Solving Process   92

    Theoretical Considerations 93
    Operational Considerations 94
    Reprise 96

PART III

THE CONTEXT

Introduction   99

10. The Community Renewal Program   101

    Origins and Expectations 101
    San Francisco's CRP 104
    Pittsburgh's CRP 108
    To the Moon? 113

11. San Francisco   114

    Decision to Model 115
    Scope and Purpose 118
    Order of Processing 120
    Theoretical Appraisal 133
    Technical Appraisal 143
    Ethical Appraisal 153
    Pragmatic Appraisal 162
    Summary 168

12. Pittsburgh   169

    Decision to Model 169
    Scope and Purpose 174
    The Models 179

Selling   205
University Participation: Research and Responsibility   208
Misperceiving the Complexity of Urban Decision   212
Summary   215

13.   The Problem-Solving Process   216

   Participants   216
   Procedures   224
   Products   228
   Addenda   229

PART IV

MEETING THE CHALLENGE

14.   Expanding the Focus of Attention: Some Recommendations   233

   The Premise Is Experimental   233
   Models   235
   Documentation   237
   Data   238
   Procedures   240

APPENDICES AND NOTES

Appendix A: Questionnaire   245
Appendix B: Code Book   249
Appendix C: Multidimensional Scaling: Some Methodological
      Comments   253
Notes   257
Index   285

PREFACE

Projects are always more difficult than the mind's eye perceives. This book conforms to the rule. Many projects become increasingly distasteful as one gets to know them. Such, however, was not true in this instance. The issues are important; the two case studies provide a fascinating account of the unintended consequences of piecemeal problem-solving; and the cast of characters is as diverse and rich in detail as one could ever hope to encounter. Hopefully, the reader will share my enthusiasm and concerns.

My debts are legion: intellectual, fiscal, professional, and personal. It is impossible to cite all my benefactors; however, I would be remiss not to mention a few.

The intellectual stimulation of Yale University must be noted. To Robert A. Dahl, Harold D. Lasswell, and Martin Shubik, for different reasons, I can only offer my sincerest thanks and the acknowledgment that without their considerable assistance, this book would not have happened.

The generous fiscal support of the Danforth Foundation's Kent Fellowship program is gratefully noted. Danforth is a true anachronism in these anxious times; it is an established institution that sincerely operates on the principle of maximum mutual trust. The National Science Foundation's sponsorship under Contract GS–2492 provided the bulk of the research money for this project. While the NSF contributed funds, all responsibility is of course entirely my own. Supplementary computer funds were provided by Joel Fleishman, formerly Yale's associate provost for urban studies and programs.

Professional acknowledgments are due all those who responded to my many questions, who took the time and trouble to relive many specific details, and who offered words of encouragement all along the way. Particular appreciation is due Maurice Groat, a civil servant of rare perception and judgment, and J. P. Crecine, a serious scholar and true friend.

Personal acknowledgments are due the many diligent and skillful editors, typists, transcribers, and keypunchers enlisted during the project. Karen Eisenstadt, Sheila Meyers, and Marjorie Roach must be thanked individually for their many important contributions: Karen for reminding me that the English language, simple logic, and matters of fact count; Sheila and Marjorie for typing.

PREFACE

While I appreciate and have benefited greatly from the unique stimulation afforded by the environment of the Rand Corporation, the views expressed in this book are mine alone and do not reflect those held by the Corporation or any of its private or governmental research sponsors.

Finally, my wife, Saundra, has endured the often tedious research process in fine spirit and in some mysterious way has always been nearby, helping, understanding, and caring. As for my children: Gay did without her daddy for lonely months while he was on the road, in the computer center, and locked away writing; and Gregory, who was not around when the project began, "participated" at its conclusion.

Garry D. Brewer

Santa Monica, California
1973

POLITICIANS, BUREAUCRATS, AND THE CONSULTANT

Introduction

The most promising answer to the challenge of complexity is not to ignore the challenge but to devise ways of meeting it.

Harold D. Lasswell[1]

Public policy-makers deal with difficult problems in our complex society every day. Unfortunately, and seemingly related to the number of facts that compete for attention, these problems are becoming increasingly unmanageable. Solutions, even when they can be formulated, regularly create unimagined new problems. Indeed, complexity challenges the very essence of effective and legitimate control in society today.

This book explores the decision-making processes in two complex urban settings and details attempts to use large-scale computer simulation models for planning and development. It is both a case study and a theoretical work on these decision systems, featuring the interplay of politics, economics, and sophisticated problem-solving.

In Principle. One of the most promising techniques for meeting the challenge of complexity is the computer simulation. At the core of the technique is the idea of setting up "models which show the workings of very complex relationships—those which are too complex to be reduced to simple conclusions by means of mathematical or statistical analysis or ordinary reasoning."[2] Piecemeal approaches to the social decision processes are intrinsically undesirable because they are inappropriate to the complexity we find there.[3] Policy-makers must integrate their intuitive hunches with the partial theories, models, and descriptive insights of specialists in such a way that the setting and theories about the setting are made understandable to practitioner and specialist alike.[4] Computer simulation models have that integrative capacity, or, as Kalman Cohen and Richard Cyert succinctly note, "the basic advantage of computer models is that they provide a language within which dynamic models can be constructed."[5] What this means in one sense is that an analytic specialist may add, delete, reformulate, and interchange various bits of information from sources of varying quality with relative ease. The method becomes a means to synthesize information from disparate

3

perspectives and sources.[6] An analogous point has been made by John Platt, in considering sets of "multiple working hypotheses" where "each hypothesis suggests its own criteria, its own means of proof, its own means of developing the truth, and if a group of hypotheses encompass the subject on all sides, the total outcome of means and of methods is full and rich."[7] In principle, a computer simulation and our understanding of a represented context can be enhanced by systematically partitioning the context into subproblems, separate relationships, and individual elements; by measuring important individual elements; by reconfiguring these into a complete set of functional relationships; by experimenting with the whole model that results to appraise and adjust it; and finally, by using the model for projective or other purposes. In practice, only much less has been possible.

In Practice. The form a model takes and how one evaluates what it produces depend delicately upon the purposes of its initiators, builders, and users. This complicated problem demands detailed attention and is illuminated in the two cases. Generally, models may be strong in some aspects, weak in others, and irrelevant in still others. Indeed, it is this selectiveness that focuses attention on important or interesting aspects of the problem context. To the extent that these purposes are ill-defined, misunderstood, unstated, or ignored, the overall utility of a model rapidly decreases.

Computers can manipulate impressive quantities of information. Since they can, they permit the building of large and detailed models that supposedly depict a complex context realistically. Such models are often overly complicated.[8] A useful distinction between complexity and complication has been suggested:

Complexity refers to substantive logico-mathematical interrelations and difficulties; *complication* can arise in almost any arrangement of facts, concepts, or thoughts. Complication is an undesirable characteristic of any construct; complexity may be an inherent feature. Complication often expresses lack of effort to give the construct its appropriate form.[9]

In general, no one knows the proper scale for a model. How small and simple must a model be to be manageable and useful? How large and complex must it be to be sufficiently realistic? One suggestion is that each model must be appraised on its own merits with respect to its own purposes and performance. This appraisal is frequently overlooked because practical constraints of time, attention, and money tend to dominate model building.[10]

It is true that models are quite flexible; however, recall that any model is only a mathematical-theoretical interpretation of social-theoretical conceptions. John Kemeny and Laurie Snell speak clearly on this point:

It is important to contrast the pure mathematical theory with its interpreted version that serves as a model. . . . [Mathematical] equations are neither true nor false, since they have no factual content. Mathematics is best viewed as the study of abstract relations in the broadest sense of the word. From this point of view it is not surprising that mathematics is *applicable to any well-defined field.*[11] (emphasis added)

Herbert Simon adds emphasis to this point in remarking, "Mathematical social science is first and foremost social science. If it is bad social science (i.e. empirically false), the fact that it is good mathematics (i.e. logically consistent) should provide little comfort."[12]

It is equally true that "a theory is defined by a set of assumptions concerning the relationships among a set of elements or variables," and a theory is "no better than its assumptions."[13] Unfortunately, these assumptions, once cast in mathematics and a computer code and embedded within a model, are seldom explicated. A model represents a theory. Acceptance of a computer program as "good" social theory depends upon one's willingness to accept the considerable assumptions of a responsible theorist. If these are unreasonable or nonempirical, for instance, the relevance of the model is decreased.[14] The relationship between reasoned empiricism and formalization is noted by James Beshers:

Prior to any mathematical work on a particular problem [I] spend a great deal of time, usually years, attempting to summarize and restate those theories and empirical generalizations that seem to have enough merit to be worth formalizing. It is so difficult to obtain any kind of mathematical representation that it hardly seems worth the effort for a bad theory.[15]

A corollary issue is the distortion introduced into a model by translating verbal, descriptive theory into mathematical symbols and computer languages. Translation necessarily involves information loss and distortion. These losses are compounded when theorist, mathematician, and programmer are not the same person.

These concerns are not trivial. Formal computer models are extremely difficult to build correctly. This intrinsic problem is exacerbated by the fact that the method is often the last resort taken after more conventional analytic techniques have been unsuccessfully tried. The enormous difficulty of specifying a model is not to be lightly dismissed despite the so-called system engineer who can "model anything, any time, any place, for anyone." Without adequate understanding of the empirical context, without full realization of the embedded assumptions, and without appreciation of exclusions and omissions, a potential policy-making user must accept a model as an act of faith.[16] This is wholly unsatisfactory when the user's purposes are serious and operational.

INTRODUCTION

Scenario: "The Appraisal Issue."[17] If we accept the *point of view* that ours is becoming a society increasingly based and dependent on knowledge,[18] if we accept the *fact* that increasing human and fiscal resources are being devoted to knowledge for its own sake,[19] and if we accept the *tendency* toward social diversification by technology-based institutions,[20] then several possible scenarios are worth considering. Let us postulate one:

- An increasing concern with complexity of society, taken with an increased pressure for problem solution, will increase the need for expert decision-making and the employment of specialized advisers.
- Decision-makers, stimulated by popular pressure, will increasingly resort to the most advanced scientific and management skills and techniques to attain problem solutions.
- Application of such techniques will be made in the name and rhetoric of science but will not be appraised by the normal standards of science.
- This "appraisal gap" will increase if left unattended and will be self-perpetuating. It will increase as the societal demands increase the scope and magnitude of problems thought to be amenable to expert solution. Self-perpetuation is assured as the form of problem solution becomes more "scientific" and more esoteric and therefore less open to diverse comment on the content of the solution.

Insufficient appraisal procedures threaten much necessary professional-technical development and the hope for eventual implementation of computer simulation techniques on a larger scale. In the near term, scarce resources will be allocated broadly and indiscriminately by well-intentioned but technically unsophisticated public officials. What will result is a dilution of some "critical mass" of research resources. In the longer run, it seems that major funding sources will contract or cease altogether their support of modeling activities. The scenario becomes even more plausible in the absence of any significant political payoff from the research. *Quid pro quo* is a fundamental fact of life ignored only at great peril.

What This Book Is All About. I begin by placing appraisal in some perspective: By what broad categories of criteria may computer models be judged? A model's intended use has a bearing on the criteria that one might employ for appraisal: What are some possible applications, and specifically what criteria are appropriate for policy-making models?

Granting that social settings and problems are complex, what is the nature of that complexity and what does it imply for the understanding and application of sophisticated analytic techniques? I examine a body of theoretical literature on social complexity and relate this to what appear to be the operational realities in two urban decision systems.

To understand these general questions, I present two specific contexts. The cities of San Francisco, California, and Pittsburgh, Pennsylvania, each participated in an ambitious, federally initiated problem-solving enterprise known as the Community Renewal Program. Each city, for various reasons, enlisted the assistance of outside experts to help with its CRP. I ask questions of the following kind: Who are the participants? What were the scope and magnitude of their various purposes, perspectives, expectations, and assessments of what resulted? What is there specifically to be learned from each example? What did the computer models set out to accomplish, and what did they in fact accomplish? What more general lessons are suggested by these cases for subsequent problem-solving and various modes of appraisal?

In my own way I have attempted to devise some new ways to meet the challenge of complexity.

PART I

THE APPRAISAL
FUNCTION

1

An Overview of the Task

Man's very soul is due to the machines; it is a machine-made thing: . . . This fact precludes us from proposing the complete annihilation of machinery, but surely it indicates that we should destroy as many of them as we can possibly dispense with, lest they should tyrannize over us even more completely.

Samuel Butler
Erewhon, 1872

Barring a second coming of the Luddites, by what means, by what institutional innovations might we exercise more positive, creative control?

As at least one scholar reminds us, the discovery of new modes of organization and procedure is of utmost importance for the current state and continuing good health of popular government.[1] One way in which this task may be accomplished is in developing comprehensive modes of appraisal which

can provide essential information about the value outcomes, pre-outcomes, and post-outcomes of any institutional practice. In this way a stream of knowledge may become available on the basis of which a higher level of disciplined rationality becomes possible for all who have access to this information.[2]

To date, individual initiative has not been adequate, nor has it been institutionalized to the point where appraisal is carried out "with comprehensiveness, competence, reliability, independence, promptitude, and economy."[3] In fact, this general point was bluntly put by a distinguished panel of the National Academy of Sciences:

Even when the proponents of a technology (whether in the government or in the private sector) seek financial support from public revenues, their own assessments still provide the basic inputs into the political system.[4]

A comprehensive general methodology of appraisal must be able to account for a great diversity of concern and richness of perspective. Specifically, for the technology known as computer simulation, at least four separate categories of appraisal are noteworthy: the appraisal of

11

theoretical adequacy, technical competence, ethical content, and pragmatic utility.

It's All in How You Look at It. To be comprehensive, an appraisal procedure must systematically consider how the simulation model handles substantive matters such as historical trends, scientific specifications, public policy impact, goal clarifications, and contingency projections for any given space-time context. Furthermore, the procedure must handle personal differences such as those that produce the "gap" between scientific-scholarly endeavors and work required by policy-makers.[5] In general, model-building analysts do not march to the sound of the policy-maker's drum. What results must be considered carefully.

Conceiving of different perspectives prompts one to consider the different degrees of effort, ranges of plausible outcomes, and standards of assessment those perspectives imply. Scientists, for example, have by and large been dedicated to rigorous measurement and theory building. This dedication often produces results that are not terribly relevant for other orientations. As Max Millikan has pointed out:

> The scientist is apt to have a strong conviction that applied research cannot be "fundamental," that there is something inherently contradictory in the advance of knowledge and the service of practical ends. . . . The researcher may face a growing conviction either that the operator has asked the wrong questions, that the questions are too vaguely or too narrowly formulated, or that as formulated they are incapable of being clearly answered.[6]

Communication failures of considerable magnitude are not exclusively age-dependent. Comprehensive procedures of appraisal must discover their nature and extent.

Theory: The Ins and Outs. A model, composed of variables and parameters in specific configurations, is a form of theory. Which variables and parameters are included represents a fundamental theoretical choice. How those entities are configured is a concrete theoretical statement. The implications of these several choices must be assessed individually. Variables for policy purposes are often selected by different criteria than those held in "purer" theoretical esteem.[7] A slightly higher order concern is the extent to which a given theoretical configuration produces convincing outputs. Mere reproduction of historical time series by a model may not be a sufficient indicator of adequate explanatory performance. In warning against the danger of premature theoretical "closure," Robert Bush and Frederick Mosteller conclude, "Almost any sensible model with two or three free parameters . . . can closely fit the curve, and so other criteria must be invoked when one is comparing several models." As one possible solution, they suggest the development of multiple models purporting to explain the same context.[8] And yet a higher order concern, related to the issue of specification, holds that a theoretical model is adequate only with respect to a specific space-time context. That is to say, it is the appraiser's burden to determine "the appropriateness of the operational indices" and to insure that they remain "chronologically pertinent to the ordering of political [and other] events as the future unfolds."[9]

Technically, How Good Is a Model? The issue of assessing computer simulations is fraught with uncertainty. While any given method or technique is "in principle capable of being comprehended and checked by anyone who acquires the requisite skill,"[10] such activities are sporadic indeed. Whether one adopts the suspicious point of view that such checks are not routinely and reliably made because of a "conspiratorial silence of experts,"[11] or is more charitably disposed, the fact remains that no more-or-less acceptable standards exist by which the technical merits of a computer simulation may be appraised.

How "Good" Is a Model? The blending of formal models with social ethics has been recognized in the work of the so-called ethical contextualists.[12] Gibson Winter, who counts himself in this group, recognizes this overlap to be particularly pronounced in the projective orientation:

The ethical issue becomes explicit fully where the sciences of man project their understanding of the past into the future as a definition of human fulfillment; these projections disclose the evaluative or ideological aspects of scientific models. The projections can be evaluated only from an ethical perspective. Science and ethics are different perspectives of the everyday world; they clarify different aspects of that world; however, they intersect as they attempt to define the course of human fulfillment.[13]

Computer models have great integrative or contextual capacity. It is this characteristic that enables one to select entities, to order them separately, and to consider them as a contextual whole. However, contextualism entails a clear-cut ethical burden. It "implies not only that values can be appraised only in a concrete setting, but also that *there is always an appraisal to be made.*"[14] That the burden exists is not in question; how a computer simulation can be used to reduce that burden is at issue. Several interesting points have been raised in this regard. The first is our inability to quantify everything of importance, particularly preferences. The second is that preferences in any situation are numerous, conflicting, and often a priori unknown. The third is that much factual knowledge is inarticulate. And finally, as Robert Dahl and C. E. Lindblom contend, mathematics and machine calculations cannot substitute for policy-makers.

Someone must control those who run the calculations and machines. Someone must control these controllers, etc. At every point there would be opportunities for attempting to feed into the calculator one's own preferences. Doubtless, pressure groups would organize for just such a purpose.[15]

These criticisms are apt. A pertinent question is not so much who should analyze what value assumptions are operating in a context:

social ethicists are specialists most admirably prepared for the task. How they gain access, and, once given access, how they might comprehend the content of the assumptions, is at issue.[16]

Pragmatically, How Good Is a Model? A model may be pragmatically appraised with respect to several possible uses. Whether a model is intended to be used as a policy-making, theoretical, data-manipulating, educational, or measurement device has fundamental implications for the criteria of assessment. To the extent that there is agreement on application,[17] and to the extent that the model satisfies criteria associated with a particular application, it may be considered "good." The question, "Is a model any good?" becomes far more meaningful when reframed to read, "Is a model feasible in the context of a specific application?"

Why Is Appraisal Important? If we accept the assertion that "whoever controls information (enlightenment) is likely to control public order,"[18] the urgency of devising procedures to ensure the proper use of information and the continuous and widespread flow of knowledge about specific institutional practices is clear.

2

Views of the World

He apprehends a world of figures here
But not the form of what he should attend.
Shakespeare
King Henry IV, Part I
act 1, scene 3[1]

Depending upon many things, not the least of which is their intellectual orientation toward it, people see the world quite differently. This observation is not especially startling; however, what is important is that each orientation constitutes a distinct observational perspective having distinct selection criteria, evidenced in the issues considered and ignored; a distinct set of prescriptions, characterized by the range of applications deemed appropriate; and a distinct strategy of research procedure.[2] Calling attention to these distinctions is not to ignore the necessary interrelatedness of the orientations. Each makes assumptions about the others, subsequently stimulating further examination and development. For example, a policy orientation that emphasizes the specification of alternative courses of action, implies some systematic knowledge about goals, past trends, interactions conditioning the flow of events, and projected paths for the considered variables. Likewise, adopting a projective or futurist orientation may be a particularly sterile strategy when the underlying conditioning factors are not well understood or are moving away from patterns determined by historical analysis.

The partial analyses routinely carried out by specialists often fail to account for the interrelatedness of orientations. To develop a comprehensive understanding of a social context, one needs to *select* according to each orientation and to *utilize* according to each orientation. In short, *all* orientations must be accounted for in the construction and operation of various models.[3]

We shall consider three stereotypical modes of viewing the world: reflective, explanatory, and manipulative. These characterizations are not hard and fast, nor are they mutually exclusive. They do illustrate general differences between those who portray and report events, those

15

who strive to understand what "causes" events, and those who daily grapple with and fundamentally create events.

The Reflective Mode

One must devote attention to describing the history and the emerging trends of any context of interest. Confounding this imperative is the general issue of "unique historical events," summarized by Stuart Bruchey as the "quality of never-quite-the-sameness":

To every event there belongs temporal singularity, a contextual particularity, and it is because of this that all historical being possesses a quality of never-quite-the-sameness. But it is equally true that the essence of a thing is not altogether its separateness. There is essential sharedness as well as essential singularity, and if this were not so, all experience would be a succession of differentiated particulars, without meaning because nothing would be recognizable.[4]

Accommodating historical and conditioning orientations as Bruchey proposes seems eminently sensible. While the empirical reality is stressed, the possibility for developing theory is left open. It is not necessary to assume that an observed sequence of events from one context must inevitably follow in a new or different context; but, as we are reminded, "evolutionary sequences often follow a regular order: either constellations of relevant factors occur more than once or variable constellations occasionally produce equivalent results."[5] Reflecting on evolutionary sequences may allow a researcher to "sum up past routines" sufficiently well that policy-makers may be able to "modify their future conduct in order to take advantage of added insight."[6] Success in this endeavor depends to a large extent upon the researcher's ability to "sum up" and then to make the necessary translations from the passive-reflective to the active-manipulative frame of reference.

Another characteristic of the reflective mode is its possibility for developing selected variables in rich detail. While writers of trends may be "limited to three dimensions: time, space, and rate," there is sufficient latitude to explicate a context, i.e. "to study the unfolding of events over time, their distribution over space, and their relative rate over both time and space."[7] As rich as much history is, there is still the problem of selectivity: information is lost in the process of constructing a single sequence of events.

The historian perceives only sequences; it is his mind rather than his eye that determines how the facts are related to each other. In a word, the criteria by which he selects some facts and rejects others as irrelevant are not inherent in the data; they are supplied by the historian.[8]

The reflective mode, nonetheless, is a useful manner in which to characterize specific contextual details; it forces one to consider the context from an explicit temporal point of view. The burden of considering other, equally plausible, interpretations of the context must be stressed. The clear implications for building theoretical models are equally burdensome. If multiple descriptions of trends are commonplace, so too are multiple theoretical explanations.[9] The practical connection between the reflective and the explanatory modes is made by the extent to which one uses case-study descriptions and historical data in constructing a process model. The problem of selectivity remains.

The Explanatory Mode

The conditioning or scientific orientation emphasizes theory construction and rigorous measurement: obtaining an explanation of contextual performance by understanding contextual components. A generally misunderstood difficulty in this orientation is that the whole context is more than the additive sum of its parts; it is fundamentally different.[10] Partial analysis, which occurs in simplifying a context, may significantly decrease understanding of the interconnections and subtle interrelationships among components. Analysis tends to destroy the wholeness of the context by limiting the researcher's focus of attention and concept of relevance. In principle, with "good" analysis, one's mind continually shifts from consideration of the individual elements to the context and back again. In practice, a truly comprehensive analysis is a rare and remarkable achievement.

Equally rare is the instance of multiple explanatory models being developed for a given context. Given the principle of selectivity, the requirement for contextual explication through appropriate space-time configurations, and the recommendation for alternative models,[11] the implications for theory building and measurement are several. Assuming that one is able to construct a logically consistent model of a contextual process, the following points must be considered. Other models exist, models that are also internally consistent, congruent with the sensory data, useful for various applications, elegant, and fundamentally incompatible with the given formulation. To the extent that *one* model is claimed to reproduce processes of interest within the context and to the extent that other equally plausible configurations are not explored, the utility of explanatory research activities for policy analysis is reduced.

To the extent that a model emphasizes state descriptions at a single point in time, its use as a projective aid is diminished. Social prediction, the characterization of "a possible sequence of events running from a selected cross-section of the past to a cross-section of the future," is not easily realized in practice.[12] The possibility of eventually attaining this capacity is not enhanced by failing to consider more-than-static configurations.

To the extent, for instance, that a model excludes specific empirical detail from a given problem context in the interests of generalization, its specific policy uses may decrease.

To the extent that noneconomic variables are ignored in the interests of measurement precision, the relevance of a model for the goal and alternative orientations may decrease.

A fair characterization of many explanatory models is that they are so predictively weak that they are of little interest to policy-makers or "manipulators." To the extent that a model is not predictive, it may lose appropriateness for use as a manipulative device.[13] The tension generated by misunderstanding the distinction between the capacity of weakly predictive explanatory models and the requirements of manipulation causes great rancor in many so-called applied social science research projects.[14]

The Manipulative Mode

No one view of the world is necessarily better or more important than the others,[15] but to understand the perspectives of those who are directly responsible for the creation and implementation of public policy calls for particularly sensitive care.

To What Ends? The discussion of contextual goals, or the "ought" of society, has long held the attention of scholars.[16] Its importance as an integral component of research has been stressed by Dahl and Lindblom, for example: "If we were concerned only with description and analysis [reflection and explanation] we should have no need to discuss values. But to appraise, one needs criteria."[17]

The goal orientation forces attention on the identification of appropriate criteria, which, when expressed as general propositions, may be compared with information about the historical and projected states of the context. Criteria are artifacts subject to adjustment and manipulation. Representative samples of general criteria commonly used would include the means to maximize freedom, rationality, security, and progress;[18] limitations on conflict and rates of social change; incentives for increased stability of economic and social systems, pluralism, consensus;[19] and general methods for increasing the dignity of man expressed in terms of the "shaping and sharing of values on a wide rather than a narrow basis."[20]

That so many generalized, abstract criteria are easily noted indicates that these are a function of one's specific purposes and orientations. It is possible to define problems so that attainment of a single goal is sufficient for solution. Unfortunately, the social context produces few instances fitting this class of well-defined problems;[21] positing and attaining a single goal or desired end state is not tantamount to problem solution. Dahl has forcefully reminded us of the inherent dangers of such a procedure.[22]

Not only are problems ill-defined,[23] but there are multiple goals,[24] and these goals are constantly changing.[25] Practically, this means that analytical attention must shift from the abstract to the particular, from one orientation to another.[26] Yehezkel Dror has summarized much of this in the following terms:

Science can point out various implications of trying to achieve specific goals, can examine the conditions under which they can be achieved, and can deal with the relationships between different goals, which can, for example, exclude, compete with, or support one another. But the values and goals themselves are outside the domain of science, and are in principle axioms that are given for the process of pure-rationality policymaking.[27]

By What Means? Formal analysis often overlooks Dror's important ideas; an indication is when operations researchers attempt to maximize or minimize a social-objective function.[28] Although policy-making stresses rational calculation and action, the problems of multiple and changing goals are seldom directly confronted by specialized analysis. Critical path analysis, as only one example, is appropriate only if a desired end state is known and if alternative paths can be rationally excluded. The question of valuation becomes as important as the problem of analysis when the path actually followed is a tentative, shifting, ad hoc resultant of many conflicting and inconsistent norms.[29] Although developing and articulating these alternatives have been the intellectual domain of the political scientist, and discussing how governments ought to select among alternatives has been the philosopher's task, navigating along the path is the responsibility of the politician, who

has to balance the myriad forces as he sees best, and the citizens judge him only to a limited extent by his accordance with their preconceived ideas. Rather, a great political leader is judged like a great composer; one looks to see what he has created.[30]

To the extent that these orientations and related concerns are not adequately understood and integrated into applied research, certain tensions are bound to develop between the various participants.

Emphasis and Tension

Considering projected states of a given context is not necessarily manipulative. Indeed a passive forecast is more properly termed reflective. However, current emphasis on planning as a means to change unwanted but anticipated futures imputes a manipulative motive to projective analysis.[31]

Tension deriving from the separate emphases of different orientations is evidenced in an ongoing debate between projective "fundamentalists" and "chartists," terms commonly used to distinguish distinct styles of securities analysts. The example is more general; for example, according to Wassily Leontieff, policy relevant predictions require a fundamental understanding of the factors explaining the context, the fundamentalist's perspective:

There are predictions by models and predictions by trends. . . . These are not symmetrical things. . . . To discuss policies not in a deterministic way, but as a problem of choice, I think you must work with models. To build policies into trends is difficult.[32]

Citing a practical constraint, Martin Shubik makes a case for the chartists:

You cannot idly dismiss the chartists, because in one sense a key to forecasting is the amount of time one has available in the decision process to make a statement about the future. A chartist can come up with some sort of fairy tale in ten or fifteen minutes. If you do not have more time, perhaps that is the best you can get.[33]

A manipulator may not have time to wait for a researcher to specify and tinker with his model. To the extent that explanatory efforts yield inflexible characterizations of a changing context, one must expect them to be of diminishing utility for manipulation. To reduce this time discrepancy, Shubik suggests

an incremental systematic process that involves, among other things, linking large data-processing procedures with models or conceptual frameworks. This would give an opportunity to link the fundamentalist with the chartist approaches.[34]

Several divergences in the interests of participants and their respective modes of activity may be summarized in terms of variations in the focus of attention: specifically, according to differences in one's intellectual attitude, time perspective, and perception of scale. Caricatured in Exhibit 2-1 are several of these general differences.[35]

Instances of divergent attitude, perspective, or scale must alert one to anticipate tension and interparticipant conflict in the model-building and model-using activities. As these tensions increase, questions of relevance, utility, and purpose may become central.[36] If the orientations of

EXHIBIT 2-1

Differences of Orientation—A Caricature

		MODES OF VIEWING THE WORLD		
		MANIPULATIVE	REFLECTIVE	EXPLANATORY
Intellectual Attitude				
	General	Contextual, rich	Contextual, selected	Partial, specific
	Logic	Intuitive, causal	Deductive, causal	Inductive, causal, and deductive
	Style	Chartist	Mixed: chartist/ fundamentalist	Fundamentalist model-building
Time Perspective				
	General	Future oriented	Past oriented	Past and present oriented
	Adjustment	Discrete: margin incremental	Continuous: long-run, expanded	Discrete: single point in time
	System state	Dynamic (change of system through time)	Dynamic	Static (state description at cross-section)
Scale of Units				
	Context	Specific context, no generalization	Specific context, weak generalization	General context, weak specification
	Unit of analysis	Multiple, small, fine detail	Mixed, variable detail	Mixed, large, gross detail
	Pathways	Multiple paths, alternative possibilities.	Single path, few possibilities	Single path, few possibilities; or fixed in space-time

(Left vertical label: FOCUS OF ATTENTION)

goal, trend, condition, projection, and alternative are not appropriately balanced in the execution of an applied social science research project, or in the construction of attendant analytical models, one must be prepared for weaknesses in the result.

A worthy objective is to strenghten the common focus of attention of the various participants by emphasizing the development of analytical tools that policy-makers can actually use.[37] Analytic tools—specifically, computer simulation models—must be systematically assessed for the "gap" between scholarly research and policy-making.

It has been asserted that such models represent theories and that the application of these models is the application of theory. As with any theory, each reflects the assumptions and biases of its maker. What questions might be asked in appraising the theoretical content of a specific computer simulation? How might one examine the several assumptions and biases that have been built into a model? These must exist, given the complexity of the represented reality. To identify and appraise their impact is another matter. Willis Harman suggests trying to assume several points of view:

By the very act of viewing the universe through a framework of events, or social descriptors, or belief-and-value systems, bias has been introduced and unknown omissions may have been structured in. The only way to check this is to use a completely different kind of viewing frame and compare results.[38]

3

Theoretical Appraisal

"The Question Is . . . "

The problem at hand is not so much to examine urban renewal or housing theory, whatever those might be. The present question is rather more limited. How can one examine the elements, expressed as variables and parameters; the structure, expressed as relationships among the relevant elements; and the resultant behavioral patterns, expressed as time series data for the variables, that are formally stated in a computer program and that stand for various theories, assumptions, and guesses about a given context? And how, once the mathematical-computer raiments have been stripped off, may we proceed to examine the criteria applied to descriptive formulations: meaning and plausibility, for example?[2]

First, it will be necessary to define a few persistently abused terms with sufficient clarity to make continual redefinition unnecessary. Second, the perpetual issue of selectivity will be discussed by way of elaborating what different orientations imply for theory building. Third, the idea of program-as-theory will be explored. Fourth, and finally, a general procedural strategy will be outlined for use in examining the subject cases.

Throughout this and what follows we keep explicitly in the center of our attention Fred Massarik's observation that the "magic of mathematics," taken in conjunction with the computer, "seem[s] to lend significance even to the trivial and credibility to the doubtful."[3] Or, to paraphrase Simon, *if it's bad social science, the mathematics don't matter.*

Concepts: Elements, Structure, Behavior

A precise definition of a system[4] is provided by Richard Bellman and Robert Kalaba:

Purely analytically, we conceive of a system as a state vector X_t, and a rule for determining its value at any time t.[5]

The state vector $[X_t]$ is in fact a nonempty set of input variables $x_{i,t}$ and parameters α_m. Variables are elements that have a definite, changeable value at any point in time; parameters are elements considered to be constant for the given analytical case but variable in other cases. The rule for determining subsequent values of the initial state vector $[X_t]$ is in fact a nonempty set of operators $[G]$, such that

$$X_{t+1} = G(X_t) \tag{3.1}$$

where,

$$[X_t] = \begin{bmatrix} x_{i,t} \\ x_{2,t} \\ \vdots \\ x_{n,t} \\ \alpha_1 \\ \alpha_2 \\ \vdots \\ \alpha_m \end{bmatrix} \tag{3.2}$$

The operators of functions $[G]$ transform the state vector $[X_{t+1}] \rightarrow [X_{t+2}]$ and so forth for the analytical period. Outputs at one point in time become the inputs for the next. The system must, of course, operate in accord with the requirements of dimensionality or dimensional homogeneity.

The structure of the system is the set of variables $[X_t]$ and the set of processes $[G]$. They represent a temporary statement, on the part of the investigator, about the phenomena of importance in the real world systems which the abstract system purports to describe. To apply the abstract system or model to one of these real world systems, measures of the $x_{i,t}$ are obtained from the real world system and inserted into the model. The model then transforms the $x_{i,t}$ to produce successive state descriptions. The time paths of the variables $x_{i,t}$ describe the *behavior* of the system over time.

In studying social systems we observe and measure only the state description of a system at a point in time or its behavior through time. The processes assumed to underlie and produce this behavior are not directly observed, but are inferred from our observations. The goal of description and measurement is to develop as accurate a picture as possible of the behavior of the system. Since no two complex systems behave in exactly the same way and no complex system is entirely stagnant in its behavior, the description of a system at a point in time will differ from the description of the same or any other system at any other point in time. The goal of theory building is to arrive at a set of processes that are simplified, in the sense that they represent some processes we infer to underlie the behavior of systems; general, in the sense that they purport to represent more than one system; and realistic, in the sense that they explain or reproduce some of the interesting behavior of the system. In short, theory building focuses on the clarification of the set of operators or processes $[G]$, and description focuses on the clarification of the behavior of the system, $[X_t]$, through time.

A computer program represents the sets of variables and processes in relationship to one another by yet another set of symbols and operators. In a very real sense a computer program is a theory. More to the point, it is an icon or totem[6] representing one's image of an underlying structure thought to be responsible for the empirical, behavioral chaos. The distinction between the behavioral context, the theoretical simplification of that context, and finally the representation of the theoretical ideas in a mathematical-computer model is worth making.[7]

Selectivity

Picking from among all possible elements and processes is largely a matter of one's way of perceiving the world, or intellectual orientation; partially a question of the immediate, practical purposes for which a simplifying image is required; and particularly a function of the slice of time and specific location in space in which a given pattern of behavior is thought to occur. In short,

the system description must select only a modest number from the set of all possible variables. In other words, the possible variables are divided into those considered to be within and those considered to be outside the system description.[8]

Depends On One's Point of View. Theoretical images from different orientations should be expected to produce different and not necessarily overlapping sets of elements and operators in formalized models. This is not to say that the behavioral or sensory data considered by each of these orientations are vastly different; they obviously are not. The process of theoretical appraisal is facilitated by recognizing that observational biases exist. One may anticipate, as we have attempted to demonstrate, the general forms of images common to each perspective. Stanley Hoffman's criticism of mathematical models in the international relations context is, by this argument, not appropriate:

> Another aberration is the mushrooming of mathematical models supposed to account for large parts of the field. Often, the *scientist* includes in his model only the variables that can be measured. . . .
>
> Sometimes the *model builders* try to measure all the important variables; but this involves some fantastic assumptions . . . . The result is quite literally a *dismemberment of reality,* due to the mistake of treating *history* . . . as a "storehouse" in which facts are piled up as separate and discrete units, and to the mistake of believing that political phenomena can be reduced to a measurable common denominator comparable to the currency unit in economics[9] (emphasis added).

Everyone dismembers reality: this is the "Principle of Selectivity." How and to what result reality is dismembered is the basic question we seek to answer by developing a theoretical appraisal procedure.

Depends on One's Intended Application. Besides fundamental differences of orientation, an observer's image is narrowed by his immediate practical purpose. Theories are not final or immutable;[10] they are undertaken provisionally, subject to revision as new problems or policies generate new questions and compel the collection of new information. Adherence to a "principle of minimum devotion," the expenditure only of sufficient intellectual, moral, and emotional energy to overcome an immediate problem, keeps open a wide range of problem-solving options and increases overall flexibility.

Time and space are disaggregations of general applicability.

Depends on One's Conception of Time. The element "time" is always a variable. How one conceives of it has a bearing on the structure and behavior of representative models. For illustrative purposes, we shall employ simple modeling terminology and conventions.

Paul Samuelson has classed six model-types with respect to time, subject matter, and treatment of random events (see Exhibit 3-1).[11] Static models, obviously, hold time constant at a single point. Equilibrium analysis and most optimizing models are static or "snap-shot" portrayals of the world. If the world were only still, the sharp, pristine images of static analysis might become as pertinent as they are beautiful. It moves, however.

Time, when considered explicitly, is conventionally represented as a continuous variable in differential equations and as a discrete variable in differential equation formulations. The former perspective implies that time-dependent system variables continuously and instantaneously adjust. The discrete point of view implies that system variables are only calculated at the interval of time selected for the analysis. For example,

---

EXHIBIT 3-1

Samuelson's Taxonomy of Models

NAME	CHARACTERISTICS
1. Static and stationary	Excludes time
2. Static and historical	Exogenous disturbances (noneconomic factors accepted in analytic period)
3. Dynamic and causal	Once initial conditions are specified, future states may be determined for any subsequent period, only economic factors are modeled
4. Dynamic and historical	Like 3 but with noneconomic disturbances
5. Stochastic and nonhistorical	Like 3 but with random or probabilistic errors
6. Stochastic and historical	Like 4 but with random or probabilistic errors

---

a year interval would mean that time-bound system variables would be averaged once for each year of the analysis. This gives a reasonable characterization of many social science contexts.[12]

When considered implicitly, time is incorporated into the model by the definition of parameters and arrangement of operators and processes in a model's structure. A parameter value is invariant with respect to fluctuations in the value of time ($d\alpha_m / dt = 0$). Allowing a set of operators $[G]$ to run unaltered for an analytical period has similar conceptual consequences: the processes are constant with respect to the value of time.

An example of the difficulty that temporal selectivity may cause is Colin Clark's daring twenty-year forecast and the antipathetic, ex post "revisitation" it received.[13] Clark's formalized image precluded both continuous and discontinuous structural changes over the range of the forecast. The precision gained by hardening the theoretical image and assuming temporal consistency caused divergences between real and modeled behavior that increased with time. Contrasted with Clark's rigid prescience is the notorious "Garrison State"[14] image. Weaknesses in its measurement precision were admirably compensated for by its comprehensive scope and vivid plausibility.

What does this matter for the appraisal of theory in formal models? Simply this: to the extent that known structural changes[15] in the context are omitted or incorrectly assumed constant in a model, a model's serviceability decreases.[16]

Depends on One's Conception of Space. Spatial selectivity is most evident in the works of specialists on social geography,[17] although specialists on innovational diffusion invoke the principle as well.[18]

Space, when considered explicitly, is conventionally represented by the subscript assigned to individual elements. For example, in the symbol $x_{i,t}$ the subscript i may stand for a country, region, state, city, tract, or grid coordinate reference. It depends upon the specific theoretical image being approximated in the model.

Ignorance of space has occurred in theoretical economics images and associated models. The normative, distributive oversights of these functionally biased images have recently been attacked by Jane Jacobs, who demands that they be replaced by transactional spatial images.[19] Regardless, the selected image of space is a distinctive theoretical choice whose appropriateness for a given context and whose implications for the analytical problem need assessment.

The "Principle of Selectivity," or the dismemberment of reality, has been presented by introducing its constituent issues of orientation, application, time, and space into the appraisal of theory. Let us develop the idea more specifically.

Theories Represented by Computer Programs

Just as theories are "not only sets of propositions about reality but they are also at the same time a special class of languages about this reality, with a very limited vocabulary and relatively few connecting rules,"[20] so, too, are the mathematical models and computer programs representative of these theoretical images.

Fundamental Issues. Consideration is due a model's derivative source. What body of extant theory is incorporated in the model? What are the particular assumptions and limitations of that theory? A careful theoretical appraisal starts with examination of the descriptive symbolizations of the context and then proceeds to more precise reformulations.

Fidelity of translation from verbal to mathematical and computer symbols is a separate and largely technical issue. Not technical is the loss of meaningful information which results in the process. It is common knowledge that "mechanisms that work, however mysteriously, get substituted for those whose virtue lies in theoretical elegance."[21] Less widely known is the fact that many, if not most, urban-related computer models are barren of theoretical insight, relying instead on strings of formalized non sequiturs. Tautological accounting identities, for example, may be valid and relevant, but they are not theory. The existence of "mysterious mechanisms" must be explicitly assessed as to its impact and relevance.

Internal consistency and empirical correspondence, logical criteria applicable to any theory, are particularly important for formalized constructs. It goes almost without saying that concepts should be well and consistently defined, interrelated, and operated; however, that the overall performance of these interrelated concepts is able to reproduce a given set of historical time series is an insufficient criterion of appraisal. The theoretical validity and relevance of each component and behavioral relationship merit attention equivalent to the overall performance of the collectivity. At our current level of sophistication, the intellectual labor expended specifying individual elements, and the marginal theoretical clarification that results, may be more important than that spent painstakingly analyzing a model's overall performance. Kaplan has commented on this:

Mathematics can spare us the painful necessity of doing our own thinking, but we must pay for the privilege by taking pains with our thinking both *before and after the mathematics comes into play.*[22] (emphasis added)

Dependence on the visceral appeal of a model's output (so-called face validity) as *the* criterion of acceptability is grossly inadequate. The simple fact is that no one *really* knows very much about the structure of the social context. An ex post facto thought, by way of appraisal, is far better than no thought at all and may facilitate subsequent analyses.

Meaning: "Neither More nor Less." The attachment of meaning to a formulation's elements and processes is a minimum theoretical criterion. For a model to typify a theoretical image and an empirical context, it must correspond with them both in all ways held to be important by the theorist. To accomplish this, elements represented in the equations must be defined in terms of real empirical attributes. Every model process or operator must plausibly replicate a theoretical process or operator abstracted from the context.[23] This suggests a few more questions. Are there correspondences between the modeled elements, the theoretical images, and the empirical context? Are the processes plausible replicates of inferred contextual processes? If either answer is in the negative, there is little reason to subject a modeled formulation to more rigorous tests, because it can illuminate neither context nor problem. Mathematical elegance and precision are not substitutes for decent social science. Analogies from extraneous contexts are not substitutes either.

Analogies, Ad Hoc Assumptions, "Guesstimates," and "Fudge Factors." An analogy may be particularly insightful at a pretheoretical level of crude approximation. Failing to know when an analogy has outlived its usefulness has certain well-known detrimental effects.

But drawing analogies between physics and other studies can result in harm. In psychology, for instance, the physical analogy has proved barren. It is not useful to think of the mind as consisting of molecules—feelings and volitions—tugging this way and that, with a resultant force which realizes itself in action.[24]

Correlations between elements from two distinct contexts may indicate commonality. But this is no guarantee that the correlations will hold for other elements or other configurations. At a bare minimum, substantiation by further observation and testing is required. No argument of the analogical pattern, or "based on this principle, can give us a good reason for believing anything. The argument from analogy is fallacious."[25]

The problem of ad hoc assumptions is primarily technical; however, it is worth noting the theoretical and behavioral consequences of such "mysterious mechanisms," to use Lowry's apt label. Ascertaining careless or promiscuous use of these assumptions gives one cause to disbelieve both the model outputs and the model-makers. Closely related to this is the incorporation in a model of vague and unmeasurable elements from a verbal image. If suitable measures are not available, one must be alert to the consequences of using counterfeit or hypothetical data. A perfectly acceptable, perhaps logically essential, verbal element may be totally intractable in a formal model for want of data. In which case, one may throw it out, assume it away, or retain and use it advisedly. In any event, the impact on behavioral outputs will be significant.

A free parameter, or fudge factor, is "sandpaper" in the hands of a totem-maker. With it he makes the beautiful, smooth, and intricate patterns that bring good fortune and spiritual peace to the clan. Reconsider Bush and Mosteller's observation: "Almost any sensible model with two or three free parameters . . . can closely fit the curve, and so other criteria must be invoked when one is comparing several models."[26] To the extent that free parameters are used to get smooth fits and the possibility of alternative formulations is ignored, one has reason to question the theoretical adequacy of a model.

It has been reasserted that a computer program represents a theory. The criteria brought to bear in appraising a program are the same as those used to judge less precise verbal images. If any processes represented in mathematical form individually lack empirical referents or collectively produce implausible behavior, then there is little reason either to test more vigorously or to trust the formulation's outputs. The outputs are likely meaningless and irrelevant for any productive purpose. The practical difficulty is extricating these elements and processes from the esoteric symbolic form in which they are cast.

Expository Procedures

Bits. Given a modeled system $[X_t]$, with sets of constituent elements and processes, one first lists all elements, then defines them, in an attempt to establish correspondences between them and attributes in the empirical context. Do the individual symbols have empirical referents? If not, determine the actual referents and the utility of continuing the evaluation. If all the symbols are meaningful and a continuation of the appraisal is worthwhile, assemble the elements with their individual structural processes and translate these into words. For example, the form (3.3)

$$x_{2,t} = x_{2,t-1} + \alpha_1 (x_{1,t} - x_{1,t-1}) + \mu \qquad (3.3)$$

where,

$x_{2,t}$ = investment in dollars at time t

$x_{1,t}$ = consumption in dollars at time t

α_1 = proportion of increment of consumption between time t and $t-1$ added to investment

μ = stochastic or random effects, measured in dollars

may be translated as follows into words:

Total investment at any time t is a function of investment in the immediately preceding period, a proportion of the increment (or decrement) in consumption between periods t and $t - 1$, and some random, exogenous effects.

In this way, one may determine that the elements have empirical referents; that the verbal statement seems plausible; and that the theory is explicitly and understandably exposed. This procedure continues for all remaining equations or statements. At any point, a strongly negative finding may be reason to abort the appraisal procedure. Similar findings should have given the theorist a reason to reconstruct and possibly abort the model-building procedure.

Chunks. Individual relationships are regularly aggregated into functional components or subroutines. Collectively these subroutines purportedly describe the overall structure of a context and contain implicit within this structure all possible variants of behavioral outputs. The makeup of any one subroutine represents a fundamental theoretical judgment of what elements and processes in fact "go together." Assuming that the test for meaning was successful, one may shift attention to individual subroutines, isolating each in the manner depicted in Figure 3-1. Constructing subroutines often demands considerable time, ingenuity, and judgment from a modeler. Ideally, one attempts to construct subroutines that are "decomposed," i.e. independent of interactions with other subroutines and exhaustive of elements having similar functions.[27] In fact, decomposability is rarely achieved, a fact of some consequence.

Once a subroutine has been isolated, one must ask: What do the inputs and outputs stand for? Is this representation plausible? Are decomposability assumptions met? What are the conditions under which the routine is called into action? Are these reasonable? Meaningful? What are the transformations performed within the ensemble? Are

FIGURE 3-1

Hypothetical Subroutine—Representation

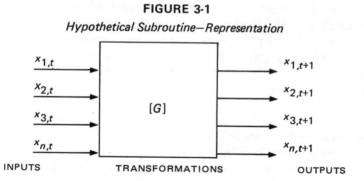

these meaningful? Plausible? If discrepancies or variances are sufficiently severe, major reconstruction may be indicated. Certainly, an ex post appraisal would terminate, and the model would be judged unsatisfactory.

Wholes. If the subroutines are "reasonable," one next shifts his frame of reference to the level of the whole model. An adequate set of subroutines must be capable of fulfilling all the functions expected from the model, and each subroutine must be included for the successful operation of the model.

If the model satisfies the consistency, meaning, and plausibility tests at each of the three distinct levels of aggregation—bits, chunks, and wholes—then one may systematically examine its behavioral characteristics from the least to the most inclusive level.

Using input values of data that are plausible as to order of magnitude and sign, one may "run through" or hand simulate the outputs of individual relationships to gain a sense of their performance. The procedure is repeated for the subroutines and then for the full model.

One is primarily interested in the *trends* and *orders of magnitude* of the behavioral output, not point estimates.[28] In this regard, common sense comes into play:

A theory or model must first of all give results which can be confirmed by common sense. . . . The coincidence of the model's results with common sense will only apply for the simplest of cases or instances. But if there is a contradiction with common sense at a primitive level we would reject the model. . . . We need not, to give an example, be highly trained economists to see that a country is not getting poorer when its National Income increases. If a model were to imply this we would reject it together with everything else it might tell us.[29]

Systematically dismantling and reinterpreting a formal model facilitates the application of common sense and other evaluative criteria.

Recapitulation. After defining and labeling terms, the idea of different orientations was reconsidered and expanded to include selectivity of application, time, and space. The important idea of program representing theory was used to develop one set of procedures that may prove fruitful in executing a theoretical appraisal. Another distinct component of an inclusive procedure is technical assessment, to which we now turn.

4

Technical Appraisal

When we mean to build,
We first survey the plot, then draw the model;
And when we see the figure of the house,
Then must we rate the cost of the erection;
Which, if we find outweighs ability,
What do we then but draw anew the model
In fewer offices, or at least desist
To build at all?

Shakespeare
King Henry IV, Part II
act 1, scene 3[1]

Appraising the technique embedded in a model is quite like appraising a piece of modern art. One "feels" or "likes" a model in much the same subjective, intuitive way that one is attracted to one work of art and repulsed by another. This is not to say that a computer model cannot be measured against appraisal criteria; it is to say that beyond several commonly accepted standards and procedures,[2] appraisal rapidly loses its objectivity.

Within the commonly recognized standards would be concern for the means by which specific theoretical ideas translate into flow charts, knowledge of procedures for specifying a model from these flow charts, bases of agreement as to the relative merits and implications of technical assumptions, knowledge of procedural techniques for obtaining gross and then fine-tuned outputs, and several performance criteria against which any model could be measured. Let us consider these in turn.

Translating Theory: Formalization

Obtaining a clear theoretical understanding of a problem context is a basic prerequisite to formalization. If the context is not well-understood or is changing, there may be no need to specify it in rigid mathematical and computer readable forms.

[Machines] perform the most monotonous and repetitive tasks at high speed and with absolute mechanical accuracy . . . , [but] the model builder can make use of this capacity only insofar as he is able to perceive repetitive temporal patterns in the processes of urban life and fixed spatial relationships in the kaleidoscope of urban form.[3]

Ascertaining whether patterns are sufficiently repetitive and stable is a preliminary step to formalization.

Representation by Flow Charts. The construction of logical flow charts has been one means of accomplishing this. Figure 4-1 illustrates some simple theoretical ideas in this form. At this level the logic of a process is broken down into manageable components. At the same time,

FIGURE 4-1

Illustrative Example—Verbal Flow Chart

> Define:
> Gross National Product at a point in time is composed of consumption, investment, and government expenditures.

> Hypothesize:
> Some portion of GNP is consumed in subsequent periods of time.

> Hypothesize:
> Some portion of marginal changes in consumption is invested (if the change is positive) or disinvested (if negative).

> Hypothesize:
> Government expenditures stay at about the same percent of last year's GNP from period to period.

some boundaries are established for the total context. In this example, we are dealing with the entities: gross national product, consumption, investment, and government expenditures. No other factors are explicitly considered, which is not to say that other factors don't matter. Indeed, many other considerations impose themselves upon and are subsumed within the gross entities selected for the flow chart; however, those selected are determined to be of primary analytic and theoretical concern for the present purpose. Within the flow chart are one definitional tautology and three behavioral-theoretical hypotheses about the interrelationships of the entities. To the extent that the whole is logically consistent, to the extent that the individual components contain, as tentatively stated relationships, all entities of primary interest, and to the extent that intercomponent relationships are logically and theoretically plausible, one may proceed with a more formal statement of the context.

At this point, however, it may be that many of the verbally stated relationships are not logically consistent, it may be that empirical evidence to support or refute the formulated relationships is not available, and it may be that the whole context has logical gaps not easily bridged by known theory and new measurement and testing. Alternative possibilities include forsaking the verbal formulation because it has neither scientific utility nor meaning, or retaining the formulation until additional supportive empirical information is developed. Should one elect the latter option, it would be foolish and unnecessarily expensive to force the verbal flow chart into more rigorous notation until the logico-theoretical problem is resolved.

Representation by Mathematics. When we are confident that a context is tractable, the next step is to specify individual relationships in mathematical terms. Words are rich in their varieties of meaning but vague when used for logical reasoning.[4] Mathematics is exact in its logic and usually void of meaning. If one is willing to accept the loss of verbal variety in the interest of rigorous logical specification, a mathematically stated version of the verbal flow chart might be constructed. One example of this is reproduced in Exhibit 4-1. Gone are the vague, albeit useful, qualifiers, "some," "a portion," "about," etc.; they are replaced by hard statements of cause and effect; gross national product at a specific point in time *is equal to* the sum of consumption, investment, and government expenditures at that point; consumption at a specific point in time *equals* a fixed percentage of gross national product from the prior, discrete point in time, and so forth. No other options, no other meanings, no other interpretations satisfy the exact conditions described by relationships (4.1) through (4.4).

Besides producing more rigorous descriptions of the context, mathematical specification enables a model builder to perform some essential "bookkeeping" chores. Checking for dimensionality and for logical

---

EXHIBIT 4-1

Illustrative Example—Mathematical Notation

$$Y_t = C_t + I_t + G_t \tag{4.1}$$
$$C_t = \alpha\, Y_{t-1} \tag{4.2}$$
$$I_t = \beta\,(C_t - C_{t-1}) + I_{t-1} \tag{4.3}$$
$$G_t = \gamma\, Y_{t-1} \tag{4.4}$$

Where,

Y_t = gross national product* at time t.

C_t = consumption expenditures at time t.

I_t = investment expenditures at time t.

G_t = government expenditures at time t.

α = proportion of gross national product consumed at time $t-1$.

β = proportion of difference in consumption invested between time t and time $t-1$.

α = proportion of gross national product expended by the government at time $t-1$.

---

*All units in constant currency.

---

completeness are two important tasks rarely carried out for social science models.

Dimensionality refers to the units of measurement assigned a model's entities. In the illustrative example, all the variables are measured in monetary terms, e.g. dollars—more specifically dollars defined in accordance with a standard accounting convention like "market" or "constant" currency. The parameters (α, β, γ) are all dimensionless or pure numbers. As a model becomes more complicated, one easily loses sight of the need to balance units, to assure dimensionality.

Any equations describing the operation of the system must be dimensionally homogeneous. The operation of the system can produce no changes that violate the requirement of dimensional homogeneity of the describing equations—a fact of enormous importance.[5]

Apples don't equal oranges no matter how elegant the relationship.

Consistency checking refers to several logical operations routinely carried out where mathematical notation is a common currency. One simple example might be illustrated by reversing the order of the relationships (4-2) and (4-3) from the sequence presented in Figure 4-1. A value for C_t must be calculated before a value for I_t may be determined; I_t depends upon or is a function of C_t. Consistency and dimension checking must be carried out for any mathematically specified context as a regular technical matter of course. To the extent that they are ignored, one must be alerted to possible errors in formulation.

Further Specification

Representation by Code. The respecification of a mathematical formulation into a computer code involves additional losses of meaning and content. A computer code or language is based on its own logical assumptions and relationships. Just as verbal languages differ in form, content, and possible meanings, so, too, do computer languages.[6] A simple illustration suggests some of these distinctions. In Figure 4-2, the mathematical notation has been translated into a form ready for computer coding. For such simple cases, the translation is easily made; for more complicated cases, each having multiple plausible possibilities for processing, achieving the best correspondence between the mathematical and computer formulations requires considerable skill. In Figure 4-3 this translation has been cast in the common FORTRAN language. Outputs of the process are shown in Figure 4-4. Even in these simple examples, the rigor of the computer code's own discipline is evident. Any technical appraisal must consider the separate requirements of the language in which a model is written, as well as the appropriateness of that language for the problem that is formulated. Certainly, FORTRAN (II, IV, G, or H versions), GPSS, MAD, SIM-SCRIPT, and a host of more specialized languages each exhibit peculiar strengths and weaknesses. The selection of an appropriate language is a very complicated enterprise and well beyond the scope of this inquiry. In general, however, the language selected is a function of the purpose one has, or the problem that is being solved.

The problem of translation does not stop with a written program. The machine, in response to stored instructions, takes the proffered computer program and retranslates or compiles those instructions into a form that is palatable to the machine. The chance of error is minimal, but the chance exists. Here once again specific, specialized conventions must be observed.

Mechanical Details. Another class of problem to be confronted is the degree to which mechanical computational characteristics and limitations impinge upon the specification of a problem. A machine of limited storage capacity and relatively slow speed may induce a programmer to take efficient shortcuts in coding a model. Such shortcuts are tolerable only insofar as they do not fundamentally alter the logic of the theoretical context. An elegant, efficient program does not necessarily capture the detail of an intended context. Discrepancies may become particularly acute when theorist and programmer are not the

FIGURE 4-2
Illustrative Example—Ready for Coding

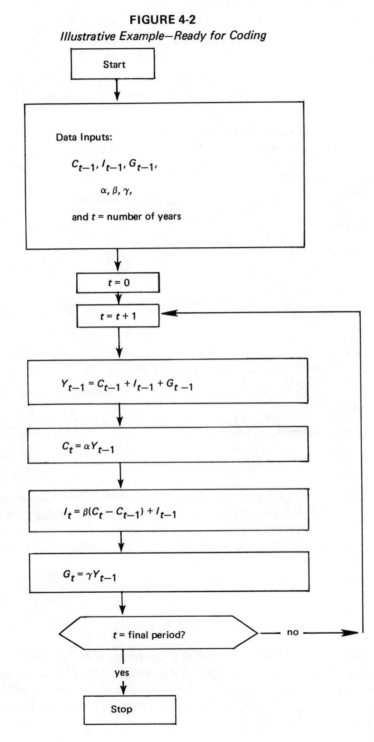

THE APPRAISAL FUNCTION

FIGURE 4-3

Illustrative Example—FORTRAN CODE

BREWER   PLS194-4159   DATE 03/05/70
    MAIN 1   -EFN   SOURCE STATEMENT   -   IFN(S)   -

```
C                   ILLUSTRATIVE REFERENCE
      INTEGER  T,TT,FY
      REAL IN
      DIMENSION Y(50),C(50),IN(50),G(50)
C  INPUT
      READ(5,1)C(1),IN(1),G(1),ALPHA,BETA,GAMMA,FY
    1 FORMAT(3F10.0,3F10.3,8X,I2)
C  DO LOOP
      T=1
      DO50 T=1,FY
      TT=T+1
      Y(T)=C(T)+IN(T)+G(T)
      C(TT)=ALPHA*Y(T)
      IN(TT)=BETA*(C(TT)-C(T))+IN(T)
      G(TT)=GAMMA*Y(T)
   50 CONTINUE
      WRITE(6,98) ALPHA,BETA,GAMMA,FY
   98 FORMAT(1H1,'INITIAL CONDITIONS'//5X,'ALPHA',F7.3,'   BETA',F7.3,
    1' GAMMA',F7.3/5X,'NUMBER OF PERIODS=', I4)
      WRITE(6,99)
   99 FORMAT(1H4,'ILLUSTRATIVE EXAMPLE'//5X,'OUTPUTS'/2X,'YR.'4X,'Y(T)',
    16X'C(T)'5X'IN(T)'6X'G(T)')
      WRITE(6,100)(T,Y(T),C(T),IN(T),G(T), T=1,FY)
  100 FORMAT(1H0,I3,4F10.0)
      STOP
      END
```

same person, and their functional priorities differ. Simple problems may be translated with little or no loss of theoretical meaning; as the context becomes more complex, the opportunities for discrepancy increase.[7] A thorough technical appraisal must explicitly consider these issues.

Assumptions

Another issue requiring technical consideration is "assumptions-made-in-the-interest-of-formalization." How well the implications of assumptions are understood or acknowledged reflects on the quality of the model. A sample of these choices is contained in the following questions of general utility:

FIGURE 4-4

Outputs from Illustrative Example

INITIAL CONDITIONS

    ALPHA 0.800   BETA   0.500   GAMMA 0.150
    NUMBER OF PERIODS=   20

ILLUSTRATIVE EXAMPLE

  OUTPUTS

YR.	Y(T)	C(T)	IN(T)	G(T)
1	900.	700.	100.	100.
2	965.	720.	110.	135.
3	1053.	772.	136.	145.
4	1171.	842.	171.	158.
5	1331	937.	218.	176.
6	1547.	1065.	282.	200.
7	1838.	1238.	369.	232.
8	2232.	1471.	485.	276.
9	2763.	1786.	643.	335.
10	3480.	2211.	855.	414.
11	4448.	2784.	1142.	522.
12	5755.	3559.	1529.	667.
13	7520.	4804.	2052.	863.
14	9902.	6016.	2758.	1128.
15	13117.	7921.	3711.	1485.
16	17458.	10494.	4997.	1968.
17	23318.	13966.	6733.	2619.
18	31230.	18655.	9077.	3498.
19	41910.	24984.	12242.	4684.
20	56329.	33528.	16514.	6287.

Linearity: Are linear specifications adequate representations of the reality context? If they are not, are there sufficient data available to specify higher order relationships? If they are not and data are not available for respecification, are systemic implications understood and reported?

Serial versus simultaneous processing: Is is necessary to solve many simultaneous equations, i.e. do events require simultaneous resolution? If yes, are these events represented as simultaneous equation systems or are they (in the interest of efficiency) processed serially by the model? If yes, are the implications for the model's performance understood?

Parameter estimation: Are parameters estimated from a cross-sectional or time series empirical data base? If cross-sectional, or taken at one or only a few points in time, are the weaknesses of the model for projective purposes acknowledged? If time series data are used, is the variation among points negligible or small enough that parameters may or should be considered fixed for the analytic period of the model? If no, are parameters redefined as variables, or is constancy assumed? Single-point parameter estimates are particularly useless for projective purposes.

Structural changes: Are subscripted entities disaggregated in the course of the analytic period, i.e. are new sectors, actors, or constraints created or destroyed in the course of the analytic period? If yes, are these contextual discontinuities incorporated in the model as they occur? Do functional relationships change as a result of outputs generated by the model, i.e. are so-called second order or structural feedbacks operating? Particularly for projective purposes, failing to account for structural-contextual changes increasingly limits a model's plausibility and utility as the time frame lengthens.[8]

Stochastic versus deterministic: Is it necessary to introduce error or random terms into the model formulation? Does this significantly add to the complication of the model's output without adding to an understanding of its structure?

Timing of events: Is the model oriented around a fixed sequencing of events, as in updating all variables quarterly or annually? FORTRAN code is characteristically used in this way. Or, does the model dynamic derive from the execution of various events, as in queuing problems? GPSS code is well suited for these problems. If the reference system is event oriented, is the model correspondingly coded? If not, and the model is tied to a "fixed clock," are the empirical consequences clearly delineated?

These are general questions, each of which suggests other more specific issues. What is important is that each set of questions implies and tests a set of assumptions made, and a larger set of plausible choices forgone. The individual and collective implications of these various, essentially technical, choices must be considered.

Running the Model—Gross Fits

Assuming that the transition from words to code has been satisfactory, attention should be turned to learning the gross behavioral properties of the model.

If at first . . . After setting the initial conditions at plausible values, correct as to order of magnitude and sign, the model is run. It will not work; the code will most probably be erroneous and will be unceremoniously rejected by the computer. The "debugging" procedure which follows is tedious, time-consuming, and often enormously frustrating. That is not to underrate its importance. Absolutely nothing proceeds until the model is debugged. Any good technical appraisal must review the inevitable modifications incorporated into the model at this juncture. For a trivial program like our illustration, it is probably not necessary to keep a formal record of these changes; however, for a program even slightly more complex, it is essential that a "debugging log" be maintained. This record serves not only to inform a programmer of his errors and their resolution, *it is an essential document* for a master modeler *to inform him of possible compromises* to the logico-theoretical context. A model that eventually compiles and runs is not necessarily useful or meaningful. Being unable to account for every single modification in the model unnecessarily complicates the assessment task. For large-scale models, it may make the task impossible.

Try . . . After the model is debugged, a general "sense" of the model's performance may be obtained through a systematic series of simplifications: Disaggregate the model into its constituent components, submodels, or subroutines. Examine each separately, setting the parameters at extreme values of, say, zero and one to determine if the outputs that are generated enter absurd ranges. Make constant those variables thought to be of less importance in order to isolate the behavior of those thought to be relatively more important. Eliminate variables that don't seem to have much impact on the component's performance. Make complex relationships linear. Increase the number and the rigidity of operating assumptions. Eliminate stochastic terms. With each of these component simplifications, the critical question is: "What difference does it make?" Specifically, to the extent that a variable has little discernible impact on a component's performance, it may be made constant, redefined, reformulated, or eliminated, and so forth. Characteristically, the initial formulation will be considerably modified at this point as the researcher gets to "know" his model better. The effects of any of these modifications must be considered.

Try, Again. After the modified individual components have been debugged again, the entire procedure is repeated for the fully constituted model. Intercomponent behavior is observed and the overall performance characteristics of the model are learned.

Up to this point it has been unnecessary to use actual data. Many reputable simulation studies have stopped at precisely this point, never having processed anything except hypothetical, albeit "plausible," data.[9]

Most of what has been suggested might be discounted out of hand as "trivial detail." Unfortunately, trivia have a way of cumulating to tragic proportions.

Trivial details such as beginning to program prematurely, badly specifying output, not deciding upon uses, failing to document adequately during programming and forgetting to note changes or to check for all of the implications of a change can wipe out any value to the program.[10]

Insofar as these trivial details are allowed to cumulate, a model-building undertaking may become hopelessly and tragically stymied. At any rate, unless this gross structural evaluation shows that the model is satisfactory, there is very little need to continue its running and fine tuning.

Should these gross runs be unsuccessful in the ex post appraisal of a specific model, there is little or no reason to continue with a more detailed appraisal.

Tuning the Model—Sensitivity Testing

These technical procedures ultimately lead to the extremely troublesome question of verification. In a sense each of the questions and issues already raised is a form of partial or preliminary verification. Technique is stressed for good reason.

In part, the reason for avoiding the subject of verification stems from the fact that the problem of verifying or validating [sic] computer models remains today perhaps the most elusive of all the unresolved methodological problems associated with computer simulation techniques.[11]

Tuning. Adjusting a model to fit an empirical data base has several purposes. First, one exposes a model to find out what it "means" in an empirical sense. Differences between the simulated output generated by the model and the experience it purports to describe are ideally attributable to the assumptions built into the model. Verification has been defined as searching and testing such sets of underlying, systemic behavioral assumptions.[12] Implicit to this ideal case is error-free data, i.e. a perfect empirical information base. Obviously, the data base used to tune a model will be to some extent incomplete and inaccurate. Differences between generated and real outputs may be attributed, therefore, to assumptions, stochastic elements, *or* imperfect data.[13]

Second, one gains insight into the general quality of the model from how well it reproduces general trends and orders of magnitude of variables in the context. "Does the model offend common sense?" is a good question that is seldom articulated and rarely answered with honesty and candor. And finally, tuning can help to indicate which of several parameters are poorly estimated.[14]

In tuning a model, one may initially assume that the empirical data are not fundamentally erroneous—an expedient justified by the cost of data acquisition. Using estimates of parameters obtained through one of many acceptable statistical techniques,[15] one may set the initial conditions of a model, and allow it to run. This is no more than a continuation of the gross fitting and structural examination carried out earlier; now, however, the model is running with real data. Once again attention is devoted to the structural properties, the embedded assumptions of the model. If this comparison of real and generated performance is not satisfactory, it might be appropriate to reassess all the behavioral relationships and to think about the possibility of systematic data error.

Determining satisfactory performance levels is a fundamental methodological problem. Recommended approaches and suggested criteria have ranged from the so-called comfort test,[16] the degree to which a model builder has intuitive subjective confidence in his formulation, to more elegant statistical tests designed to measure variations between generated and actual data. In the latter category, Cohen and Cyert have used both factor and regression analyses on the computer-generated and actual time series data: satisfactory fit is defined as some acceptable minimum discrepancy between regression statistics or factor loadings for real and generated data.[17] And Henri Theil has even created a special purpose statistic in this regard, the "Theil inequality coefficient," shown in (4.5)[18]

$$U^2 = \sum_{i=1}^{T} \frac{(P_i - A_i)^2}{\sum_{i=1}^{T} A_i^2} \qquad (4.5)$$

Where

P_i = prediction of the ith term

A_i = actual i^{th} term

T = number of time periods

At issue is the precision, the amount of variation that is acceptable before a model is termed unsatisfactory. Recall our initial point that technical appraisal rapidly loses its objectivity as science yields to judgment—and maybe even to metaphysics.

If, after obtaining more and better measures, re-estimating parameters, readjusting suspect relationships, and rerunning the model, the results are still unsatisfactory, one has good reason to reassess the overall research strategy.

Sensitivity. If, on the other hand, the results are satisfactory, one may proceed with a series of sensitivity tests. Sensitivity analysis examines what difference a small change in a single initial condition, in a parameter, in the value of a variable at the start of the analysis, or in an

45

underlying unchanging rate or threshold which governs the operation of the model's processes, makes in output variables of particular interest. Thus, it provides insight into the structural relationship of inputs to outputs. Alternatively, a sensitivity analysis may be used to compare a datum or reference run for all output variables against those generated under the influence of altered initial conditions and parameters. In the former case one is most concerned with the identification of the amount of specific response to the amount of specific stimulus; in the latter case the emphasis shifts to a comprehensive comparison of differences between the time series of the reference and modified versions of the model. The former stresses understanding of the internal structure of the model; the latter stresses elaborating alternative descriptive possibilities of performance from the model.

The major limitation of a sensitivity analysis is its cost in time and money. The range of plausible variations is unbounded. For each relationship there are a large number of possible qualitative alternatives, and for each data input there are a large number of possible quantitative alternatives. Furthermore, for quantitative variations in inputs there may exist scale effects or thresholds, beyond which responses disproportionate to stimuli are generated. The research burden is to determine the implications of each unique combination of relationships, initial conditions, and parameters. It is an impossible task in one respect, but it is important that it nonetheless be carried out. A model cannot be used with any confidence if one does not know what it responds to. Particularly, it is essential to sort out the trivial from the tragic implications of variations in the model's entities.

To the extent that large input variations produce marginal or negligible changes in the outputs, one may assume either that the model is too crude to register these differences or that the relationships are not particularly sensitive in the real world. The former implies that the model may need re-examination and perhaps respecification; the latter indicates that the selected entities possibly may not have much intrinsic interest and may be redefined, aggregated, or omitted.

To the extent that small input variations produce unexpectedly large changes in the outputs, one may assume either that the model contains fundamental mathematical or programming errors or that the reference system is in fact sensitive to small variations. The former demands that the model be re-examined and corrected and is the usual case; the latter indicates a potentially critical leverage point in the reference system and is the rare case. Programming errors of this type (where the model compiles and runs but produces "strange" outputs) are enormously difficult to find, even when systematic error-checking routines have been constructed in the model. Tragic—that is to say, high-impact—parameters and relationships are best retained in a model only after considerable extra effort has been expended to insure that the reference system in fact behaves that way.

What can a well designed and executed sensitivity test tell one about the technical worth of a model? A great deal.

Criteria

After one has frequently applied the "common sense" test and modifications have been investigated, the so-called Turing Test might then be appropriately used. Does the output of the model offend the common sense of expert persons versed in the reference system? If yes, there may be cause to reconsider the entire undertaking. If no, there may be cause to proceed cautiously to more detailed tests.

Richard Cyert has suggested several specific criteria in this regard that are worth summarizing: [19] (1) Do the number, timing, and direction of turning points in the generated data correspond to the reference data? (2) Are the amplitudes of fluctuations similar in direction and magnitude? (3) Do the average values for the variables approximate each other? (4) Do the turning points for each variable correspond as to time and direction? (5) Are the distribution, standard deviation, and variance of generated and real variables roughly equivalent? These are reasonable questions worth posing as appraisal criteria.

For the considerable effort involved in a thorough technical appraisal, the potential rewards are considerable.

5

Ethical Appraisal

The scientific penchant for precision is rightly called to task for losing "sight of the importance of intentional analyses which unfold some of the richness of human meaning and valuation." Those specialists concerned with the normative status of society may indeed have "a special obligation to criticize such imperialism in the sciences of man,"[1] but to a large extent they have failed to do so because they have isolated themselves, contented to play empty formalistic games. Let us briefly consider the nature of this isolation and outline several possibilities to introduce an ethical component into the construction, utilization, and assessment of formal social science models.

The Value of Context—The Context of Values

The isolation of social ethics—the empirical study of moral conduct[2]—from social science, if one rightly interprets Abraham Kaplan, should never have occurred. "Political morality . . . is intrinsic to all policy whose decisions significantly affect the value placed on things human. Public morality is the morality of public policy."[3] A specific obligation of social ethics to aid understanding of public policy is to call attention to the multiple dimensions of complex social contexts.

The problem is that there are many ways of projecting order. . . . in science the normative element is inescapably present. . . . It is right there because you are proposing a legitimate order. . . .

The difficulty with simulation models, with functional analysis . . . the limitation with these things, the breaking down into parts and the projecting of a kind of order, is that it presupposes an answer to the problem . . . [being addressed by the model].[4]

One easily recognizes a legitimate function for the social ethicist: identification of scientific simplifications that have embedded ethical assumptions that bias possible outcomes. The widespread failure to discharge this societal responsibility is partially explained by the preoccupation of the ethics profession with transcendent doctrines of moral absolutism; that is, "the pretense that the right and the good are unequivocal and certain, and that they are realizable in every case by unswerving adherence to high principle."[5] By now, one hopes, the message is clear. *Values are contextual, not absolute.*[6] Values can only be appraised with respect to a concrete setting: ". . . a description of a value of a commodity refers to that commodity in its environment. Value is not a property of the commodity in abstract, but of the commodity *in situ.*"[7] It may be that social ethicists, through the medium of contextual analysis, can begin to recover a sense of social responsibility. Winter, for one, has boldly sketched out this important task:

Policy has to do with man's problems in coping with his future. . . . Policy brings to statement what is judged to be possible, desirable, and meaningful for the human enterprise. In this sense, policy is the nexus of fact, value, and ultimate meaning in which scientific, ethical, and theological-philosophical reflections meet.[8]

Some political scientists know that this convergence of fact, value, and meaning quite likely will occur in the creation and implementation of public policy:

And if it [political science] is to make the contributions it should to the pursuit of public policy—and here I become dogmatic—it must deal with ethical questions. It must refuse to back away from the process of evaluation.[9]

However, most political scientists have been so preoccupied that Pennock's imperatives have been overlooked.

Convergence: Manipulation, Projection

That man continually orients himself to an imagined future has profound implications. Man, as Kenneth Boulding points out, responds not

49

to an immediate stimulus but to an image of the future filtered through an elaborate value system. His image contains not only what is, but what might be. It is full of potentialities as yet unrealized. In rational behavior man contemplates the world of potentialities, evaluates them according to his value system, and chooses the "best."[10]

Approximations of rationality operate at the level of an individual's abstracted and much simplified view of the world, or his "image" of it. Even if this simple view is hardened into a formal model, the fact that other images exist should not be overlooked.

A human must choose or decide on the system requirements. He may derive them from the needs the system is to satisfy or by computations from more primitive information about what is wanted. He must order the requirements as essential and less important.[11]

Ethicists must be alert to identify particular value-laden elements embedded in such hardened and narrow personal approximations.

As a projected time frame expands beyond the immediate, marginal present, the number of possible states both real and modeled systems may assume increases. Likewise, so does uncertainty about which discrete state from among many possibilities a system will in fact assume. That is to say, as one peers farther into the future, rationality rapidly yields to intuition.[12] In reality this has meant that a policy-maker "muddles through," doing the best he can at the margin of time.[13] It has meant, in one intellectual context at least, that sophisticated mathematical models have rightly been downgraded from a pretentious predictive role to a more honest educational one.[14] It has also meant appeals for the construction of alternative means to study the future,[15] and for the construction of explicitly normative models.[16] While these needs are only now beginning to be articulated (and one may interpret this as a refreshing wave of humility),[17] the several possibilities for specialists in social ethics seem obvious. Foremost is the development of alternative desired and desirable end-states for both individual variables and whole systems under consideration. For example, this might mean devising a fulfilling image of man that considers more than his profits or his power.[18] Another possible function is to alert participants in a social system to the potential and inevitable value shifts and discontinuities that result when certain systemic goals are achieved or closely approximated.[19]

It is in the future, in our attempts to manipulate the state of the social system through purposive activities, that a convergence of social science and social ethics seems most likely and most necessary. As Winter reminds us all,

it becomes apparent that historical fulfillment is the decisive perspective for evaluating social policy. The problem of policy is ultimately how the future is grasped and appraised. The essential meaning of responsibility is accountability in human fulfillment in the shaping of the society's future.[20]

Problems Impeding Ethical Integration

Obscuring Winter's vision of accommodation and rapprochement are several common problems whose notoriety allows summary consideration. This is not to underplay their seriousness, however. For until we, as scientists, have begun to resolve these issues, convergence will most assuredly elude us.

In the absence of any commonly accepted social accounting scheme,[21] much of what passes for policy analysis necessarily concentrates on qualitative variables of illusory character. Confronted with this fact, a builder of formal models resorts to one or a few simplifying tactics. He may rely primarily on "hard" indicators, usually expressed in monetary or demographic metrics, thereby ignoring the qualitative imponderables;[22] or, despite the lessons of the utilitarians,[23] he may attempt to quantify these "soft" variables. Practically, what is certain is that a model-builder will not spend much time or devote much attention to these troublesome qualitative variables and the heroic assumptions made for the sake of elegance and rigor. For policy purposes, Jeremy Bentham's narrow-minded hedonism is *still* an inadequate representation of the social problem context.

A corollary to the quantification issue is the slightly more subtle problem of different, conflicting, and unknown preferences in the social context. Preference scales are not stable; they are not wholly—or even approximately—determinate. Indeed, to the extent that the familiar political processes of goal elucidation and consensus building are not somehow reflected in the construction and use of a policy model, the exercise may be rather academic. Quite typically, political officials are unable to articulate their *own* preferences, except in vague platitudes, much less have an awareness of what *anyone else's* relative preferences might be.[24] This is not all-unfortunate, for as we are reminded,

when the theorist attempts to make policy judgments as he would theoretical judgments, he simply becomes a naive policymaker. . . . The theorist who fails at policymaking operates with a bad theory, as it is bad theory partly because he has tried to keep it *explicit, articulate, conscious,* and *orderly.*[25]

Which is *exactly* the point at issue in the construction of a formal computer-mathematical model, as was indicated with various technical criteria. The evaluative shortcoming is simply stated: In the absence of clearly specified information about the preference lists of policy-makers or segments of the population, a model-building analyst will, in the interests of technical efficiency and tractability, substitute his own simplified, explicit, and orderly preferences into his formulation.[26]

A related issue of incomplete contextual information has received scant attention. There are several kinds of incomplete knowledge worth noting: (1) information known to participants that is not introduced, whatever the reason, into the analytical process; (2) information that is known and introduced but is omitted by the analyst as irrelevant or intractable; and (3) information that has simply not yet manifested itself. In all cases, to formalize the model-builder is forced to make hard technical choices, and the resultant effect for his model is approximately the same. The model increasingly diverges from its reference system and loses both predictive and policy utility. Models and the information supporting them are crude, limited, and extremely fragile.

Responsibilities of Ethical Appraisal

An appraisal procedure that explicitly considers valuative issues contributes another sense of experiential order to the ongoing analytic task. Ethical appraisal has, besides this function of expanding perspectives, several other contributions to make to a responsible analytic enterprise.

"Keeping the analyst honest" is a multifaceted and unending function. What are the analyst's own operating norms? Which among these are reflected in his models? Is he made conscious of them?[27] Are analytical efforts being expended for discipline-relevant rather than policy problem-relevant rewards and deprivations? "Social science has its own policy imperatives that are defined by the state of its discipline. It has its own history as a community, it has its own possibilities . . ."; however, "what is rewarded is not policy relevance, rather it is discipline relevance."[28] It is essential to insure that a policy analyst is responsive and responsible to the policy problem as his primary source of reward and deprivation. To the extent that the model becomes reified in the interests of an intellectual game, the analyst and the enterprise must become suspect. Someone, somehow must be alert enough to note this shift and to call it to the analyst's attention.[29] A variant on the theme of misplaced relevance is the case of the problem-solving consultant or research corporation. To the extent that "problem solutions" are claimed for and sold by such commercial interests, one needs to consider a range of interesting ethical questions. More will be said about this later.

Estimating a model's normative possibilities is another aspect of a thorough ethical appraisal. By this is meant filtering through alternative value networks the possible normative choices contained in an analysis, adding or deleting where appropriate, ordering these new choices, and comparing the new possibilities with the old ones used in the analysis.

Discrepancies create the basis for serious discussion and resolution between the scientist and the ethicist. The key problem is to determine the adequacy of the values chosen with respect to potential options.[30] Other options and orderings exist; how they may be determined, combined, and brought to bear in a specific context is crucial.

> Each style of science is, in this sense, implicitly an ontology which unifies meaning in its totality from a particular perspective. By the same token, each style of thought is implicitly an ethic, since it makes some proposal of the unity of process and value, present possibilities and future realization.[31]

And, finally, ethical appraisal must be explicitly charged with the continuing assessment of what moral implications flow from an overall research activity.[32]

Integrating a Perspective

The emerging functions of the social ethicist, as his special enterprise begins to converge with social science at the analytical context, are several and include: the identification of gross scientific simplifications, the identification of values and norms in the modeled "images," the development of end state specifications for a system, the elaboration of potential systemic value shifts and discontinuities, the explication of operating preferences for all concerned participants, and the assessment—in general terms—of the moral implications of an ongoing research activity.

It has been asserted that the fundamental problems confounding the execution of these functions have arisen from the professional diversion into formalistic and scientistic modes of discourse, the lack of even minimally quantifiable social elements, the existence of multiple, changing preference orderings, and the omission of much essential factual information. "Keeping the analyst honest" is in several senses a summary slogan indicating the need for increased personal, professional, and societal responsibility.

This book intends to call attention to these problems and functions and to stimulate enough thought that they may one day be resolved and implemented. The cases that follow will be tested by several of these evaluative functions. A related purpose is to create better modes of normative appraisal. This is clearly in the common interest.

> We must either leave science alone altogether and forgo its transformation of means, or else integrate it with our moral aspirations and forgo the fixity of traditional ends. A belief is not scientific because it has been "proved" but because it is continuously tested and tested by conformity to experience rather than to axiomatic truths.[33]

Let us turn our attention to several forms of experiential testing.

53

6

Pragmatic Appraisal

American culture treats computing and romantic love in the same way. Much is made of outstanding success, but more is promised to the average man than can possibly be delivered. As a result, adventures in both fields are prone to end in recrimination and disillusionment.

Earl Hunt
American Psychologist,
March 1969

Philadelphia's redevelopment administrator, Edmund Bacon, made these telling comments about his experience with several of the "newer" methods:

I think that the time has come when we have discovered, by trying it, that studying the problems of underprivileged neighborhoods through such methods as space systems analysis and creating simulated models does not work. I think that we are entering a new era in which we see the city itself as the laboratory for our experimentation.[1]

A modification of this rather absolute position might be: to date, no simulation models have been useful to Mr. Bacon or others in formulating urban policies. This is probably correct, but it is not the same as saying, "creating simulated models does not work." If the intended application of a model is policy-making, then there must at least be some correspondence between the model and the problem context, i.e. its "reference system."

Significant correspondence means that the outcomes of policies fed into the computer, on the one hand, and of policies adopted in the real world, on the other hand, resemble each other *in all respects important to the policy-maker in the real world.*[2]

Clearly the general class of models known to Mr. Bacon and other practitioners has not been significantly correspondent with any operant reference system to be helpful for policy-making. And *for their uses, this is the critical consideration.* Still, for other applications a given model may be quite adequate. Underlying the problems of proper application is the more general tension between the manipulative and reflective orientations described earlier. I shall elaborate some special evaluative criteria of models intended for policy-making; but first, consider what specialized criteria are needed to understand and appraise models intended primarily for data manipulation, measurement, theory building, educational, and other distinct applications.

Data Manipulation Applications

While not as sophisticated as its more esoteric progeny, Wassily Leontief's well-known input-output analysis suggests one basic use for a model qua data manipulator: consistency checking of variables thought to be inter-related.[3] This application develops "more or less automatic procedures for the checking for logical consistency and completeness in models," thus imposing "order and clarity over a diverse and poorly coordinated set of data and informal concepts."[4] This is a valid end in itself and is often discounted in the rush to build more intellectually satisfying devices.

Examples of models employed primarily as data manipulators would be found in the many area transportation studies of the last decade[5] and to some extent in the political survey simulation, *Candidates, Issues and Strategies.*[6]

Generally such models may be characterized as emphasizing "housekeeping" chores, employing input-output matrices or strings of tautological accounting identities to these ends. This is not to understate the importance of reliable and efficient "housekeeping." In many instances it is necessary to institutionalize data collection requiring the expenditure of vast quantities of resources. Models have been useful tools in this regard. While this class of models is noteworthy for its sparse theoretical content, it nonetheless represents a necessary precondition to the design and construction of richer theoretical structures. It is highly desirable to have one's data sufficiently under control that attention may be devoted to more difficult concerns.

One evaluative criterion is the extent to which variables are processed in accurate, standard, and consistent reporting units. Data management often involves vast quantities of time, money, and talent. A model may become a major aid to efficient data management.

Measurement Applications

One aspect of the explanatory mode stresses the rigorous measurement of system variables. Emphasis is on precision and on the advancement of technique for its own sake. Policy-making concerns are clearly subordinate.

Representative examples of this type of model are found in any standard econometrics text, in Kalman Cohen's fine doctoral dissertation,[7] in the Brookings Institution's econometric model of the United States,[8] and in George Fishman's tightly written piece on measurement and analysis of synthetic data.[9]

Characteristically, models applied as measurement devices rely on nearly error-free data: the cleaner the better, which, for Fishman, meant manufacturing his own. These variables may be configured together in numerous individual relationships, as in the case of the Brookings model; however, the individual relationships are often structured simply and limited to a few distinct variables. Finally, these models often operate in a "one period change" mode; parameters are reset after each iteration to force observed data and model outputs to correspond. For measurement, the richer the data environment, the better.

To the extent that one has *much, good, clean* data on well-defined variables, measurement considerations may predominate. To the extent that the variables have some policy implication, there may be cause to extend a measurement device somewhat into policy-making—as has been the Brookings' experience. It is worth noting that policy relevance derives less from the elegance and rigor of that device than from its Keynesian theoretical underpinnings, which "provided a set of causal laws whose independent variables were accessible to action in the immediate present."[10] Most measurement exercises do not benefit from profound theoretical insight. The usual case is the one Millikan relates, in which a measurement specialist discards

those aspects of the problem which do not interest him [on the grounds] that there is no point in his doing research on problems which are inherently not researchable. The higher his standards of scientific research, the narrower will be his selection of problems and the greater the eventual frustration of the customer with the result.[11]

Theoretical Applications

Closely related to the measurement application is a concern for theory building. For some, separating these may seem stiff and unnatural; but the distinction is useful. Recall, however, that theory building and measurement are constituent characteristics of our explanatory intellectual mode. Using a model as a theoretical device may be a reasonable strategy in an impoverished data environment or in the instance of conflicting, equally plausible theoretical points of view. We have considered means for appraising a theory that is embedded in a model. The present question is how a model might be employed to enhance our theoretical understanding.

Guy Orcutt and his associates have led the way in increasing theoretical competency, particularly at the micro-analytic level.[12] Geoffrey Clarkson added considerably to our theoretical understanding of a class of investment behavior.[13] J. P. Crecine did much the same thing for municipal budget decision-making theory.[14] And finally, preliminary efforts have been made to build contextual theories of modernization and mass political-behavior processes.[15]

No one claims that these theory-building attempts are directly applicable to a specific policy context. In general, these efforts are characterized by their concern for replication of some specific structural processes thought to be producing observed behavior. Empirical referents predominate over concerns for "error-free" or easily measured data. Although these examples are all logically consistent, their predictive power is either weak or untried.

A model may be theoretically feasible if one is primarily concerned with the description of processes and the development of contextual interrelationships. It should be flexible enough to permit the redefinition of theoretical-behavioral elements and relationships without destroying the overall processing or operation of the model. It may be constructed in functional or logical modules that facilitate understanding and "tinkering" with larger-scale subsystems or subroutines. It does not have to be data dependent; emphasis is on the complexity of the internal workings and their rich, derivative behavior, not on the manipulation and reduction of quantities of data.

Educational Applications

In a real sense, all models have an educational application. However, a model may be built specifically to satisfy instructional or heuristic requirements.

The most visible proponents of educational applications in the urban context are Richard Duke[16] and Alan Feldt.[17] Duke's METRO game-simulation is an elaborate teaching device of considerable scope, utilizing component parts and routines of his own and others' design. Its purpose is to create an "urban-like" environment in which decision-makers and students may learn about the complexity generally thought operating in a hypothetical urban context much like East Lansing, Michigan.

Feldt accurately characterizes most educational applications as "highly effective teaching [heuristic] and communication devices," whose "utility for prediction and replication tends to be low."[18] One might elaborate by noting the limited scope, gross detail, and necessarily small or outdated data bases associated with most educational applications.

Assessment criteria for this class of models are minimally restrictive, given a general definition of educational application: any model produces *some* educational benefits. Adopting a more restricted conception of education would underscore the criteria of *interest, manageability, flexibility,* and *economy.* A model should be intrinsically interesting for the phenomena it considers or extrinsically interesting for the details of its design (or misdesign); it should be easy for unsophisticated users to set up and run, i.e. it should be fully documented and should have input and output formats that are easy to comprehend; it should be flexible enough that individual relationships can be altered and whole subsystems can be replaced; and it should be relatively inexpensive to run in terms of computer time and supporting personnel. After all, it is only a game.

Policy-Making Applications

Specifying, assisting, or informing policy is not a game, although these uses include many concerns that are common to other potential applications. The difference between a theoretical application and a policy application, for example, is not incremental or quantitative, it is discontinuous and qualitative. Accordingly, more thorough consideration will be given to this application category.

Some Possible Uses. Formal models, and the research supporting them, may be used for several distinct policy purposes. Let us postulate that the specialized requirements of each potentially demand specialized models as well. At the least, individual differences among intended usages must be considered when deciding whether there is "significant correspondence" between the policy-maker's needs and the model's capabilities.

A model may be used *to validate a decision already made.* In this context, model as propaganda device, stringent scientific appraisal criteria are relied upon only to the extent that the model should not be patently bogus. This is a question of degree, actually, because all models are in one sense "fake." In another policy context, the model-building process might be used *to slow down or avoid making a decision.*[19] It is conceivable that a problem of the magnitude of urban renewal, for example, could best be confronted politically through an avoidance strategy. This might include a large data-collecting and model-building component intended to produce, at some unspecified future date, ameliorative recommendations based on the best "scientific" findings.[20] Other possible policy uses would include *descriptive clarification,* the determination of the present state and past trends of the problem context; *unconditional forecasting,* the identification for policy-makers of impending areas of concern in the context; *normative specification,* the creation and examination of various desired end states for the context; and *program evaluation,* the assessment of the effectiveness of various prior public interventions.

In general, there are few applications of existing models that one can identify as being policy specific, whatever the level or means of classification.[21] Several explanations for this seem plausible.

Policy Models: A Scarce Commodity. Recalling an earlier discussion of different intellectual orientations helps to characterize models for policy application. In general, these models reflect the biases of the policy-maker as caricatured in Exhibit 2-1. The models deal with specific, well-designated contexts, have finely detailed variables, and consider multiple developmental pathways from the projective perspective. To the extent that the "clash of interest and utility" between researcher and policy-maker is resolved in the former's favor, one may predict that policy applications will be slighted.[22] To the extent that a model is biased toward "purer" scientific characteristics of measurement and theory building, it may lose its appropriateness as a tool for policymaking. For example, the well-known *ceterius paribus* assumption of theoretical social science, while aiding enormously in clarifying the structure of a context, limits the possibilities of system change to one or a few potential paths. To the extent that a model depends upon such an assumption for its explanatory elegance, its usefulness as a policy device may diminish. Let us turn our attention to other general questions reasonably posed in appraising the suitability of a model for policy-making purposes.

Policy Criteria: A Suggested Checklist. In the ex ante situation, where one is contemplating construction of a formal model, concern for the *analytical question* has rightly been cited by Merton, and others, as fundamental:

Experience suggests that the policy-maker seldom formulates his practical problem in terms sufficiently precise to permit the researcher to design an appropriate investigation. Characteristically, the problem is so stated as to result in the possibility of the researcher being seriously misled as to the "basic" aspects of the problem which gives rise to the contemplated research. This initial clarification of the practical problem, therefore, is the first crucial step in applied social science.[23]

"What's the question?" is to a large extent dependent upon the researcher's skill, interest, and sensitivity in understanding the policymaker's problem.

After the question has been mutually agreed upon, subject to marginal reformulation as the research progresses and participants "learn," it is worth resolving the extent to which answering the question will be useful to the policy-maker. Utility might be determined in terms of the policy-maker's control over the variables encompassed by the question.

THE APPRAISAL FUNCTION

Catherine Bauer cited this for the planning context: "What the planner wants to know is the specific effect of a particular factor in the environment over which he has some *bona fide* control."[24] If there is agreement that an answer to the question would be useful and that the policy-maker does indeed have a measure of control, then one might begin asking more scientific questions.

No set of questions or criteria can provide the final word. However, the following questions might serve as a point of departure for more intensive examinations of the feasibility and desirability of producing a computer simulation model for policy purposes. Quite different criteria, overlapping only incidentally with these, would be required for different purposes, e.g. theory building, education, data manipulation, and so forth.

1. Are the variables related to the question accessible and measurable at acceptable costs?
2. Is there a good data bank containing these variables already? Is it accessible? Are the variables in a flexible, usable format?
3. Is there sufficient reliable theory concerning the question to enable the construction of a model that will have a good representation? Or, are the phenomena encompassed by the question well understood?
4. Will it be necessary to consider alternative theoretical possibilities? If so, are there data or are the prospects for obtaining them acceptable, relative to their cost?

To the extent that these issues are not resolvable, computer modeling for policy application may be a waste of time and other scarce resources. Alternative approaches may be more appropriate and potentially more productive.

Questions of general policy appropriateness that might be asked after the fact of model construction would include the following:

1. Is the distortion between the model outputs and what the policy-maker is looking for so large that the model can be pragmatically rejected out of hand? Can the distortion be reduced? At a reasonable cost in time, effort, and money?
2. Are the model's output and input generally intelligible; are they in a form that is familiar to the policy-maker?
3. Does the model offend "common sense"?
4. Are elements of the identified question excluded out of ignorance or in the interests of generalization or precision?
5. Is the model static and descriptive in the interest of simplification?
6. Is it possible to include submodels or to change individual behavioral relationships that appear to have a bearing on the question without destroying the processing or the logic of the model and without significantly increasing its operating costs?

7. Are variables of direct relevance to the question, as determined empirically and by sensitivity testing, omitted in the interest of precision?

8. Is the model able to at least predict, through reconstruction, the time series upon which it is formulated? Has it been able to predict time series from the reference system that has been developed subsequent to the model's formulation?

9. If there are known structural changes in the empirical problem context, are provisions made in the model to capture these? That is, if there are increasing numbers of disaggregations, changing parameters, or precipitating discontinuous events in the context, are these taken into account? Or are these events ignored or assumed away?

10. Are the policy interpretations of various model entities, and their recommended changes, consonant with the ethical-moral and professional standards of the policy-makers and the affected population?

To the extent that these questions are not satisfactorily answered, the model is not suitable as a policy-making device.

Public officials can be led to expect far too much from social science research in general, and from simulation activities in particular, concerning the answering of a class of difficult questions that are not scientific in the commonly accepted sense. Unfortunately, these are political questions, such as, "What should the goals of the city or the nation be? What should we politicians do about them? To whom should we do it?" Expectations become inflated in the absence of information on the limits and the possibilities of present-day social science. For example, prediction is expected even when the crudest understanding has not yet been achieved. This particular misconception is widespread and not limited to any special group of individuals.

Policy-making and Computer Simulation.[25] Simulation might be used when (1) it is either impossible or extremely costly to observe certain processes in the real world; (2) the observed system is too complex to be described by a set of mathematical equations; (3) no straightforward analytical technique exists for solution of appropriate mathematical equations; and (4) it is either impossible or very costly to obtain data for the more complicated mathematical models describing a system.

Simulation should not be used when (1) simpler techniques exist; (2) data are inadequate; (3) objectives (the "Question") are not clear; (4) there are short-term deadlines; and (5) the problems are minor or trivial.

At the very best, simulation can help to answer questions that seek useful insights about simple structures and gross interactions in a moderately well defined context. As important as those activities are to a juvenile discipline and an infantile methodology, they are patently unsatisfactory for the purposes of making public policy.

THE APPRAISAL FUNCTION

The tragedy with many innovations is that as an innovation diffuses, it becomes distorted, abused, or exploited for private gain. Quite typically the early claims for miracle curatives have given way to bitter disillusionment. Partial acceptance, based on a more realistic assessment of the true worth of an innovation, proceeds, if at all, only after much careful matching of need and capability. This book is directed to the difficult but critical task of generating a set of criteria by which a particularly promising innovation may be realistically measured. Perhaps in time disillusionment will yield to enlightened acceptance, and then we may all get on with the more pressing tasks at hand.

Synopsis

Various aspects of an appraisal function, including fundamental distinctions between several intellectual orientations, summarized as reflective, explanatory, and manipulative modes; various theoretical, technical, and ethical choices, characterized as inclusions and omissions of content and procedure; and various potential applications, described in terms of measurement, data processing, theory building, education, or policy-making, were elaborated in some detail. Hopefully, several major, substantial issues have been raised.

Each of these aspects may be represented as a choice, as an opportunity or set of opportunities taken and forgone. In constructing a formal model, one intellectual orientation is stressed at the relative expense of unstressed orientations. Including some theoretical notions implies the exclusion of others. Acceptance of the consequences of certain technical assumptions and procedures implies the rejection of others. Finally, the clear specification of one application may necessarily exclude other potential applications.

These choices are essentially simplifications that imply certain costs, and require appraisal as to their more general effects with respect to specific questions and purposes.

Speaking to the relatively easier issues, it goes almost without saying that it is in one's general interest to minimize technical deficiencies—that is to say, to optimize those choices over which one has greatest control. A badly constructed or plainly erroneous model is of little value at all. A more difficult consideration is the degree to which one uses theoretical information to construct a model. Weaknesses in the general theoretical fabric must be acknowledged; undue confidence in models configured from dubious or speculative theories must be guarded against; and the use of nonempirical and otherwise untested structural conjectures must be avoided. A computer model represents a theory. Applying the model is the same as applying the theory. Finally, one needs consciously to establish priorities for what is to be lost by pursuing one application as opposed to any other. Certainly no one should expect an abstract, elegant, theoretical construct to be directly useful as an applied policy-making device; scientific-intellectual satisfaction ought not be substituted for pragmatic satisfaction—the basic criteria are considerably different.

What has been a common thread in this discussion is simplification. How simplifying choices are made and what results must be carefully considered.

PART II

COMPLEXITY, SIMULATION, AND THE SOCIAL PROCESS

Introduction

The nature of man is intricate; the objects of society are of the greatest possible complexity; and therefore no simple disposition or direction of power can be suitable either to man's nature, or to the quality of his affairs.

Edmund Burke
*Reflections on the
Revolution in France*[1]

No serious social scientist would deny the proposition that political and social systems are complex. One manifestation of systemic complexity, in the words of a political theorist, is that "the operation of no one part can be fully understood without reference to the way in which the whole itself operates."[2] Stated differently, the significance of each element of a system is defined by the structure of other elements in the configuration. There is no single suitable definition of complexity, although Herbert Simon's rough approximation is at least a serviceable starting point. For him, a complex system is

one made up of a large number of parts that interact in a nonsimple way. In such systems, the whole is more than the sum of the parts, not in an ultimate metaphysical sense, but in the important pragmatic sense that, given the properties of the parts and the laws of their interaction, it is not a trivial matter to infer the properties of the whole. In the face of complexity, an in-principle reductionist may be at the same time a pragmatic holist.[3]

Confronted with this complexity, social scientists have reacted in the only way possible: we have simplified, emphasizing some aspects of social phenomena to the exclusion of others. Richard Bellman and Robert Kalaba have remarked in this general regard that

it is ironical in science that in order to understand, we must throw away information. We cannot, at least at this level of our intellectual development, grapple with a high order of complexity. Consequently, we must simplify.[4]

The Need to Simplify: Theoretical Considerations. Underlying the need to simplify is the pragmatic constraint of man's limitations as an information-processing device. If one understands, as George Miller has persuasively demonstrated, that man's "span of absolute judgment and the span of immediate memory impose severe limitations on the amount of information that we are able to receive, process, and remember,"[5] then the consequences are more comprehensible as well. Indeed, limited human capacity "has made it necessary for us to discover ways to abstract the essential features of our universe and to express these features in simple laws that we are capable of comprehending in a single act or thought."[6] Unfortunately, the subject matter does not usually lend itself to such intellectual operations.

Earlier we pointed out the "in principle" desirability of integrating various orientations, perspectives, and partial theories to improve the explanatory power of social theory. The payoffs from such integration are many and mostly obvious; to accomplish it we must deal with "organized complexity," a term fashioned by Warren Weaver in 1948 to characterize and distinguish social from natural phenomena. Problems of *organized complexity* "involve dealing simultaneously with a *sizable number of factors which are interrelated into an organic whole.*"[7] Jay Forrester has described complex social systems as being "high-order, multiple-loop, non-linear, feedback-structures," whose significance is in the

interactions of the psychological, the economic, the technical, the cultural, and the political [intellectual disciplines]. The interactions between these are often more important than the internal content of any one alone. Yet, if they are isolated in our study and thinking, the interactions will never come into view.[8]

One partial explanation of this isolation in thought and interaction in reality has been advanced by Simon as a theory of nearly decomposable systems "in which the interactions among the subsystems are weak but not negligible."[9] Christopher Alexander has gone one step farther and suggested that urban social phenomena are not so easily decomposed; rather, in set theoretical terminology, "a city is not a tree," a root with clearly defined branches. On the contrary, cities are filled with complex overlap and in structure more accurately resemble a semilattice of many interconnected points.[10]

The attempt to discover decomposed, simple, treelike structures where interconnected and overlapping structures exist has given rise to overly simple theoretical accounts and sophisticated symbol systems. Simple utopian concepts, for example, are nonetheless utopian whether cast in computer or mathematical codes and symbols.

Operational Considerations. Efforts to grapple with governmental problems increasingly turn to technical expertise as a means of integrating technical with what we might imprecisely label "political" information. Technical professionals are thought to be skilled in understanding the complexity and uncertainties of an environment. For this supposed skill, they are accepted and trusted by those in positions of political authority and control; the result is an often reluctant but nonetheless increasing faith among political men in scientific explanations of both complexity and uncertainty.

While politicians are identifying more strongly with the professional experts, the loyalties of the experts are unclear. Professional values and relationships tend to supersede public ones. Furthermore, as the problems and the institutions set up to solve them become larger and more complex, it becomes increasingly difficult to assign overall responsibility. A complex problem is divided into smaller parts; each participant in the problem-solving process is responsible only for his small part. The degree of fragmentation in a problem-solving effort is an important operational indicator of the complexity of the problem.

While the professional-political relationship is not very well understood, from past experience it is reasonable to assume that we shall be seeing more, not less, reliance upon specialists and specialized methodologies in government. In the defense sector, extraordinarily complex tasks have for many years been routinely parceled out to highly specialized organizations and individuals for analysis and recommendation. Increasingly, domestic problems are being handled in the same manner.

This inquiry will look at the efforts of several specialized problem-solving institutions, assessing their impacts on public decision-making in two urban environments. However, we defer this matter until Part III. First, we explore briefly the general, abstract nature of organized complexity, with an eye toward the implications of complexity for the process of solving problems of public policy.

7

On Size and Organized Complexity: Some Theoretical Considerations*

The subtility of nature is far beyond that of sense or of the understanding; so that the specious meditations, speculations, and theories of mankind are but a kind of insanity, only there is no one to stand by and observe it.

Francis Bacon
Novum Organum, Book I[1]

Insanity is easily attributed to weaknesses of the intellect. The extent of the affliction is great and debilitating; the practical implications for theory building and understanding are devastating.

Human Limitations

"Man is a miserable component in a communication system," asserts George Miller in his essay, "The Human Link in Communication Systems":[2] "He has a narrow bandwidth, a high noise level, is expensive to maintain, and sleeps eight hours out of every twenty-four." Not only that, but he is guilty of "constantly taking information given in one form and translating it into alternative forms, searching for ways to map a strange, new phenomenon into simple and more familiar ones."[3] Moreover, as Jean Rostand suggests, regarding the physical limitations of the eye:

---

*Portions of this chapter have been presented in a modified form as "Analysis of Complex Systems: An Experiment and Its Implications for Policymaking," in Todd R. LaPorte, ed., *Organized Social Complexity: Challenge to Politics and Policy* (unpublished MS).

[The eye] has only a restrictive field of vision. Thus it may not be able to take in an entire phenomenon and may have to disperse and divide its attention by darting from place to place. *Each act of concentration on a given point simply means lack of attention to other points.*[4]

Or as von Neumann postulated, in connection with some quirks in the internal processing of information in the brain itself:

[Because of the brain's simultaneous reception and processing of information], the logical approach and structure in natural automata may be expected to differ widely from those in artificial automata.[5]

The nervous system is thought to be statistically oriented, which implies that it operates on frequencies of periodic pulses not discrete markers, a supposition which accounts for system reliability *and* imprecision.[6]

What results is consistent: As an empirical context increases in absolute size, the accuracy with which any one element is perceived rapidly decreases beyond some inelastic limit of human capacity.[7] The limit of one's *span of absolute judgment* is not great, "usually somewhere in the neighborhood of seven . . . unidimensional judgments."[8] As this limit is surpassed, we must devise means to recode individual elements into "larger and larger chunks, each chunk containing more information than before."[9] Recoding is however limited by the ingenuity required to create new codes that correspond to some realistic reference system. The divergence between codes and the reference systems in complex contexts was noted by Bacon 350 years ago:

The human understanding, from its peculiar nature, easily supposes a greater degree of order and equality in things than it really finds; and although many things in nature be *sui generis* and most irregular, will yet invent parallels and conjugates and relatives, where no such thing is.[10]

We are grossly imprecise but fairly reliable empirical devices. It is understandable that contexts of simple structure have yielded to our limited theoretical penetration. It is also plausible to assume that more complex, organized structures will be more resistent to probing. If we persistently "suppose a greater degree of order and equality in things" than there really is, should we expect otherwise?

Organized Complexity

Imagine a continuum extending from zero to a very large number, say one million. Problems at the low end of the continuum (numbering from 1×10^0 to some absolute upward limit of 1×10^1 elements) may be characterized as "problems of simplicity." Newtonian physics and the physical sciences prior to 1900, according to Weaver, represent this class of problem.[11] Force equals mass times acceleration with reassuring regularity. Problems at the upper end of the continuum are characterized by their disorganization and distributional properties, factors leading to statistical management. The problem of "disorganized complexity"

is a problem in which the number of variables is very large, and one in which each of the many variables has a behavior which is individually erratic, or perhaps totally unknown. However, in spite of this helter-skelter, or unknown, behavior of all the individual variables, the system as a whole possesses certain orderly and analyzable properties.[12]

Examples of disorganized complexity would include gas problems in chemistry, actuarial problems, and celestial mechanics. The greater the number of elements, the easier it is to discern patterns and to measure aggregate, average systemic behavior. Largely unsuccessful are analytical experiences with problems in the intermediate range of the imaginary continuum. These problems, which feature discernible aspects of self-conscious organization or purposiveness, Weaver labels "organized complexity." The term includes most social phenomena.[13]

Organized complexity is little understood. In fact our repeated attempts to force ill-suited statistical analyses on these problem contexts has obscured their special character. This is not to say that some statisticians haven't been aware of these technical limitations; one need only consult Kendall's melancholy presidential address to the Royal Statistical Society, "Natural Law in the Social Sciences," to obtain a measure of their impotence.

The sheer shortage of information and the intractability of multivariate complexes compel us to deal with summary data. The result is that we are in some danger of generating by the averaging process patterns which are not really there . . . [14]

Powerful statistical techniques do not prevent us from making the pedestrian errors of simplification that Bacon noted; modern methods only obscure these hoary patterns of thought. Patterns of organized complexity

are just too complicated to yield to the old nineteenth-century techniques which were so dramatically successful on two-, three-, or four-variable problems of simplicity. These new problems, moreover, cannot be handled with the statistical techniques so effective in *describing average behavior in problems of disorganized complexity.*[15]

Three characteristics of organized complexity that are somewhat known deal with matters of size, nonlinearity, and aspects of structural composition.

Elements of systems of organized complexity surely fall within the middle range of size on the imaginary continuum. Furthermore, the number of temporal states or orders that must be accounted for in describing systemic behavior is large. Forrester suggests a range between tenth and hundredth order,[16] a consideration partially constraining an infinite temporal regression alluded to by Stuart Bruchey:

The conditions of any event . . . must beat their way back into the past via a process of "infinite" regression until they disappear in the mists of the unknowable.[17]

Concern for an expanded temporal order quite clearly diminishes the acceptability of cross-sectional description at a single point or a few points in time. The analysis of specific contexts by time series data must take precedence.

A complex system contains many nonlinear relations and both positive and negative feedbacks, characteristics that allow extremely rich and diverse behavioral patterns to be generated from apparently "simple" structures.[18] Attention, it would seem, could be profitably diverted to the attainment of understanding of these structures. This assertion has not been lost on Gabriel Almond, for one, who notes:

The principal advantage of the system concept is that it analytically differentiates the object of study from its environment; it directs attention to the interaction of the system with other systems or its environment . . . [19]

How one differentiates environment, system, and constituent subsystems is a separate issue not rigorously considered by Almond.

Decomposability

The implications of decomposability, the extent of disconnectedness among systemic elements, have been rigorously studied by Ando, Fisher, and Simon. Simon and Ando summarize their work in terms of dynamic systems represented by nearly decomposable matrices:

We have seen that such systems may be viewed as composite systems, constructed by the superposition of: (1) terms representing interactions of the variables within each subsystem; and (2) terms representing interactions among the subsystems. We conclude that, over a relatively short period, the first group of terms dominates the behavior of the system, and hence each subsystem can be studied (approximately) independently of other subsystems. Over a relatively long period of time, on the other hand, the second group of terms dominates the behavior of the system . . . [20]

The point is this: A system may be broken down into clusters or subsystems of relatively frequent interaction and heightened interdependence.[21] The greater the complexity of a system, the less likely is it that it can be decomposed and the more likely that short-run behavior of any one subsystem will ramify throughout the entire system. To the extent that a system may be broken down into clusters or nearly decomposed subsystems, we may separately analyze their behavior to enhance our understanding of the behavior of the whole. Decomposed and nearly decomposed systems are analytically smaller and less complex than the whole.

Recall our illustrative example from chapter 4. Alternative representations of its structure might be depicted as in Figure 7-1.[22] The matrix

FIGURE 7-1

Structural Representations of Illustrative Examples

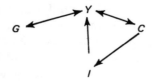

[Direction of arrow represents causal order.]

INPUTS

		Y	C	IN	G
O U T P U T S	Y	0	1	1	1
	C	1	0	0	0
	IN	0	1	1	0
	G	1	0	0	0

format contains either values of *zero*, signifying the presence of a direct structural link, or *one,* standing for the absence of such a link between input (column) variables and output (row) variables. It is a square matrix because the system is closed. Time subscripts are ignored although inputs logically precede outputs. The representation does not signify the strength of interconnections; all it describes is the presence or absence of a direct link. In the illustration, the government element is least connected to the others. Although not decomposed, its connectedness is less than that of the others. The system has seven direct interconnections. If we operate the system through time, the number of indirect links increases dramatically. Even for this very simple system,

FIGURE 7-2

Chain of Indirect Structural Connections for "Y"

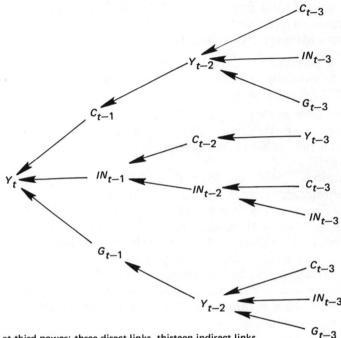

"Y" at third power: three direct links, thirteen indirect links.

by the fourth power of the matrix,[23] *all* variables are linked with forty-two indirect interconnections. Figure 7-2 represents this process. By the tenth power of the matrix, the number of interconnections has increased to 1,431, and the specter of Bruchey's infinite regression begins to confound the analysis. To the extent that a model's elements are interconnected, it becomes increasingly complex. Decomposition is a partial management tactic. To the extent that a system may be decomposed into subsystems (either by function or by location, for example), we may analyze each separately.

Social systems exhibit properties of organized complexity. Their structure contains overlapping interaction among elements, positive and negative feedback control loops, and nonlinear relationships, and they are of high temporal order. These characteristics largely account for the observable diversity of social behavior. Man's limited intellectual apparatus, however, persists in discerning simple, ordered, and sterile regularity in the face of the perverse empirical evidence. Our images are poor proxies for the behavioral reality; our theoretical representations but reflect these defective images.

Images, Totems, and Utopias

In his survey of ideal communities, Thomas Reiner calls our attention to traditional images operating among urban specialists.[24] In general, his review bears witness to Alexander's assessment that men,

trapped by a mental habit, . . . [and] limited as they must be by the capacity of the mind to form intuitively accessible structures, cannot achieve the complexity of the semi-lattice in a single mental act.

Therefore, they must propose and build cities structured like simple trees,[25] devoid of overlapping elements, rigid in structure, and changeless through time. Should one expect more of man's formalizations of these images?

Assumptions[26] following from the treelike perspective are *common to every formal model of the urban social context.*

The tree's *symmetry* is everywhere evident. "Cities look as though they were laid out with straight-edge and T-square." Utopia often is imagined as a vision of an orderly city—clean, neat, harmonious.[27] This conception of "city-as-utopia" has persisted since Aristotle's time at least.[28] Deriving from the geometric, nonoverlapping assumption of order is the practical concern for *boundaries.* Social contexts are usually bounded, often in bizarre ways; however, Utopian imagings seldom take this into account.

It is a curious fact that most people who portray their vision of an ideal political system ignore the limits imposed by the existence of other political systems. . . . political utopias are usually portrayed without the troublesome limitations imposed by foreign relations, which are eliminated by either ignoring them entirely or solving them according to some simple plan.[29]

As it is irrational and conflictful to consider foreign relations, utopian images understandably ignore or "solve them according to some simple plan." Utopian images are *rational* and as *free from conflict as possible.*[30] And "since there is no conflict, there is no need for hidden motives. Men are quite plastic and manipulable, and willing to be manipulated."[31] Related to the assumptions of symmetry, rationality, and order is the temporal bias toward static *equilibrium.*[32] The limitations of the concept are regularly overlooked. Although we "know perfectly well that we shall not find facts in a state of equilibrium,"[33] we are seduced by the irresistibility, the orderliness, the symmetry of the idea of harmonious equilibrium. After all, if the "theories of mankind are but a kind of insanity," the assumption of equilibrium is but one additional dimension of that insanity.

The common operating assumptions of urban model building are utopian in the senses we describe here. Models and systems of planning are just as "utterly visionary in concept and disappointing in execution"[34] as the classical utopias because they suffer from the same conceptual and intellectual shortcomings. These new utopias may even be less satisfactory than the old ones. To the extent that the "humanitarian bent has disappeared," and has been replaced instead by a "dominant value orientation . . . best described as 'efficiency' rather than 'humanitarianism,' "[35] they *are* worse.

The question of size has direct bearing on these issues of complexity. Increasing the size of a social context increases its intrinsic complexity and analytical difficulty. Let us increase the size of some small systems to demonstrate the point.

Orientation, Purpose, and Simplicity

The issue of size has long held the attention of students of society. In the urban context, for example, Plato reportedly assigned a population of 5,040 to his ideal polis.[36] While the conclusiveness of the number is open to discussion, the motives that prompted its creation are not: How large must a social context be to afford necessities and amenities and how small must it be to avoid general diseconomies?[37] The present question is of similar form. How large must a formal model of a social context be to be realistic and interesting, and how small must it be to be understandable and manageable? Neither form of the question of size is easily dismissed; however, we shall concentrate on certain dimensions of the latter in an effort to understand a common class of models represented in our two case studies.

The size of a state vector $[X_t]$ is a key determinant of a system's complexity. The greater the number of states, the greater the potential complexity. Ashby has noted,

in the concepts of cybernetics, a system's "largeness" must refer to the number of distinctions made: either to the number of states available or, if its states are defined by a vector, to the number of components in the vector (i.e. to the number of its variables or of its degrees of freedom . . .).[38]

The number of states is the number of values that components or elements can assume. The number of components is the number of variables and parameters in the state vector. For simple models it is often possible to apply mathematical techniques to obtain a set of solutions for any variable $x_{i,t}$ at time t in terms of a set of parameters and initial conditions. Such solutions, highly prized and comforting to many analysts, become more difficult to achieve as the quantity and form of relationships respectively increase in number and difficulty.[39]

Once again the orientations and purposes of policy-maker and scientist conflict. A policy-maker's interest is in increasing the chance of attaining a specific desired outcome (alternatively—avoiding undesired outcomes) in a specific space-time configuration. The scientist is more concerned with the verifiability of his theory in many contexts. Crudely, a formal theoretical model, which one is able to solve by establishing and applying *existence* theorems, and, even more scientifically satisfying, *uniqueness* theorems, will be stripped of "robustness" to the point where its utility to a policy-maker is nil. If one's purpose is manipulative, a robust theory comprised of elements that are interesting and accessible to policy-makers is preferable to simpler, sparser, but solvable formulations. This powerful assertion is made on the assumption that one's primary concern is problem-solving and on the condition that the theoretical criteria of consistency, meaning, and plausibility are met.[40]

It is undeniable that this trade-off is profoundly difficult to make. Arguing for simplification, Mario Bunge contends that "the falsity of simple theories is usually easier to expose than the falsity of complex theories, on condition that they are falsifiable at all."[41] The tension between explanatory and manipulative orientations is again called to our attention by forcing a choice from among alternative theoretical images:

[Because] any number of testable systems can be invented to cope with a given set of empirical data; the question is to hit on the *truest* one—a scientific problem—and to *recognize the signs* of approximate truth—a metascientific problem.[42]

For systems of organized complexity it is usually necessary to abandon mathematical techniques to deduce system behavior. To accomplish these deductions, one specifies values for each of the initial conditions and parameters and calculates the values of these variables for the next and all subsequent time periods in the analysis. To deduce the qualitative performance of a given system, it is necessary to repeat these calculations for each unique set of initial conditions and parameters and to examine the results separately. Simulation, the procedure just outlined, is far less powerful than mathematics, but it can be used to explore *larger*, more *robust* systems—a fact of fundamental consequence for policy analysis.

Dimensions

Using our simple example once again, the question of model size may be examined with respect to the inclusion and representation of time, numbers of elements, forms of relationships, degrees of interconnection, and uncertainty.

Time. As the projected time frame expands beyond the immediate, marginal present, the number of possible states a system may assume rapidly increases. This state of affairs contrasts sharply with that of history, in which a single behavioral trace from among all inherent possibilities has been divulged. Projecting into the future involves the selection, from among an extremely large number of possible traces, of that *one* having the greatest likelihood of developing. The greater the extension of the time frame and consequent increase in potential states, the less the likelihood of anticipating the system's behavior. Static analysis of a model is a simpler task than the analysis of a system for a number of historical periods and infinitely simpler than the analysis of that same system for a like number of projected periods. Expanding the temporal frame of reference increases complexity.

Elements. The size of a system may be increased by considering new variables and parameters, by increasing the number of sectoral disaggregations, or by improving the quality of measurement. The addition of variables and parameters makes possible extra system states. Assume that population affects the illustrative example. Then hypothesize that the level of population at any point in time is equal to the population and the net result of births and deaths for the prior period.

$$N_{t+1} = N_t + (B_t - D_t) \tag{7.1}$$

where,

N_t = total population at time t.
B_t = births at time t.
D_t = deaths at time t.

Assume also that the ratio of births to deaths is relatively fixed for the analytical period and can be adequately represented as a percentage rate of growth, then

$$N_{t+1} = (1.0 + PR) N_t \tag{7.2}$$

where,

PR = average percent rate of natural increase of population

The old system has been increased to five variables and four parameters and is larger even though the new elements have not as yet been structurally connected to it.

The illustration may be enlarged by considering disaggregated sectors which, to begin with, are assumed to be structurally identical and devoid of interchanges among sectors. Sectors are often represented with a letter subscript as follows:

$$[X_{i,t+1}] = G\ [X_{i,t}] \qquad\qquad (7.3)$$

This disaggregation could stand for separate economic or social functions, but in the models considered here it represents a distinct spatial location. For example, a two-sector model might separately consider the city and its surrounding countryside in a given context: a convenience when rates and values of elements are empirically disparate or where aggregated behavior offers insufficient detail for a given problem. In any event, increasing sectoral disaggregations, *ceteris paribus*, increases both analytical size and inherent complexity.

Reconsider the idea that increasing the number of time periods increases system size. Now it is easier to accept the subtler point that a "system may also be made larger . . . if, the number of variables [elements] being fixed, each is measured more precisely, so as to make it show more distinguishable states."[43] Given the poor quality of data in most social science contexts, this point concerns us least.

Relationships. Just as the elements increased the size of the system, so, too, did their interrelationship. The system was made larger by the addition of two elements *and* one relationship in the previous example. Alternative functional forms may also increase size. Population growth, for example, is frequently represented as a complex logistic function rather than the simple linear function given in (7.2). The use of such nonlinear forms, all other things being equal, will increase a system's complexity.

Connections. Complexity also varies with the degree of connectedness among elements as implied in the set of processes $[G]$. We have considered nearly and completely decomposed systems to be those in which interactions with other systems are negligible or nonexistent. A decomposed system, by this reasoning, is less complex than one that is nearly decomposed; in other words, the greater the number of interconnections among subsystems, the greater the degree of overall complexity. Similarly, the greater the number of connections between elements within a subsystem, the greater the subsystem's complexity.

In our example, let us increase connectedness by hypothesizing that appropriate variables are per capita measures rather than totals. Relationship (4.2), and others, now take on one of two forms, either as in (7.4),

$$\frac{C_{t+1}}{N_{t+1}} = \alpha \frac{Y_t}{N_t} \qquad\qquad (7.4)$$

or, equivalently, as a fixed proportion of income in period t, times the proportionate increase in population in (7.5).

$$C_{t+1} = \alpha Y_t \frac{N_{t+1}}{N_t} \tag{7.5}$$

The connectedness matrix indicates the impact of this one simple change. Recall that the original matrix had seven direct interconnections; by the fourth power of the matrix all variables were interrelated by forty-two indirect interconnections, and at the tenth power, there were 1,431 such links. The addition of two elements, one relationship, and one hypothesis yields an initial matrix of eleven direct links, seventy-eight indirect links at the fourth power, and 2,770 indirect links at the tenth power.[44] Complexity indeed varies with the degree of structural connectedness.

Another aspect of connectedness is the effect of thresholds below which relationships connecting elements are insignificant and above which they must be considered.

Thus there exist factors, such as "height of thresholds" . . . which can vary a large system continuously along the whole range that has at one end the totally-joined form, in which every variable has an immediate effect on every other variable, and at the other end the totally-unjoined form in which every variable is independent of every other. Systems can thus show more or less of "wholeness."[45]

As Ashby's formulation in terms of thresholds suggests, the degree of connectedness depends upon the magnitude of cause and effect as determined by the values of the elements.

The simple connectedness matrix has not taken thresholds into account and has implicitly assumed a binary case: either a connection exists or it does not. Assuming the operation of thresholds, identical structures will differ in their degree of complexity from case to case depending upon the magnitudes of specific elements.

Uncertainty. System size increases as the amount and kind of uncertainty increase. It is useful to distinguish between uncertainty of measurement and uncertainty of specification or stochastic processes.[46]

Uncertainty of specification and stochastic disturbances has been represented symbolically by μ in relationship (3.3), reproduced here.

$$x_{2,t} = x_{2,t-1} + \alpha_1(x_{1,t} - x_{i,t-1}) + \mu \tag{3.3}$$

where,

μ = stochastic or random effects measured in a consistent unit.

Specification error derives from incorrect or oversimplified structural representation. Stochastic effects are exogenous contextual events not accounted for by the model.

Measurement error may be represented in a simulation model by disturbing the specific values of a model's initial conditions by some factor from a random distribution. For example, the initial value of $x_{1,t}$ from relationship (3.3) might be known within a margin of error of, say, plus or minus 10 percent. We could represent this by generating a random number, scaling it to the dimensions of the initial value, and recomputing a new value within the margin of error.

Conscious consideration of these kinds of uncertainty increases the inherent complexity of the theoretical context and the analytical difficulty of the formalized representation of that context. Uncertainty about the reality context remains; deciding if and how to draw uncertainty into replicates of that reality is at issue. To the extent that one supersedes determinism to account for errors of measurement and specification and to consider stochastic processes, a system becomes larger, more complex, and analytically more difficult.

Summary

Size and its several composite dimensions of time, elements, relationships, interconnections, and uncertainty provide a means to examine fundamental methodological, philosophical, and pragmatic issues in the social sciences.[47] Our present purpose is concentrated on the last issue. What dimensions of size seem most critical in complicating a model and rendering it analytically unmanageable? And restating our opening questions: How large must a model be to be interesting or realistic? How small must it be to be tractable for purposes of analysis and appraisal? Is it, in short, possible to imagine and represent a given social context without "killing" it in the process?[48] We shall consider these questions after discussing what implications size might have on the operational context in which the solution of urban problems is attempted.

8

On Size and Organized Complexity: Some Operational Considerations

> ... the history of scientific progress tells us of complex organizations found precisely where we looked for simple order.... If the human mind had devised the world, it would be a dead world.
>
> Bertrand de Jouvenal
> *The Art of Conjecture*[1]

Introduction

Fragmentation is one common result of increasing the size and complexity of problems confronting organizations. By breaking such problems down into their constituent parts, one may gain some insight into their difficulty and may even occasionally solve one of them. However, in the process, accounting for who is responsible for what aspects of the problem that produce what outcomes is made extremely problematic. Fragmented, rational, individual behaviors tend to produce somewhat irrational, unintended, and often undesirable collective outcomes.

Let us distinguish between the research process and the institutional context in which the research is being done.

Fragmented Problem Solving

Increasing the size of an institutional setting potentially increases the number of decisions and outcomes, increases the level of uncertainty about which possibilities will in fact be selected, and, through fragmen-

83

tation, ordinarily decreases the chances that any one individual will either know what is going on or take responsibility for it.

With increased institutional complexity one should expect the quantity and the diversity of available and potentially competing system interpretations to increase. Depending upon the general stakes at issue and the perceptions of possible threats and payoffs held by concerned participants, these diverse interpretations may seriously hinder the institution's operation. One might argue that up to some manageable limit such diversity is a positive attribute. Problem-solving behavior requires the consideration of a number of plausible alternative courses of action and the selection of the course having the greatest probability of success.[2] In more operational terms, the division of labor among specialists may allow more and more representative common interests to be heard and selected from. But on the other hand, specialists may only serve to confuse or distort these common interests. Practically, it seems that the "manageable limit" is surpassed regularly with dysfunctional consequences in many institutions.

Concisely, I argue that specialized professional concerns, manifested in several ways, are seriously impeding policy-making.

Academics. Academic specialists respond to the problems of central interest to themselves and to their professional colleagues. Publication of scholarly works to gain the approval of one's peers is a legitimate academic goal, whose utility for any specific policy problem is at best incidental and at worst misleading. While it is a perfectly legitimate academic concern to do pioneering theoretical development or basic experimentation, the utility of such activities to policy-makers is often not entirely clear. To the extent that discipline and policy imperatives diverge, what results from academic activity may well not benefit policy-makers.

Salesmen and Builders. Entrepreneurs serve as an important catalyst between policy-makers and those who possess highly specialized talents and skills. To the extent that brokerage dominates a problem-solving activity, confusion and distortion between the research and policy-making processes may be sufficient to defeat the effective prosecution of both.

Contracts are let to solve policy problems within a period of time for an agreed-upon amount. When time and money are used up, a report containing the "answer" to the problems must be produced. Unfortunately, to secure the contract an entrepreneur's vague and overoptimistic self-assessments frequently confuse what the problem is and distort expectations about what an answer might be.

Entrepreneurs are not necessarily evil or pernicious. Moreover, such undesirable types of behavior are rather easily detected and dealt with; the real problem is subtler and consequently more difficult to understand. Salesmen of problem solutions are seldom versed in the technical intricacies of the products they sell. It is probably unreasonable to expect a simulation salesman to be an expert computer technician. Likewise, one does not expect an automobile salesman to have an engineering degree. There are critical differences, however. When one buys an automobile, questions about the technical proficiency of the designers and the excellence of manufacture are more or less resolved because of external professional standards that guide the former and quality-control procedures that assure the latter. Such is not the case with "simulators" and simulations. Not only are there few discernible scientific standards available to aid in one's evaluation of a computer simulation, there is little agreement among professionals in the trade as to what standards are pertinent or ought to be developed. Certain low levels of misfeasance and abuse are tolerable for a profession; however, as the stakes increase, such laxity may become too costly by any measure. For example, building a large-scale simulation and then reselling all or part of it to other users and clients is rational entrepreneurial behavior whose more general consequences may be intolerable. Without adequate standards and procedures for quality control, efforts to maintain proprietary control over a computer simulation may only mask and perpetuate an ill-conceived and poorly executed product. A rational entrepreneurial desire to build a general-purpose urban computer simulation is no guarantee that one can or should be built.

Another result of the fragmented problem-solving process involving users, builders, and entrepreneurs may be a "can do for fee" syndrome.[3] A user buys a complex model or simulation, but he or the person who inherits it does not necessarily understand the whole model, if he ever did. At some point the user wants the model to do something he thought it could or should be able to do, but, for a variety of reasons, he finds out that it cannot. Then he must go back to the salesman and his model-building team, who respond by writing a modification, or an extra subroutine, or entirely new models . . . for a fee. The procedure has an open-endedness that assures the salesman continuing business; however, it appears that it is the user who is getting "the business."

The essential point is this: *Any entrepreneur worth his salt will behave in these ways if he expects to stay in business.* Salesmanship may well be the undoing of what promises to be a highly useful problem-solving technique.

Users and Managers. Because the problem-solving process is complex and fragmented, users essentially come to rely heavily on the simulation-builders. Not understanding precisely what a model can or cannot do, a user has to accept the simulation "black box" on faith. The more faith replaces understanding, the more a user is a prisoner of the builder.

A "good" manager can be technically incompetent. Being an efficient, conscientious, and honorable public servant does not mean that a manager will have any idea of what is happening in the design, construction, and use of a computer simulation. Furthermore, it is quite unreasonable to require public institutions to maintain the amount and diversity of technical talent necessary to meet all the problem contingencies that confront them.

And here, gentle reader, is the rub. The world is complex, and it is important that decision-makers learn to manage their own little segment of it. However, to do so increasingly requires a trusting dependence on specialists whose own rational behavior does not necessarily serve the decision-maker well. Unless and until top decision-makers discover new procedures to understand specialists and what they produce, realistic and creative mastery of the complexity of urban decision-making will continue to be more goal than actuality.

Misperception of the Difficulty of the Task

The problems addressed in the two cases under consideration are monumental. What is known about the underlying mechanisms and processes of urban development is minuscule as compared to what must be learned. Little wonder there is such a divergence between in-principle promotional arguments and what has been realized in practice. Besides the intrinsic difficulties of the problems, management of large-scale computer simulation and model-building projects is also far more demanding than one might imagine. The complexity of both substantive matters and procedures for their management severely confounds the problem-solving task.

Promises and Harsh Reality. We all are exposed to and understand sophisticated promotional techniques. What is not so well understood is the fact that promotion may produce some serious costs, including distortions of reality, losses of control over a context, and gaps in credibility.

"Operational models" that are neither theoretically based, well tested, nor understood, but nonetheless gain the attention of decision-makers, may result in either poor or harmful policy and will eventually earn the decision-makers' enmity for all those who produce computer simulations.

Good specialists, oversold by their capabilities and successes in one area, often believe that what they know is generally applicable. It is self-deluding and probably wrong to assume that what was learned by simulating a military logistic system or a problem from physics will transfer to dissimilar contexts. The warning to beware of the model-builder who can simulate virtually any problem or context is not meant to deprecate the desire to do something to manage hard problems. It has to do with the difficulties of modeling, specification, data gathering, validation, sensitivity analysis, documentation, and question formulation. These are all nasty, hard, and boring subjects that make the difference between the advertised illusions and actually having produced a viable, useful simulation.

Large-scale Simulations Provide Their Own Complexities. Model building is an extraordinarily difficult and normally unpredictable activity. Even when theoretical insights about a given problem are available, it is still far from a sure thing to be able to specify those insights in a productive way. To imagine that such can be accomplished within the constraints of a short-term contract, of say a year or two, for a prespecified amount of money, is illusory. Nothing is strictly "impossible"; however, the probability of building a large-scale urban simulation within prespecified constraints of time and money is so low as to be essentially negligible. This view is asserted for several reasons.

Why is a model being built? There is little understanding of the many reasons why a simulation project is undertaken in the first place. Users may desire to have a model built for other than scientific purposes, a point we have touched on, but serious attention needs to be directed to these other possibilities. Four come to mind, although others doubtless exist.

- Models may be used for advocacy purposes to rationalize a choice that has already been made.
- When problems are particularly difficult, sensitive, or transitory, resort to model building may delay or relieve a user from the onerous task of making a choice.
- Working on routine and noncontroversial problems using modeling methodologies may serve to occupy the time and talent of one's staff. This is a simple fact of bureaucratic life, especially so when a sizable investment has been made in computer equipment and where unevenness in the number and importance of operating tasks necessarily occurs.
- Another political-bureaucratic factor is the need to demonstrate one's progressiveness and the desire to give the appearance of using the most modern management techniques to solve problems. The innate "sexiness" of computer simulation makes it a prime candidate for this purpose.

These are serious matters, because the question of validating a model depends directly and delicately upon the initiator's intended purpose or projected use of a simulation.

Given what appears to be a current lack of interest in documentation procedures and standards, reinvention of the proverbial wheel is a likely outcome for many large-scale simulation activities. Documentation gets overlooked because salesmen and model-builders are less interested in it than they are in producing, for a prespecified sum, an operating model on schedule. Most users do not know or appreciate the importance of documentation. Cumulation of knowledge and effective utilization of a model are both unnecessarily impeded by lax or nonexistent accounting through all aspects of its initiation, promotion, contractual specification, execution, appraisal, and termination.

Besides aiding communication among technical specialists, good documentation helps the processes of external evaluation and is a necessary first step toward the integration of specialized knowledge.

The Urban Problem-Solving Game. Poor documentation is only one operational symptom of fragmentation. Other features of the urban problem-solving game need to be mentioned.

Proposal writing is an art. Not knowing what a "good" versus a "bad" proposal looks like, the most well-intentioned public official is hard-pressed to choose between the vague, jargon-filled, and equivocating menus offered for his approval. Faith and intuition replace intelligent and technically informed selection criteria. The issue is even more pervasive. Without general, professionally held standards and lacking many examples of credible "solutions" to urban problems, research tends to lack direction, except to do more research for its own sake. If no one really knows what an "answer" looks like, much less how to achieve it, should we expect otherwise?

When reports and simulations purportedly bearing "answers" are produced at contract's end, the user again crashes into a knowledge barrier. What were the specialist's various assumptions, both stated and unstated? What do the conclusions mean in terms of "what we are going to do"? What can a model be expected to do? What are its necessary weaknesses? How do the promises articulated in the proposal compare with what is delivered? Is the work any good? For what? For whom? Having insufficient skill to begin asking such questions, having few or no disinterested, external professional sources to rely on, and having to rationalize the simulation or reports to superiors and public alike, the user has at present several options: (1) take the work purely on the faith that it does what the builder contends; (2) take it based on the reputation of the researchers or the firm producing the work; or (3) take it and hope that it does not cause the grief or embarrassment of critical comment—an eventuality more or less assured because of the existing poor documentation and inadequate professional review. Faith is an extravagant luxury, if a user's interests and purposes are serious and operational. Faith is one thing if the task is to rationalize a decision that has already been made, but it is quite another matter if the task is to use a simulation scientifically and operationally to muster evidence for or against policy choices.

Remember, this is a self-sustaining game in which all the players behave rationally but the aggregate outcomes are virtually guaranteed to be less than rational.

"What's the Question?"—"What's an Answer?"

There are some basic, tough questions that are seldom asked in this particular problem-solving process. Besides these, there are several operational tests that are also infrequently employed.

Some Questions. What is the problem? What does an answer look like? In those few examples (in the military sector mainly) where simulation was "successful" and worth the effort, common properties appear to be that one or two well-defined questions, the answers to which were important, were asked early. Not only were answers important, the principal users and builders were intelligent enough to recognize an answer when confronted by it. After deciding on the question, it helps to know what an answer might look like so that it does not go unnoticed if and when it subsequently appears.

Who is the *real* user? Does anyone have any idea what he wants? Can he get it? At what costs? Is there a cheaper, easier way to proceed? These questions are related to a model's initiation, promotion, and specification and often are not asked, if at all, until a great deal of time and effort have been expended building a model. They are, of course, absolutely critical for several obvious reasons, not the least of which is selecting appraisal criteria appropriate to the stated use of a model.

Who is the "master modeler"? Who on the design and production side really knows from start to finish *all* of a model's eccentricities, strengths, and weaknesses? These questions relate to the execution phase of the decision sequence in a model's "life." Without continuity of authorship and control, everyone involved may evade responsibility for whatever deficiencies in a simulation result, and no one in effect really knows or is liable for what the model produces.

Who appraised the model? Who gave final approval? Who used the finished product? With what results? Were these documented and made publicly available? These questions are all related to the appraisal and termination phases of the process and are seldom asked, much less acted upon.

Two Operational Tests. A suspicious point of view holds that the urban problem game is played partly to create a market for the talents and products of the salesmen-builders. One might be less persuaded by this argument if it were possible, in the role of private citizen or of interested professional bystander, to obtain reports and other substantiating papers, computer programs, manuals, and cost-accounting information. Unfortunately, such is seldom the case. Indeed, the explanation that this kind of information is unavailable is distressingly common.

A second operational test is to require that a model transfer from where it was built to comparably configured locations. At present this is often either impossible or only partially possible, at great expense in time and technical talent. There are two major reasons why models should be made to transfer if at all possible: one is scientific and the other is pragmatic.

Scientific standards demand faithful replication of procedures in diverse locales. Initial failure to replicate makes suspect the findings of a discovering person or organization. Repeated failures to replicate tend to confirm such suspicions. If a salesman or a model-builder is to borrow from the general reputation of science to justify himself and his product, then he must be prepared to subject himself to the standards and procedures of science. Simulation models that do not transfer, or are designed not to (whether intentionally or otherwise) essentially negate this key scientific requirement. It is a matter of consequence, not lightly dismissed or excused away with, "It's not adequately documented," or "It's undergoing modifications," or worse yet, "It's proprietary."

The pragmatic reason is the obvious one of controlling unnecessary duplication and redundancy of effort. The scientific reason concerns cumulating knowledge.

The Context of Research Is as Important as the Research Itself

It is useful to distinguish between research and the political-administrative context in which the research is conducted.

"Business as Usual." During initiation, promotion, and contract specification, it often happens that a group of model-building specialists has been, in the jargon of the trade, "wired in from the start." Such dominance of the process by a single one or group of salesmen-builders follows naturally where competing groups are small in number, where the user is not sufficiently technically skilled, and where few external professional controls exist. On the issue of who actually writes the request for proposal (RFP), user-contractors often resort to consultants, hiring from the small pool of available specialized talent to outline and "conceptualize" what the work will be. (The procedure is routinely carried out informally by telephone or in private conversation.) Even at the level of specifying what the problem or question is, users are compelled to rely on the fragmented problem-solving process already noted. What results is often a grant for a "sole source" contract to the predominant group. Without external appraisal and adequate documentation, such relationships may continue unperturbed over periods of time.

Who Is Using Whom? Bureaucrats and politicians may have their own reasons for hiring out problem-solving.

It is clearly in a bureaucrat's interest to be able to point to a stellar list of "name" researchers who are currently employed. The bigger the name and the more of them, the better. Distinguished academics, for instance, are quite visible in the initiation and promotion phases of a model-building project's life. It remains to be seen, however, who it is that actually executes and subsequently appraises the same project. The "mix" of the cast of characters appears to change during a project's life, and our hypothetical bureaucrat, playing the "name game," has little reason to be much concerned about *who actually does* the job once he gets credit for securing stellar services.

Politicians, one might imagine, could be satisfied merely by presenting the impression of using science and sophisticated management techniques to attack one of the many problems confronting them. In an area where image is often more telling than actuality, such could easily be the case. As long as the work progresses quietly and presents results that are either neutral or supportive of a politician's own preferences, there is little reason for political intervention or disruption of the research "business as usual."

To the naive or the uninitiated all of this has a rather cynical cast, but then, so too does the existing process.

9

Disentangling the Problem-Solving Process

The student of government is confronted with great difficulty in determining specific units, and with many variable factors which may make the accurate interpretation of a result very difficult and perhaps impossible. Political situations are usually complex, containing many factors which it is difficult to isolate successfully. The relations of the variables are not always readily disentangled, and their confusion may be the source of the most serious error.

Charles E. Merriam
New Aspects of Politics[1]

There are two basic levels to the problem-solving process: theoretical and operational. Theoretical considerations focus on the problems of specifying, constructing, operating, and validating scientific models about complex contexts. Operational considerations concentrate on the interactions of those who are participating and interacting in the context. It is, once more, the key distinction—which formed the basis for arguments in chapter 8—between the research and the context in which the research is being carried out.

Considerations of complexity have long been at the root of much social science theory. How various simplifying choices are made at a very abstract level along various dimensions of size has considerable impact on the efficiency, economy, and efficacy of one's formal symbolizations.

The operational consequences of dealing with complex problems in a large institutional setting are numerous and subtle. The urban problem game, as presently configured, is not particularly structured to illuminate either questions or answers or to cumulate our general knowledge and understanding of mistakes and successes in the field.

Theoretical Considerations

Understanding a formal symbolic model, the theoretical image it replicates, and the true context purportedly described by the model and the image declines rapidly as size increases. One loses control. Certainty about the symbol system's structure decreases as the number of elements, interconnections, and relationships and the degree of uncertainty increase. The central point is essentially this: If at some level of size for a given model we decidedly lose the ability to make structural revisions, i.e. to improve the model theoretically, it might be prudent to minimize complicating the formulation with extraneous elements and concentrate on the structuring of individual relationships and decomposed subsystems. A data-dependent model, even given *all* the necessary input information, does not necessarily provide adequate theoretical interest, technical precision and flexibility, and pragmatic utility. A more productive strategy, recommended by this analysis, calls for fewer observations on more distinct variables configured in empirically satisfying relationships.

How large should a model be? Small enough to be useful theoretically, but large enough to be realistic.

> The dilemma of the scientist is to select models that are at the same time simple enough to permit him to think with the aid of the model but also sufficiently realistic that the simplifications do not lead to [highly inaccurate] predictions. . . . The more complex the model, the more difficult it becomes to decide exactly which modifications to make and which new variables to introduce. Put simply, the basic dilemma faced in all sciences is that of how much to oversimplify reality.[2]

The disorganized-complexity perspective implies that one obtain a large number of observations on a few variables at single points in time. One way of accomplishing this is to increase the number of disaggregations of a fixed number of variables. What results is a bias toward fine spatial detail in urban models[3] or, in another context, a bias toward simple aggregated measures of many nations at a cross-section in time.[4] In either case, one's ability to understand individual differences and behavior through time is slight. The essential point is that the analytical context is made complex by increasing the number of conceptually undifferentiated elements to satisfy a preference for a larger sample size. Conversely, the recommended organized-complexity perspective implies that individual differences do matter. Time, interconnections, various conceptual elements, and diversity of structural configurations are each more important than the number of observations of one or a few elements. What are some implications deriving from the latter perspective, given the information generated in our theoretical discussion?

Acquiring and managing data to support a finely detailed model probably cost more in time, money, and human attention than any conceivable benefits that might somehow be obtained.

Decision-makers do not operate with a large number of elements; they can't, if one believes George Miller and his associates. Perhaps research could be productively expended determining what elements and processes they do use under various contingencies. In other words, strive to develop different explanations for "coded" elements, i.e. aggregated macroelements used by the policy-makers and others participating in a context over time. Write and model protocols. Decision-makers are visceral theorists. We need to look seriously at their ad hoc operating theories.

Functional models (e.g. population, economic, government) might for short periods of time—of, say, less than five years—be used to satisfy both explanatory and manipulative demands for precision on the one hand and relevance on the other.

Spatial models for individual, highly particular locations of demonstrated *policy interest* might be devised and continuously updated with survey or direct measurements. In other words, concentrate research resources on the continuous collection of detailed information for one or a few spatial sectors that have high and continuing utility for policy-makers.

Using formalized versions of the macro-, aggregated concepts and processes that decision-makers routinely employ, it seems potentially profitable to explicate the hierarchical links down to the higher particular spatial models mentioned. The meaning of the higher level is not accounted for by analysis of the lower. In other words, how are the results produced at the aggregate level (asymmetric control totals) linked to more specific, contained spatial configurations?

Expanding the analytic time frame confounds analysis and greatly reduces predictive power. The role for preferred end state specification at future cross-sections in time seems viable. In other words, precise predictions at expanded time periods are highly speculative anyway; therefore, use the model as a means of indicating what general structural modifications and behavioral implications will be needed to achieve some future state. A present configuration is directed toward some desired future configuration. The role for explicitly normative models is quite clear.

Operational Considerations

If nothing else, the reader has been alerted to the possibility that individual rationality, behavior that is even steadfastly moral in a strictly normative sense, may produce overall collective behavior that is undesirable or deficient in several aspects.

The undesirable features of the "bigness" phenomenon hold for organizations more generally. These features have been referred to as the "artichoke effect":

> . . . . a proclivity to add features, add functions, and add interfaces—layer upon layer—onto existing systems. Each succeeding layer has less and less useful or tasty substance on it, until the outside layers merely add weight, complexity, and a prickly hinderance to reaching the core of the problem that someone wants solved.[5]

No solutions to the problem are readily apparent; however, understanding that it exists is a first step. Resorting to crude description and characterization to sketch what appears to take place indicates the sad inability of existing political and administrative theory to account for the scientific-operational interface. Questions such as "Could the examined projects have turned out otherwise?" or "What difference would better or at least different project or output designs have made?" are essentially unanswerable, although one suspects they hold keys to the disentanglement of the present situation.

What is certain, however, is that it is dangerous to keep the amount of scientific and operational interconnection so low; that is to say, fragmented problem-solving bears costs that are worth taking into account. The needs for better coordination, documentation, and studies of use and validity at the theoretical, technical, political, and administrative interfaces are great. As only one example, expending resources to ensure that appraisals are carried out on how previous simulation-based studies were initiated, developed, and used might be a wiser, more important choice than funding additional studies.

A recommended means to carry out inquiries on use and validity would be to trace the life of a computer-based study from its earliest initiation, to promotion and implementation, and on through appraisal and termination. Who wanted it? Who sold it, on what grounds, for what purposes? Who conceived of it in abstracto? Who built it? Who used it and in what ways? Who appraised it? Who decided to renew or retire it? The progression through the social decision process or "life" of a simulation study is doubtless complex; nonetheless, understanding the sequence is the key to disentangling and understanding the operational problem.

In the final analysis, one needs to be alert to establish new procedures and expectations to assure that the game will be played differently. In effect, what is proposed is a reasoned examination of what appears to be the present state of affairs. Coordination, standards, communication, independent appraisal, review, and accounting are all necessary precursors to a healthy and promising professional development.

This effort is directed to these ends.

Reprise

Complexity of several varieties underlies both social theory and social process. Having developed several themes from the theoretical literature, the reader is hopefully prepared to begin understanding how one existing process operates.

It is important to distinguish between individual participants, who are for all practical purposes behaving rationally and somewhat successfully, and the more inclusive process, which is not.

Let us turn our attention to two illustrative examples of the process in action.

PART III

THE CONTEXT

Introduction

"Appraisal" . . . *describes the degree to which official policy has been realized (or failed of realization), and the degree to which officials played a determining role (taking all other significant factors into account).*

Harold D. Lasswell
Rutgers Law Review[1]

In using our "Appraisal Function" to evaluate the two case histories of model-building that follow, it is essential to understand that the general deficiencies and limitations we find are more properly attributable to gross underestimation of the extent and difficulty of the overall task—integrating the computer into the urban decision process—than to any individual or corporate maliciousness or perfidy. Indeed, the open and thoughtful manner in which most respondents discussed these cases supports this contention.

It is accurate to say that most participants sincerely believed in what they individually were undertaking. Incredible efforts were expended to accomplish what even the most enthusiastic promoters hoped could be done. In both cases one senses, but can only imagine, what great excitement attended these projects. The enthusiasm and professional dedication demonstrated by many participants are truly remarkable. Neither rogues nor fools, no one in these particular casts of characters is to be blamed for having to play out a strenuous scenario to its unhappy conclusion. It is absolutely essential that the reader keep personalities separate from the processes in which they operated. This is a tall order, but remember that even so great an actor as Sir Laurence Olivier has performed in plays that "bombed," and so it is with the dramatis personae who made their debuts in San Francisco and Pittsburgh.

San Francisco and Pittsburgh have been singled out for several specific reasons:

1. The projects were large-scale, ambitious, and highly visible undertakings.
2. Both were conducted under the auspices of the Community Renewal Program of the Urban Renewal Administration during approximately the same time periods. Comparisons are therefore enhanced.

99

3. Most of those who were directly involved have moved on to other responsibilities and were willing to provide more detailed information than might otherwise be expected.
4. The projects are more or less officially terminated, i.e. the entire decision sequence of intelligence, promotion, prescription, invocation, application, termination, and appraisal has nearly been completed.
5. However, no comprehensive appraisal has yet been carried out.

The problems encountered in these projects appear to be so general that their thorough appraisal can only in the long run be beneficial. The mistakes are worth explicating; they are not worth repeating. I have presumed to execute the appraisal function in hopes of establishing a continuing and "competitive flow of appraisal statements made available to elite and rank and file opinion elements throughout the body politic."[2]

A forewarning on the manner of presentation is in order. My general attitude has been that if an individual or organization is willing to promote publicly, appraisal should be straightforward, unequivocal, and likewise public. But where it seems inappropriate or needless, pointed references are minimized. I am willing to acknowledge errors of judgment on this issue; however, I am not willing to be cowed, because our central problem—instituting systematic appraisal procedures—is too important.

Besides using the criteria developed in Part I to consider in some detail the models produced for each city, attention will be focused on several constraints that inhibit more effective integration of complex procedures into the urban decision process. To this end I shall examine the views of people who participated in the research or problem-solving aspect of that process. One such person put the point succinctly: "I think that the first step to a cure is diagnosis. Unless you are really willing to lay out how bad it is, we are never going to get anywhere. I think that's the missing ingredient, you see?"[3]

If we are successful in providing a small measure of the "missing ingredient," then hopefully we will have begun to make headway in managing the central problem as well.

10

The Community Renewal Program

The time has come, the Walrus said
To talk of many things:
Of shoes—and ships—and sealing wax—
of cabbages—and kings—
And why the sea is boiling hot—
And whether pigs have wings.
                          Lewis Carroll
              Through the Looking Glass, 1892[1]

One planner discerns three distinct sources and styles in the intellectual heritage of his profession: architectural, reformist, and technocratic.[2] It is the technocratic style that concerns us particularly, for its espousal of "faith that technical analysis is superior to the political process as a means of arriving at decisions," and for consequent desire to reallocate "many questions from the politician to the analyst."[3] In a sense, this inquiry takes the measure of several such analysts and their techniques.

As it was within the compass of the Community Renewal Program that these analysts received both license and latitude to operate, this program requires some discussion.

Origins and Expectations

The Community Renewal Program (CRP) was created by Congress in 1959 as an amendment to the Housing Act of 1949. As a result, grants to local governments for the preparation of renewal plans were to be made by the Housing and Home Finance Agency. Such plans were to be comprehensive, including all federal, local public, and private renewal activities, and time-phased, accounting for governmental actions in decreasing detail over time. CRPs do not order the bulldozers to roll; rather, they serve as authoritative planning guidelines for local government officials. An underlying philosophy of the CRP is that it helps such officials to examine analytically and thoroughly alternative courses of action and attendant consequences before launching into uncoordinated, piecemeal renewal projects. Simply stated, the CRP represents an attempt to institutionalize comprehensive problem-solving at the local level of government.

Two threads in the history of the CRP help explain the decisions of San Francisco and Pittsburgh to seek assistance from experts with sophisticated and specialized skills.[4] One thread may be characterized as political; the other is technical.

Political-Bureaucratic Thread. The need of public officials for more and better planning information increased dramatically after the passage of the Housing Act of 1949. As planners sensed the inherent possibilities of the act and shifted from simple, single-project, site and survey studies to comprehensive planning, information requirements for new and varied data grew, along with a new concern for acquiring information about entire urban areas. The scope and magnitude of these data included (1) the number, location, and condition of the residential housing stock, with attention to the number, size, and income of families using the stock; (2) local housing-market activity, with emphasis on demand patterns that would result from relocating families; (3) the existence and participation of interest groups, including owners, residents, and public and private organizations;[5] (4) the identification and measurement of blighted areas; (5) the determination of resources available to facilitate renewal; (6) the identification of potential renewal project areas and determination of types of remedial actions for each; and (7) a scheduling of these actions to renew the urban area.[6] The list has proven elusive. In short, public sector functions increasingly required more and better information to formulate comprehensive and long-range plans for entire cities.

Writing in 1964, Robert Weaver noted another relevant phenomenon—increased federal concern for the interconnection of the environment:

Another charge frequently leveled against urban renewal is that it suffers from "projectitis," a vision which does not extend beyond the limits of a single development. The Federal Government already provides assistance for planning comprehensive community renewal programs. These are programs in which urban renewal activities and capital improvements can be coordinated. From the start we encouraged as many cities as possible to take part in this planning, because in order to be successful with urban renewal, a city must know where it is going.[7]

His sentiments parallel those of William Slayton, who, as commissioner of the Urban Renewal Administration, told Congress in November, 1963:

[A CRP] embraces the renewal problems and needs of an entire city. The objective is a long range urban renewal program that is coordinated with all other renewal related local programs—with total needs in balance with total resources.[8]

Slayton had expectations for solving these problems:

Both the CRP and the GNRP [General Neighborhood Renewal Program] help to create a much sounder basis for local urban renewal decisions and, therefore, help to make more effective use of Federal assistance for renewal projects.

The broadened planning base for local renewal programs, particularly under the community renewal program, permits a community to mesh its renewal planning with the planning of other programs . . . [9]

The public sector spokesmen acknowledge the insufficiency of the single-project approach, admit concern with the complexity of the environment, and reflect a growing restiveness—these statements were made about five years after the CRP was enabled—and sentiment to solve renewal problems.[10]

Technical Thread. Among other governmental responses to the depression of the 1930s was the institutionalization of technical rational planning efforts. Commencing with the creation of the National Resources Planning Board in 1933,[11] and flourishing in the form of successful wartime operations research activities,[12] present-day technocratic planning is composed of at least three strands, corresponding to distinct sets of activity.

One of these has evolved out of sustained government concern for the planning of highway and transportation networks. A considerable assemblage of skilled and experienced talent has been well nurtured over the years by a continuing series of transportation studies.[13]

Another strand in the technical thread is conventionally tied to the research and training activities of the University of Chicago's planning school. Among its significant effects, it has shown how city planners might

use the personnel and approaches of other disciplines, including operations research, decision theory, cost-benefit analysis, input-out studies, information theory, and simulation models as well as sociological and manpower analyses for understanding the behavior, attitudes, and ends of the clients of planning.[14]

As always, how successfully these specialists and their particular skills are utilized by the planner is an open question. Regardless, this variety of planning is typically solidly grounded in the social sciences.

The third strand leads to a group of technique-oriented experts— many of whom identify with the operations research profession, and most of whom typically do not have much training in the social science professions. A trend toward increased participation of these specialists in urban problem solving is noted in the remarks of Philip Morse, a prominent operations researcher:

THE CONTEXT

During the past five years [1961-66] an increasing number of experts have become persuaded that the procedures of *operations research would be effective in solving some of the problems of the public sector,* such as those in urban operations, in public health, and in education for example. Operations research professionals, noting the *success of applications in* the *industrial* and *military sectors,* became convinced that many of their methods, such as system modeling, computer simulation, mathematical programming, and the application of the theory of stochastic processes, could be useful in public affairs—indeed, *that the public sector urgently needed this kind of assistance.*[15] (emphasis added)

In fairness to Morse, and to other socially conscious technicians, when the problem is right, these techniques can be used very effectively, e.g., certain well-defined allocation problems. However, determining whether a problem is "right" and what techniques are appropriate is extremely difficult when the persons who have the substantive social knowledge are not those who have the technical virtuosity. Morse is keenly aware of this difficulty; many others are not.[16]

Catalysts and Reactions. Martin Meyerson's "seminal" keynote address to the American Institute of Planners in 1956, in which he called for the building of a "bridge" between short-term decision-making on individual projects and long-term, frequently utopian planning,[17] must rate as the call to arms for comprehensive analytic planning efforts. That, taken with the ongoing "planning revolution" created in part by the 1949 Housing Act,[18] set the stage for the model-building activities we describe.

Political and technical threads joined when San Francisco and Pittsburgh enlisted expert technical assistance to execute their own comprehensive Community Renewal Programs. It is essential to note that these two efforts are relatively *atypical* of the more than 150 other CRPs undertaken as of 1966. A routine CRP dealt in quite conventional ways with physical, relocation, legal, and financial issues—a sort of planning "business as usual."[19] Indeed this inquiry is prompted by the unfulfilled potential represented by these atypical cases. It is to the promise of "a new wave of innovations in the urban renewal process," deriving from "new and powerful techniques potentially useful for urban analysis and planning in general,"[20] that we direct our present efforts.

San Francisco's CRP

The Housing and Home Finance Agency approved the City Planning Department's CRP application in October, 1962.[21] The twenty-six month program was budgeted at $1,019,651. The federal cash grant was for two-thirds, or $663,245, and the local contribution accounted for the remainder, or $356,406. A third-party contract for $520,000 between the Department of City Planning and the Arthur D. Little Corporation (ADL) was signed on February 18, 1963. The final report was expected from them on April 1, 1965.

The decision to do a CRP using computer simulation techniques was not clear-cut. According to the initial program manager in the Department of City Planning, "We just got swept along."[22] The city had been in the throes of selecting its electronic data-processing equipment. During that period of time, i.e. before the CRP was formulated, a computer systems consultant circulated within City Planning a management information study that he had previously prepared for a Los Angeles client. The report was inspirational. "It was a copy of this report that [Stanford] Optner did for Los Angeles that inspired us. As a matter of fact, he came up here because he was interested in installing our EDP system."[23] Another city planner, whose prime responsibility was research, was so inspired that during 1960 he began, through conversations and internal memos, "advancing a systems-oriented CRP, largely an information system, a decision-making system based upon a management information system. . . . His prime candidate for consultations was Stanford Optner."[24]

At approximately the same time, the mayor's urban renewal coordinator, in the process of casting about for ways to launch the city's CRP, began informal discussions with a personal friend who was a planning staff member with Arthur D. Little.[25] After this, according to the project manager, the City Planning Department was drawn into these discussions but failed in its attempt to

get both this guy Optner and A. D. Little together. (Neither one of them wanted to get married.) Finally A. D. Little went out alone with the concept of the model. They had [name] and two or three other high powered brains from the Cambridge office who were both knowledgeable on planning matters and on systems analysis and data processing matters. . . .[26]

Informal discussions between members of the ADL and City Planning staffs about the feasibility of using such sophisticated techniques to do the CRP eventually led to ADL's submission of a formal prospectus. On reflection, the matter seemed ironic to the program manager:

Then they took over and under their house funds, or what not, they actually wrote us a prospectus which then became the . . . [pause] and this is ironic, after we got this thing, pretty much reflecting what we had been persuaded was what we wanted to do, then we threw it open for proposals. . . . We had about five or six, but we finally did choose Little.[27]

The prospectus itself lacks the sharp specification of project objectives that are contained in ADL's August, 1963, report, "San Francisco Community Renewal Program—Purpose, Scope, and Methodology." As the research design phase of the study had been completed in June,

1963, one may surmise that the following abstracted comments represent ADL's realistic perceptions of the problem, study objectives, and research methods.

General Political-Bureaucratic Needs and Purpose.

. . . there is a need for new and improved methods to enable City officials to deal with problems of this type. This situation is not unique to San Francisco; City officials everywhere have a similar need. The underlying purpose of the Community Renewal Program in San Francisco is to provide City officials with new and better tools to cope with the problems of urban change.[28]

More Specific Purposes.

It is *comprehensive,* in that it will deal in an integrated fashion with all public and private actions which must be taken to provide continuous and sound maintenance and development of the City's land and buildings.[29]

The program will be concerned with both residential and non-residential areas, thus transcending the "housing-bias" of renewal efforts to date.[30]

. . . attention will be paid to studying and forecasting the growth prospects in the Bay Area and, in particular the markets for space in the various cities within the Bay Area . . . [31]

. . . it will include *all* government actions which affect urban physical change, planned together for maximum effect, and designed to eliminate gaps and overlaps in treatment.[32]

Time Frame for Action.

No program, even the most highly integrated and efficient, could hope, in just a few short years, to solve the grave problems facing the City. While the upper time limit of the Program has not been fixed, it will probably span a 20-year period.[33]

When completed, the CRP will indicate the *kinds* of renewal actions that are needed, *when* specific renewal activities should be started (as a part of the total program) *where* such actions should be taken and by *whom.*[34]

This is a rather large bill of particulars; doubtless, the Department of City Planning and other city officials could have benefited handsomely from this kind of information. Much of it was to be produced by using a large-scale computer simulation model:

Technical Methods and Promises.

If further investigations demonstrate that the systems approach is feasible, San Francisco will have a unique tool for solving its renewal problems. The model will help, for example, to structure the thinking about the problem and to guide the planning of the research and the evaluation of results . . .

The testing and evaluation of specific proposed plans will be an added benefit of the model and computer. Furthermore, through the knowledge gained from testing alternative plans, the integration and coordination of public programs and policies will be enhanced and the obstacles that might hinder the efficiency of the overall system will be identified.

The fundamental objective of the CRP is its programming function; that is, the establishment of a schedule of actions, both private and public, on a time-phase basis. . . . The system concept, utilizing a mathematical model adapted to electronic

106

computers, offers the most promising method of dealing with the complexities involved.[35]

Thus, the consultant's statement of purpose, scope, and method identified the general problems and specified an approach for their solution, indicating that such a solution must be comprehensive, unbiased in its consideration of more-than-housing matters, unencumbered by restrictive political boundaries, wide-ranging with respect to governmental decision-making, and inclusive of a twenty-year time frame. To achieve solution, "a mathematical model adapted to electronic computers" was advocated.

An Operational Model. ADL's exact words give an unequivocal statement of what they expected this solution device to do:

Based on the model, urban development trends and future renewal requirements will be forecast. The model will be used to run a series of special tests designed to determine and measure the effects of introducing changes in the model by altering one or more elements in the existing situation. The factors in the model will be changed to test different assumptions, conditions, and policies and their consequences.

The consequences of different renewal programs, priorities and time schedules will be analyzed and tested against the financial, relocation, administrative, and other resources available to meet the City's renewal needs. . . .

These tests may point up the need to alter certain renewal objectives, or to reschedule certain renewal actions, or to remedy certain deficiencies in finance, administrative organization, research, etc. . . . [36]

There can be little doubt that this was to be a policy-making device, to be used, according to the definitional distinctions made in chapter 6, "Pragmatic Appraisal," for both unconditional and normative forecasts.

Participants. The people who were charged with the production of the model for the CRP are identified in Exhibit 10-1. They were identified by Arthur D. Little as "staff members of Arthur D. Little, Inc., and its consultants who are directly involved with the Program and members of the Citizens and Technical Advisory Committees."[37] These committees were required as part of the CRP and were respectively intended to ensure local popular participation and to provide a pool of on-call expert talent for plan formulation.

Three primary actors are relevant: the consultant, the city, and the federal government. We shall subsequently discuss each group in some detail.

Hopefully the reader has some tolerance for the wearisome recitation of professional and contractual detail. Establishing the exact rules under which the research game was played is important. What was happening in Pittsburgh was remarkably similar in the underlying process involved, and yet it was different in particular details and constraints.

EXHIBIT 10-1

Participants—Expert Advisers

ARTHUR D. LITTLE, STAFF AND CONSULTANTS

Staff

Dr. Ira M. Robinson	Project Director
Dr. John W. Dyckman	Project Consultant
Francis Hendricks	Urban Systems Analysis
Sheila Spaulding	Social Surveys
Martin L. Ernst	Operations Research
Dr. Harry B. Wolfe	Operations Research
Dr. Robert L. Barringer	Operations Research
Harry G. Foden	Industrial Economics
Dr. Cyril C. Hermann	Regional Economics
G. Thomas Kingsley	Urban Planning
Judy Piper	Data Retrieval

Consultants

Professor Martin Meyerson	Organization and Administration
Dr. Jack Lessinger	Metropolitan Space Markets
George Williams	Organization and Administration
H. Milton Patton	Organization and Administration
John O. Ganter, Jr.	Investment

TECHNICAL ADVISORY COMMITTEE FOR THE
COMMUNITY RENEWAL PROGRAM[a]

Professor C. West Churchman
Mr. Hall Dunleavy
Mr. Joseph Esherick
Professor Donald L. Foley
Mr. Maurice I. Gershenson
Mr. Irving M. Kriegsfeld
Professor Ralph Lane
Professor William Massy
Mr. Richard S. Peterson
Professor Philburn Ratoosh
Professor Robert C. Stone
Professor Anselm L. Strauss
Professor Paul Wendt
Mr. Alan R. Winger
Professor Catherine Bauer Wurster

Source: "Purpose, Scope and Methodology," p. 27.

[a]*Ibid.*, p. 28. I was unable to find the exact composition of the Citizens Committee, but for the immediate task this is of little consequence.

Pittsburgh's CRP

In December, 1960, Pittsburgh applied for a $408,876 federal grant to do its three-year CRP.[38] The two-thirds federal share of the project was approved on February 10, 1961, but at a reduced level of $200,000 and for a shortened time frame of two years.

The viability of the program was questioned by one participant:

In terms of how the money was to be used for the readiness of that community to begin to engage in the kind of planning and programming activity that was contemplated as part of a legitimate CRP . . . it was a pretty bleak outlook . . . As a matter of fact, I can recall advising the Urban Renewal Commissioner Slayton . . . that I thought it was a waste of money at this point.

Not the least of the city's problems were deficiencies in talent and motivation:

[Pittsburgh] didn't have a staff, had no incentive to move ahead in this project—it just inherited the damned thing. So the whole thing was a big political deal at the beginning and Pittsburgh got . . . a couple of hundred thousand dollars to tackle its CRP. A whole year went by [February, 1961-February, 1962] and nothing happened.[39]

In the spring of 1962, Pittsburgh hired Calvin Hamilton as its new director of city planning. The general conditions of his appointment are described by Hamilton: "The terms of reference under which they hired me were to provide a master plan and to produce a plan and strategy for urban renewal and a plan to help the decision process."[40]

Hamilton's reputation as an innovative, creative planner was well known and probably facilitated his appointment. One young planner recalls, "he came in as sort of a wild man, that is, unorthodox, unusual kinds of ideas, lots of enthusiasm, not much technical knowledge at all but a willingness to trust people."[41] The specific conditions of his appointment evidently included political support from important local quarters for any efforts that he might make to "shape up that City Planning Department, hire a new cast of characters, and unload some of those that were unable to carry their own freight, and get that program going. . . . So he did just that."[42] To assist this rebuilding, Hamilton hired an outside planning advisory service to recommend improvements for the about-to-be-renewed City Planning Department (improvements he later instituted). In the midst of all these changes, the CRP began to look more like a large windfall and less like the symbolic albatross.

Cal also saw the great potential leverage that was represented in the CRP—it wasn't at all likely that he was going to be able to wheedle much in the way of resources out of city government, but here was a Federal package, $200,000, that was half spent already on nothing. It wasn't going to solve his problems, but if he could come up with some kind of exciting package, he might well be able to land a sufficient bundle of dough to be able to attract the kind of people to the city to be able to engage in effective planning.[43]

By October 5, 1962, the city had requested an additional $558,809 from the Housing and Home Finance Agency. The city's additional contribution (one-third) totaled $390,078, most of which was in the form of noncash credits: salaries, rent for space, etc. Total resources for the project from all sources were $1,148,887. The period of the amended CRP extended to February 10, 1965.[44] After receiving HHFA approval in March, 1963, the Department of City Planning contracted with the Center for Regional Economic Studies (CRES) of the University of Pittsburgh to "supplement, assist, help guide the work of the Department, and evaluate the results of the program," because "there are certain areas within the CRP for which the Department does not have the requisite skills."[45] The price for assistance, guidance, and evaluation until December, 1964, was *$215,000.*[46] CRES had been established in July, 1962, to continue a regional economic analysis program originally done by the Pittsburgh Regional Planning Association under Ford Foundation auspices.[47] Although CRES maintained ties with the Pittsburgh Regional Planning Association, *"The contract with the City of Pittsburgh is* [March, 1963] *the largest research effort of the Center's current program."*[48] To provide specialized computer skills it did not have, CRES in turn subcontracted with the CONSAD Research Corporation.

Mayor Barr spelled out what the revitalized CRP was to do in his "Amended Application" statement to the federal officials. Pertinent portions of that and other documents establish the general perceptions of the problem, objectives for the study, and methods of solution. In these matters, the extent of correspondence with the San Francisco context is remarkable.

General Political-Bureaucratic Needs and Purposes.

The Community Renewal Program provides the means to undertake a comprehensive analysis of the general conditions of the entire City and to establish priorities in an over-all approach to the City's problems. The CRP provides the opportunity to review and up-date accepted forms of measurement of the urban structure, to utilize recently developed techniques, and to develop new ones as needed.[49]

More Specific Purposes.

To determine the most effective organization of the various public and civic agencies to conduct a comprehensive renewal program.[50]

To determine the geographical areas within the City which must logically remain in their existing predominant land use, such as residential, industrial, commercial, or appropriate combinations, and the actions necessary to stabilize and encourage such uses.[51]

A spatial emphasis on the city, to the relative exclusion of the surrounding six-county region, is evident. This point is contrary to the regional, Bay Area perspective called for in the San Francisco proposal. Coordinative purposes were the same, however:

To devise a system which will promote the coordination of renewal activities among the agencies supporting the renewal program and the private sector of the economy.[52]

110

Time Frame for Action.

[An "Optimum Renewal Program"] will schedule renewal projects for the next six years to coincide with the City's Capital Improvement Program, with progressively less detailed programs for the following six year periods.[53]

The terminal year used for purposes of projection and analysis was 1980.[54] The analyses were intended to develop and test alternative programs and criteria for

... schedules of cost and anticipated benefit for those redevelopment areas where alternative land uses and densities are under consideration.

... differential property tax upon different types of land.

... the effects of such governmental actions as code enforcement, community facility improvements ...

... optimiz[ing] the marginal return to the city on its urban renewal investments.

Specifically, the CRP was to "determine the exact nature of the specific criteria ... to establish the priorities of action to be recommended."[55] The prose may have been murky, but the promise was not.

Technical Methods and Promises. The Center for Regional Economic Studies, "because of its special qualifications," was to provide the following services for the CRP:

[development of] a simulation model that will assist the Department of City Planning in predicting and evaluating the consequences of alternative renewal-planning policy decisions.[56]

And, under the final terms of the agreement,

... completion of data collection efforts, computer programming, quality control checks on the inputs of the experimental design, and several operational runs of the completed model using selected problems which will be designated by City officials.[57]

CRES was also responsible for developing "projections of selected measures of economic activity for the City of Pittsburgh." These were to include projections of the population, by expected changes in age, sex, and race; of the level of employment, by various industrial classifications; of amount of income, by changes in per capita ranks, social class, and industrial origin; and of use of land, including total industrial, commercial, and residential demand and the allocation of these projected demands. As a part of this same agreement, CRES contracted to do market studies—consumer demand, location, etc.; to execute a municipal revenue-expenditure study; and to assist the Department of City Planning with the use and improvement of its computer system.[58]

An Operational Model. The Pittsburgh CRP's computer models were to make both unconditional and normative forecasts that could be used for policy-making purposes.

THE CONTEXT

Through the use of this technique, combining computer simulation and human problem-solving, the department plans to pretest the effect that planning decisions would have on the city before they are actually put into action. . . . The different effects of important policy alternatives can be seen by the decision makers using the results of simulations. Thus their decisions are more soundly based on facts with a much clearer understanding of the implications of any one given policy decision.[59]

Participants. Primary responsibility for the production of the models was delegated to personnel affiliated with CRES and their subcontractor, the CONSAD Research Corporation. Most of these persons are listed in Exhibit 10-2. Once again, statutory requirements led to the creation of a CRP Technical Advisory Council, which was composed mainly of public figures and administrative personnel from related renewal agencies and enterprises. There is no evidence of a formal committee to guide the development of the simulation models, per se.

EXHIBIT 10-2

Participants—Expert Advisers

CENTER FOR REGIONAL ECONOMIC STUDIES, UNIVERSITY OF PITTSBURGH[a]

Dr. Edgar M. Hoover	Director of Center
Dr. Benjamin Chinitz	Associate Director of Center[b]
Dr. William C. Pendleton	Associate Professor Economics and Senior Economist—CRES
Dr. Charles L. Leven	Associate Professor of Economics and Center Staff Member

Plus: "Other members of the staff of the Center and Graduate Research Assistants."

CONSAD RESEARCH CORPORATION

Dr. Wilbur A. Steger	President and Adjunct Professor of Economics, University of Pittsburgh
Mr. Steve Putnam	Staff Member
Mr. J. P. Crecine	Staff Member
Dr. Nathan Grundstein	Consultant

CRP TECHNICAL ADVISORY COUNCIL[c]

Mr. George Duggar	
Mr. Patrick Cusick	
Mr. Aldo Colautti	Executive Secretary to Mayor Barr
Mr. Bernard Loshbough	
Mr. Edward McGee	Allegheny Conference
Mr. John Mauro	Urban Renewal Coordinator
Mr. Robert Pease	Urban Redevelopment Authority
Mr. Elmer Tropman	
Mr. Sherwood Pine	
Mr. Leroy Little	

[a]Memo, Chinitz to Jalbert.
[b]Chinitz "will be responsible for the overall execution of the contract." *Ibid.*, p. 2.
[c]CRP Technical Advisory Council Meeting, "Minutes," July 29, 1963.

However, at one point in time—November 7, 1963—a one-day seminar composed of several distinguished academic and public notables was convened to hear discussions and to elicit recommendations for model development. Aside from the publicity given the seminar, it appears to have generated little in the way of continuing feedback.

To the Moon?

The Community Renewal Program is one degree of freedom in the boundless urban equation. It is neither more nor less. But when a city is paralyzed, impotent, and dying, one must hold out hope that less can somehow be more.

Hoping for more, two cities tried to shoot for the moon. They used consultants and computers and told themselves that comprehensive plans and time-phased programs would chart their course to a decent future. But where were they headed? "The City thought we were on our way to Alpha Centauri . . . we knew we'd be damned lucky to even get to the moon."[60]

II

San Francisco

*Arthur D. Little, Inc., has shown modern com-
puter technology to be an effective tool for
finding practical solutions to city problems . . .
simulation models provide a continuing method
for finding answers and predicting results as
recommendations are followed and programs
for revitalization continue.*

Arthur D. Little, Inc.
Community Renewal Programming,
1969[1]

San Francisco is, of course, widely known for its many esthetic delights: precipitate hills, quaint cable cars, magnificent bridges, phantasmic fog. Less widely known is the extent to which commonplace, ugly, urban ails have consumed "The City," as it is widely known to local chauvinists. Urban renewal is one of the more important restorative efforts, and the fate of the city is very much intertwined with its success or failure. We are not directly concerned with renewal activities per se; however, we shall specifically consider the degree of success attained by the Community Renewal Program in planning for these activities.

Enlisting the support of expert advisers and sophisticated techniques represented a departure from the norm; any outcome could be expected to have exaggerated effects.

Sadly, despite considerable, commendable postproject effort on the part of members of the Planning Department, San Francisco does not have an operating computer simulation model that can be reliably or routinely used for renewal policy-making. All claims to the contrary, the model is still nowhere near completion and has been set aside by responsible civic officials. The model built under the CRP contract will be considered in terms of its scope and purpose, order of processing, theoretical content, technical adequacy, ethical potentialities, and pragmatic applications.

Decision to Model

The decision to build a computer model involved several members of the City Planning Department, the mayor's urban renewal coordinator, and representatives of the Arthur D. Little Corporation.

Politicians and Bureaucrats. Three factors apparently explain the city's willingness to participate in this major research and model-building project—*money, politics, and naiveté*.

Under the regulations of the CRP program, the city contributes only one-third of the total cost of its project, and this may be in local, noncash credits. The rationale for in-kind contributions is a fairly simple one: Cities do not have much surplus cash. The practical implications are more subtle. By interpreting local credits as work that would be done regardless of whether the project were undertaken or not, the city could conclude that the CRP would cost it nothing. Feeling little or no fiscal obligation, the Board of Supervisors and the mayor had slight reason to appraise seriously the merits of the proposal as to feasibility, method, or possible impact. In one participant's somewhat earthy terms, should the program go awry, the Board of Supervisors had a hedge and could always tell critics, "Go screw yourselves. We never wanted this anyway. The only reason that we were sold on this is because it was free."[2]

San Francisco's Department of City Planning had often found itself competing with and losing to the local Urban Renewal Agency in terms of the size, financing, scope, and magnitude of its projects. But the planning, as opposed to renewal, bias in the CRP made City Planning the logical recipient of this particular federal program. If Planning could "capture" the CRP, it would be a major political-administrative coup for the department: "[City Planning] wanted this to be their show. MacCarthy [then Director] made the decision to go on with this new business, to go with the ADL crap. He was going to play it for what it was worth."[3]

The department found the idea of using computer techniques generally beguiling, but its sophistication and understanding about model building did not match its enthusiasm. As one consultant put it:

[The Department of City Planning] was as naive at times as you could possibly encounter anywhere. They had what I would call the "Pinball Machine Syndrome." They were fascinated by bright colored lights and prestige considerations, and they had no clear idea of how they wanted to use this thing at all.[4]

Large-scale model building typically requires the active participation of many sophisticated individuals. Apparently unaware of this, or for whatever other reason, the Planning Department assigned one administrator-manager and one research staff member to the project. The manager was to keep the accounts straight and the researcher was to serve as liaison with ADL's staff. (The researcher left the project early and was replaced by a junior planner who had no prior technical experience.)

Technocrats. The consultant's willingness to take on such a project is explained by institutional and reputational considerations.

In the year prior to the signing of the CRP contract, the consulting firm had made major changes in its San Francisco regional office:

This [ADL/San Francisco] had been principally a physical sciences office. You see we do lab work here, chemists, what have you. We also had a regional urban planning group . . . At about that time it was decided to pull the labs back to Cambridge, expanding the urban and regional economics side of it. This [CRP] was to be a major project. I guess that it was one of the reasons that the office was expanded.

Later in the same interview, the stake of the firm is noted. "It was our hope . . . our hope that this would be a springboard situation."[5] The institutional stake in the CRP as a means to create a saleable reputation in an expanding segment of the consultant's business is reasonable and easy enough to understand. However, the idea of *selling* apparently underscored not only the consulting contract, but also the concept of building models.

[Name of planner in ADL] essentially sold the City on this vague idea of maybe building a mathematical model to accomplish the purposes of the Community Renewal Program. [He] was not involved at all in the structuring . . . in the detailing of it. This is a typical case, I think, of something being sold without a hell of a lot of understanding on the part of the client.[6]

Unfortunately ADL's planner-consultant, who had engineered most of the early negotiations and had taken charge of drafting the proposal, left for an academic position approximately three months after the CRP contract had been signed. The city's project manager reflected on this unanticipated turn of events:

Everybody, including Arthur D. Little, was kind of upset. Their Western manager said to us, "Believe me, when we accepted the contract we weren't cognizant of this." . . . I think they [ADL] were quite genuine, judging by the way that they were sputtering. I don't think they knew that he had apparently been negotiating with [name of university] for a long time.[7]

To fill this discontinuity in management, another well-known planner was hired by ADL. His assessment of the project's status is indicative of many ensuing problems:

[The planning director] was a very traditional guy in terms of planning. He wanted, very much to his credit in the initial phases, to be innovative and so on and thought that this was maybe the way to go. He never did understand it. Let us be honest, we really didn't even know what the hell we were going to do.[8]

With a contractual commitment, an expanding institutional base, and a reputation for sophisticated problem-solving competence at stake, the consultant turned to its experienced pool of operations research personnel for support. Actual responsibility for executing the vague promises that had been sold in the proposal fell to a group of three or four skilled technicians, who were assigned as a "model team."

Initial Design. Recounting the early design phase helps explain the form that the model eventually took. Lacking working-level access to the client—except through the two technically unsophisticated individuals attached to the project—and failing to obtain an unambiguous statement of the problem from any of its own planning personnel, a senior operations researcher from ADL's Cambridge office assumed parental responsibilities.

He was the father of it. He gave birth to the concept. He came out here [from Cambridge] and spent two days talking with [the present and former planner-project leaders] and some others. So out of this two days of interviews, [he] sat down and said, "What are the significant relationships; what are the determinants?" He laid them out in a five page memo.[9]

According to the reports of the designer and others, the model's eventual structural details conformed to this original formulation.

The basic structure I think I developed in about a week of work . . . to give you a feeling for it. Thereafter I played a large part in discussions of matters of that sort [redesign] , but we never varied too much from that structure thereafter.[10]

The detailing task was left to operations researchers resident in San Francisco, whose prior professional experiences are as noteworthy as are their personal expectations for the project. One of the principals relates both, for instance:

My background has been primarily in private work: inventory control, simulation models, statistical and analytical studies for private companies. I was real excited in the prospects of using some of the same or similar approaches in the area—for the public good in the public sector.[11]

A Summary of the Decision to Model. The essential points to be made are these: The client was neither accessible nor technically sophisticated—facts of enormous consequence that prompted one operations researcher to remark, "Without a knowledgeable client . . . one could communicate with, from whom one could get directions, we were in effect the people who made all the decisions."[12] The planner who, to a large extent, had been responsible for "selling" the principle of computer modeling had detached himself from the project, and his replacement had neither adequate technical skill nor sufficient time to build computer models. In the opinion of one skilled operations researcher,

at the time we did the job, the planners [ADL and the city] by and large knew little if anything about models or computers or any of the quantitative methods.

117

They thought, I think, that they saw in the model an opportunity to do a lot of things that planners had always wanted to do . . . [13]

And finally, the consultant had a contractual obligation, immediate self-interest, and a professional reputation for problem-solving to uphold. Building an operational model within the given period of the contract became a major motivating factor.

The computer model that resulted from this critical sequence of events is reported in ADL's "San Francisco Community Renewal Program: Model of the San Francisco Housing Market."[14] This will be a key source for our inquiry—not because it is an especially good example of documentation, it is not; but because it is one of the few extant technical and public detailings of the model.[15]

Scope and Purpose

The original ambitious claims related in ADL's "Purpose, Scope and Methodology,"[16] in August of 1963, were scaled down as the difficulty of the problem and the inhospitality of the local environment became apparent. Hopes of producing the comprehensive, more-than-housing, Bay Area-wide, decision-assisting, forecasting device alluded to in the initial stages of the project gave way to the reality of a somewhat circumscribed residential model of San Francisco's housing stock. The policy-making, forecasting purpose remained.

Scope. Not only did a data reconnaissance and field study of city information resources fail to produce any reliable, consistent, or suitable data sets for use in model construction and testing, but two prime sources of land-use data, the Assessor's Office and the Board of Education, refused for "political reasons" to share their files.[17] Having no other recourse, ADL decided to rely primarily on Bureau of Census data from 1960. Additional data, surveys, and special studies were undertaken to supplement the information developed for ADL by the Census Bureau in a special cross-tabulation of the 1960 data.

By February of 1964, the industrial and commercial sectors had been officially deleted from the model for lack of data. The shock of finding so little data had caused the project leader to despair, "Our CRP really should not be concerned in a direct way with economic and social goals—these are not legitimately in our current purview."[18] And by May, 1965, the rationalization process had proceeded so far that one researcher could write:

Since the important focus of the Community Renewal Program is on residential housing (and since data are more available in this area) the model focused on the residential housing sector. In this connection, attributes such as condition, number of rooms, neighborhood amenities, etc., are important attributes and this very strongly influenced the choice of attributes with which the Community Renewal Program is concerned. Other attributes, such as transportation and accessibility are less important in this connection, at least in San Francisco, and are therefore not considered explicitly.[19]

These opinions are inconsistent with the stated purposes of the Community Renewal Program[20] and with events in the local context. They do indicate how far the scope of the project had narrowed.

Reality deflated expectations even more when the pitiful state of housing-market theory was discovered. In spite of a passing mention of the well-known "Herbert-Stevens Model,"[21] and a perfunctory, though erroneous citation of "the empirical work of Black [sic] and Winnick,"[22] there are no explicit indications of the incorporation of extant social or housing theory in the model. No doubt, the scarcity of "an adequate theoretical framework within which the complex and baffling characteristics of the housing market can be properly viewed,"[23] had profound effects on the model-building enterprise. If the theoretical image is uncertain, partial, and changeable, building a computer model of that image may quite understandably be impossible. It is important to recall the distinctions developed in Part I between policy and theory building purposes for the models. Without sufficient reliable theory, building models for policy applications may be a waste of time and other scarce resources. One can, of course, ignore the consequences and plunge on, as ADL did.

Purpose. Although the scope of the model-building activity had narrowed, the purpose remained remarkably consistent with the stated, contractual purposes: construct a device for use in forecasts of policy alternatives. To appraise properly, it is important to establish clearly the stated, intended purposes for which a computer model is being built. Ex post facto restatements such as: "We were developing theory," or "It was a good experiment," are necessarily discounted. Just as in the game of pool, one is interested in comparing stated purposes with actual outcomes. Did the balls fall the way the shot was called, or not? We have already reviewed the 1963 version of the model's purpose. The thinking of the project leader on these matters in August, 1964 is revealed in this observation:

As all of us are aware, our major focus in the CRP is with the operation of the private real estate (or investment) market. The mathematical model aims to simulate the working and functioning of this market in the City of San Francisco. The objective is to create a replica of the actual conditions with respect to the land and building space market of San Francisco on which renewal actions—both private and public—can be tested and their implications evaluated. By simulating the behavior of the market, we hope to develop a tool for testing the effects of public actions on the workings of the private sector . . . [24]

And finally, in the 1966 technical description of the model, purposes are characterized:

The Model is currently available to study any series of possible broad patterns of action that could be taken by the City of San Francisco to improve its residential housing. . . . Results can be provided in terms of the relative stocks of housing of various types provided for different population groups, or in a variety of other forms. It is, therefore, a tool immediately available for use in studying the implications of different City policies.[25]

Because the purpose is consistently clear, our appraisal of the output in relation to the purpose must be similarly unequivocal.

Order of Processing

There are three distinct versions of the model. MOD I, a simplified formulation employing hypothetical data, was run in December, 1964, and is partly discussed in ADL's "Technical Paper #1—Simulation Model for Renewal Programming."[26] The difference between MOD I and MOD II is considerable, according to the city's technical representative:

[ADL] took the step to go with MOD I, which was not complex. It had something like eight location categories and a limited number of family choices. The big decision came between MOD I and MOD II. Unfortunately, I was at the time decidedly in favor of a disaggregated, highly complex version of MOD I.[27]

The "big decision" to complicate the model was made by January, 1965. Some disagreement about this choice apparently existed:

The decision to run MOD II was not a foregone one. As far as [ADL management] was concerned, I believe that MOD I would have been an acceptable product. However, [several members of the model team] were concerned that the product would be neither applicable nor accurate and urged that MOD II be given an opportunity to "prove out."[28]

Because this decision was made less than six months before the termination of the contract and because the remodeling proved considerably more demanding than expected, ADL's final recommendations for a CRP were not developed with the model. In fact, the final Community Renewal Program was developed along conventional lines in the final weeks of the contract. MOD II was eventually turned over to the city in late summer, 1965.[29] It is the version that we shall appraise. After a one-year hiatus, work on a third version of the model was undertaken.[30] During this period the city acquired a new planning director, who wanted resolved whether the model could be made to run in a useful manner or not. At his initiative work on MOD III began. Because MOD III is not the version that has been publicized, is little known outside of a small group that tried to salvage MOD II, is not what the consultant contracted for and delivered, and embodies mostly marginal structural refinements over the second version, we shall delay its consideration for the moment and concentrate primarily on MOD II.

General Characteristics. The model attempts to replicate demand and supply activities in the housing market. Population, elaborated in "Households" according to household type, number of members, race and age of the head, income, and rent-paying ability, is predicted exogenously to the model for each time period; these disaggregated household groups are the fundamental elements of the demand. The supply of housing is specified initially by house type, condition, and location, and is then processed internally by the model for each time period. Housing (supply) is matched with Households (demand) according to the latter's preference list for housing, which is simply determined by the ability to pay. If demand exceeds supply in a given period because of increases in the number of particular household types or their ability to pay, housing may be constructed, rehabilitated, or improved in subsequent periods. How many of each housing type is determined by a set of operators designed to calculate expected improvements in investment return, given the type and amount of excess demand. With the exception of a "bandwagon effect," which allows overbuilding house types for which there is no longer adequate demand, the model is driven by the assumption that the private real estate market maximizes returns on investment.

Public sector activity takes three forms in the model: as direct intervention into the marketplace—accomplished by exogenously changing variables representing purchases, sales, or site improvements; as implicit intervention—by exogenously changing model parameters representing rents, taxes, or subsidies; and as intervention in the market's inclusive environment—by exogenously changing parameters governing code and zoning ordinances.

The market operates by comparing the stock of available housing with household preference lists. If demand exceeds the supply of stock, for a particular type, the price is forced up, unallocated households are placed in less desirable housing types (according to their preference lists), and pressure is created to add more housing to satisfy the demand. The model responds to the pressure by adding and deleting housing in accord with its cost calculations for new or improved housing, attempts to meet unsatisfied demand, and recomputes indices of demand pressure, rent levels, and vacancy rates.

While the matching of household and house type in the simulated market proceeds, the housing stock is made to deteriorate in accor-

121

dance with a fixed-schedule aging routine. In the model's terms, deterioration primarily means that a house type is able to attract only poorer households and consequently returns less on its investment. The model did, however, make an allowance for small numbers of more affluent households acquiring deteriorated stock. This was managed by selecting higher income households to fill as yet uninhabited, deteriorating stock after first preference matches had been made.

The model operates based on a two-year period and was iterated through nine full cycles to produce an eighteen-year forecast of the housing stock.

In summary, the model can be characterized as a housing-stock accounting scheme that keeps track of an initially specified housing inventory as it ages through time and is acted upon in the marketplace by a predicted population, unspecified private investors, and public policy.

Elements. In 1960, San Francisco had something on the order of 310,000 individual households, which the model aggregated into no less than 114 different categories or groups of household types, henceforth distinguished by the label "I groups." Each demonstrates a distinct demand for housing. These 114 groups were created by disaggregating the total population of the city according to four attributes: general household *type*—no children, head over sixty years; no children, head under sixty years; households with children; *color* of the household head—white, black, Oriental, and other; household *size*—(1, 2, 3+), (1-2, 3-4, 5+), or (1, 2, . . .) depending upon color and type. Each household type and color category was further disaggregated according to one of three sets of annual *income* classes:

$0 - $2,000	$0 - $4,000	$0 - $4,000
2 - 4,000	4 - 6,000	4 - 6,000
4 - 6,000	6 - 8,000	6 - 8,000
6 - 8,000	8 - 10,000	8 - 12,000
8 - 15,000	10 - 15,000	12,000+
15,000+	15,000+	

This variation of size and income classes among racial categories severely hinders intergroup comparisons.[31] The number of households in each group was calculated as a percentage of all households, based on percentage distributions of the four attributes found by the special cross-tabulation of the 1960 census data.

Preference lists were derived from the same empirical source by a method that is not clearly presented in the descriptive accounts.[32] In general the list was developed from the percentage rates of occupancy of house type by household types according to the 1960 census. The "Hendricks-Barringer Aspiration Index" (named for two members of the model team) assigned arbitrary weights to these percentages to indicate toward what housing type any given household would aspire. The criterion is economic and static, i.e. fixed once and for the entire eighteen-year period of the analysis, and produces an ordering of fifty alternative housing preferences for each household group.

The census tabulation was also used to infer a "rent-paying ability" for each of the 114 groups. Maximum and minimum rent values for each group were determined and are read in as data. The ability to pay is distributed normally between maximum and minimum values for all households, except for the very rich and the very poor. These households are skewed log normally toward a maximum rental value. The reasoning for this is that wealthy households choose to spend more on housing than would normally be expected on the average for the group; the very poor have to spend more. Distributing rent-paying ability normally also forestalls sharp discontinuities in the rent-paying abilities of household types and facilitates calculation. No empirical evidence is presented to suggest that rent-paying ability is either normally or log normally distributed. The hypothesis is merely asserted and then employed.

The supply of housing is located in 106 "neighborhoods," the elementary land unit in the model. A neighborhood is characterized by three elements: *income range, racial composition,* and mean *household type.*

Neighborhoods roughly correspond to 179 enumeration district boundaries used in the 1960 census, not to census tracts.[33] Census tracts were not used, according to a city planner, "because enumeration districts were smaller and would allow us to maximize differences between neighborhood groups. Neighborhoods are really pretty arbitrary."[34] The procedure by which 179 enumeration districts were compressed into 106 neighborhoods is also arbitrary.

Each neighborhood was to be classified with a "location number," "L," to be derived from a substudy of the "Amenity Attributes of Residential Locations."[35] The thirty-six possible amenity classes were distributed among characteristics of "functional quality," "urban character," "topography," and "historic status."[36] But the "amenities" study was intractable for the purposes of the model, and only the "topography" characteristic survived. Finally, the "L" number for each neighborhood was created from census enumeration district data on topography, modal housing type, and average rent.[37]

The difficulty of settling on a basic scheme for the "L" category illustrates the frequent mismatches between the imaginative definitions of a problem and the harsh realities of building a working model. The theme is fundamental.

Within each neighborhood, residential land was assigned to one of 4,980 *fracts,* a special unit of analysis developed by ADL:

TABLE 11-1

Location Numbers in San Francisco Model

L	TOPOGRAPHY	MODAL STRUCTURE TYPE	RANGE OF MEAN MONTHLY RENT
1	Hilly	SF	$0-140
2	Hilly	SF	140-275
3	Hilly	SF	275+
4	Hilly	5+	$0-75
5	Hilly	5+	75-115
6	Hilly	5+	115+
7	Level	SF	$0-125
8	Level	SF	125-175
9	Level	SF	175+
10	Level	2-4	$0-75
11	Level	2-4	75+
12	Level	5+	$0-75
13	Level	5+	75-115
14	Level	5+	115+

Source: ADL, "Technical Paper No. 8," January 1966, p. 16.

In order to keep inventories of dwelling units commensurable among different housing types, and *to keep the inventory of space for the City within the memory capacity of a large computer,* we invented for Model purposes a land unit that we call a "fract."[38]

Each fract contains housing of the same type and condition at a given constant population density and encompasses approximately two acres of space. The fract is an artifact: a summary statistic, having no spatial referent, which has been devised to accommodate computer capacity limitations. The total number of fracts within a single neighborhood is constant; however, neighborhoods do not contain equivalent numbers of fracts. Fracts do not necessarily contain contiguous parcels of land, and it is impossible to identify the location of any fract, except to say that its parts are spread about within a given neighborhood. Construction, demolition, and rehabilitation involve fracts, not single houses.

Within the fracts, the fundamental element of housing is the "dwelling unit."[39] Each unit was classified according to its *tenure,* number of *rooms,* and *structure* type. This produced thirty mutually exclusive "J" or housing types represented in Table 11-2 (several of which subsequently turned out to be nearly empty).

The housing stock is also characterized as to condition ("C" categories) as either *sound,* in need of *minor repairs, deteriorating,* or *dilapidated,* based on Bureau of the Census ratings. The initial assessment of condition and the determination of aging or decay rates of the housing stock are critical factors in the model. Several substantial theoretical

TABLE 11-2

Housing or "J" Types in San Francisco Model

J	STRUCTURE	TENURE	ROOMS
2	Single Family	Rent	1-2
3	Single Family	Own	1-4
4	Single Family	Rent	3-4
5	Single Family	Own	5-6
6	Single Family	Rent	5-6
7	Single Family	Own	7+
8	Single Family	Rent	7+
9	Public Structures		
10	Vacant Land		
12	2-4	Rent	1
14	2-4	Rent	2
15	2-4	Own	1-4
16	2-4	Rent	3-4
17	2-4	Own	5-6
18	2-4	Rent	5-6
19	2-4	Own	7+
20	2-4	Rent	7+
22	5+	Rent	1
24	5+	Rent	2
25	5+	Public Housing	3-4
26	5+	Rent	3-4
27	5+	Public Housing	5+
28	5+	Rent	5-6
30	5+	Rent	7+

Source: ADL, "Technical Paper No. 8," January 1966, p. 17.

issues are embedded in the decay process, but we shall defer comment until the "Theoretical Appraisal" section of this chapter.

Thus, housing units are grouped into 4,980 artificial units—fracts—which are in turn contained in 106 neighborhoods. Household types ("I" groups) demand, according to derived preference lists and constrained by inferred rent-paying abilities, housing possessing various structural ("J"), conditional ("C"), and locational ("L") characteristics.

Processes. A simple flow chart summarizes the processes by which demand and supply interact. There are nine logical steps in the operation of the model.

Step One is housekeeping. Data are read in and stored, machine and program controls are filed, etc. The quantity of data involved necessitates the use of overlays and some very clever packing and unpacking routines to enable the model to run within the limits of computer capacity.

Step Two ages the housing stock in one of three ways: improvement, "normal" aging, or "accelerated" aging. The stock's condition may be *improved* through private market action, prompted by a demand-

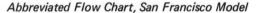

FIGURE 11-1

Abbreviated Flow Chart, San Francisco Model

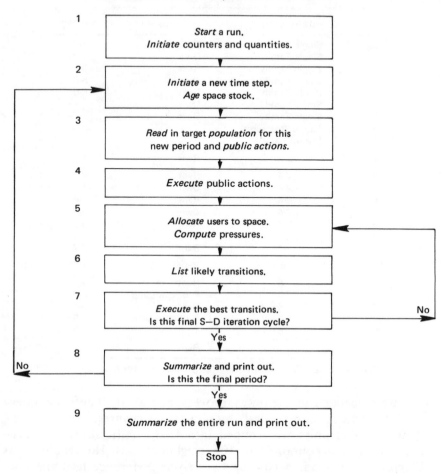

Source: ADL, "Technical Paper No. 8," January 1966, p. 34.

induced sequence of events; through private initiative induced by public funds, i.e. rehabilitation; through new private construction, motivated by profit concerns; or through the construction of public housing. On the other hand, the housing stock may age or decay. Aging, the process by which a building becomes obsolescent and deteriorates under conditions of normal maintenance expenditure is simulated through the application of a first-order Markov process. The Markov process describes the proportion of houses of any given condition—sound, minor repair, deteriorating, or dilapidated—that decay to a worse condition within a given period of time. If demand for a certain type of housing is sufficiently high, it may be in a simulated investor's interest

126

to undermaintain, thereby increasing his profit margin. In this case, an "accelerated aging" option or branch is taken in the program and the housing condition is made to deteriorate more rapidly than it would "normally." The Markov process terminates in a fifth, or absorbing, state, which replicates the removal of stock from the market altogether. While "Technical Paper #8" reports that values for the aging matrices were derived from the 1960 Census of Housing,[40] an earlier report indicates that the data come from a WPA special real-property survey conducted between 1937 and 1939.[41] One must assume the earlier paper to be correct because it is devoted exclusively to the aging issue and it was noted in several separate interviews as the prime source. We shall consider the appropriateness of these data momentarily.

Step Three inputs exogenous population predictions for each "I" group for each period of the analysis. It also reads in any public actions that are to be executed in the given period. Because the model's purpose is to assist policy-makers, let us mention what public actions are considered. All of these actions are exogenously determined.

- Zoning—Each neighborhood is tagged with two zoning numbers representing the maximum number of fracts that are available for either high-density (5+ units) or medium-density (2-4 units) development. Changing either of these parameters could significantly change the characteristics of a neighborhood. The only aspect of zoning that can be handled is density. This point is not made in the technical literature but is obvious from the program listing itself.
- Location category—Because "L" categories are data assigned to neighborhoods, these data may be altered. ADL's assertion that "it is possible to simulate a change in the amenities of any given Neighborhood by changing its Location category"[42] is hard to comprehend because the "L" categories are such poor indicators of amenities.
- Assessed and Rental Values—Both may be manipulated to produce more or less investment return for a given house type (JcL—house category, condition, location). ADL's interpretation of what a change in these parameters means is neither clear nor particularly plausible.
- Capital Improvement—A fract may be removed from the private residential market by altering its "J" category to #9, signifying "for public use." Liberal interpretations of what this means include the construction of freeways, parks, and public buildings. Recall, however, that a fract is a summary bundle of homogenous houses, and it is not precisely locatable within a neighborhood.
- Code Enforcement—A percentage of substandard fracts may be brought up to sound condition; the particular fracts affected are chosen randomly.
- Construction Costs—Construction cost estimates are critical elements in the algorithm that reconciles supply and demand. It is possible to alter these estimates at any period. ADL interprets these changes as subsidies or "special aid" to induce construction.
- Aging Rates—Because the probabilities for the Markov process are read in as data, they may be changed, causing the housing stock to decay at a greater or lesser rate.

- Rent-paying Ability—The range or distribution for any household group may be altered at will, to reflect public subsidy, for example.

Step Four executes the public actions by altering parameters for a period's run. Each fract has six binary (yes-no, on-off) "flags" associated with it which indicate peculiar attributes:

1. Transition—A fract may be operated on once per time period. This flag indicates whether a transition has already occurred or not.
2. Public Property Designation—"On" implies public use only; "off" means that the fract is acceptable for private use.
3. Private Market Residential Use—Publicly owned property may be open to private residential use. This is interpreted as a "grace period" during which private residents may use public land.
4. Codes—When "on" the market is forced to bring substandard fracts up to sound condition. It effectively shunts profit criteria normally used to determine improvement odds and uses the best of unprofitable transitions instead.
5. Rehabilitation—If "yes," the cost of transitioning a fract's cost to an improved condition state is reduced an arbitrary 10 percent.
6. Redevelopment—If "yes," the cost of transitioning a fract to an improved condition state is reduced an arbitrary 20 percent.

So much for the public actions, all of which are mechanically injected into the ongoing processing. In fact, the model's treatment of public sector activities is best characterized as crude, but imaginative, bookkeeping.

Step Five allocates the housing supply to household demand according to individual preference demand lists. For each house type (JcL), a *rental value* and a percentage representing a *minimum yield* are read in as data. Yield, defined by

$$JcL = \frac{\text{Rental Value}_{JcL}}{\text{Market Value}_{JcL}} \tag{11.1}$$

or,

$$MV = R1 \ / \ YMIN1^* \tag{11.1a}$$

is best thought of as a return on investment. Market value is not measured directly but is calculated from rental value (derived from the 1960 census tabulation) and yield rate (determined by a special ADL real estate study). In the model, a temporary assignment of demand to housing supply is made without market interaction. That is to say, as many matches as possible are made at the beginning of each simulated

---

*FORTRAN notation: $R1$ = initial value of rent; $YMIN1$ = the yield for that rental value; MV = market value, at initial rental. The notation may be rather tedious to follow; however, I have attempted to reproduce faithfully what was listed in the computer program.

period. *The model reallocates every single household every two years.* Marginal adjustments in response to in- or out-migration or to house construction, etc. are not possible.

After households are allocated initially, excess (unallocated) demand is translated into "rental pressure" by means of a "rent-pressure relationship." If pressure is sufficiently large (i.e. if predetermined parameter values are exceeded), indicating that a different housing use would return a better profit, fracts may be transitioned from one housing type to another. ("A transition represents the change of one fract to a different 'J' type or a different condition.")[43] Fluctuations in pressure may only be great enough to cause rents to change without forcing a change in housing type. One fundamental assumption underlies this phase of the model's operation—profit. "We [ADL] feel that in the long run, however, land-use decisions will respond more nearly to the value of economic yield than to any other individual indicator."[44] "Normal yield" is defined in relationship (11.1). "Transition yield," the anticipated return for a new housing use, is calculated in one of two ways depending upon the anticipated change. In either case a yield ratio (transition yield / normal yield) is calculated. If the ratio is greater than unity, a transition is allowed. Yield ratio calculations are given in FOR-TRAN notation for *new construction* (11.2) and *rehabilitation* (11.3).[45]

New Construction: †

$$YIELD = (R2/YMIN2) / ((R1/YMIN1) + COST) \qquad (11.2)$$

Rehabilitation:

$$YIELD = (R2-R1) / (YMIN2*COST) \qquad (11.3)$$

where

$YIELD$ = yield ratio
$R2$ = rental for new use
$YMIN2$ = rate of return on new use
$R1$ = rental for old (present) use
$YMIN1$ = rate of return on present use
$COST_{(11.2)}$ = total amount to construct project of new type
$COST_{(11.3)}$ = amount needed to change from one condition or type to another: difference
$*$ = multiplication sign in *FORTRAN*
$/$ = division sign in *FORTRAN*

The interpretation of the new construction relationship is straightforward. Substituting from (11.1a), $YIELD (CONST) = MV2/(MV1 +$

---

† For clarity, relationship (11.2) could be distinguished from (11.3) by subscripts, e.g.
$YIELD (CONST) = (R2/YMIN2) / ((R1/YMIN1) + COST (CONST)) \qquad (11.2)'$
$YIELD (REHAB) = (R2-R1) / (YMIN2*COST(REHAB)) \qquad (11.3)'$

COST). If this yield ratio, the ratio of expected to present market value plus construction costs, does not exceed unity, no transition can occur.

The interpretation of the rehabilitation relationship is not so simple. Substituting and altering symbols for the sake of clarity, one can easily see that,

$$YIELD = \frac{MV2}{R2} \cdot \frac{\Delta R}{\Delta C} \qquad (11.4)$$

where,

$$YMIN2 = R2/MV2 \qquad (11.5)$$

or, the yield ratio for rehabilitation is a direct function of the new market value and the difference in rents, and an inverse function of the expected rental and the difference in costs. Whereas the yield ratio for new construction is determined by simple total-cost comparisons and would be expected to produce stable values for the index, the yield ratio for rehabilitation is determined by differences in rents and costs and would, except for a narrow range of ($\Delta R/\Delta C$), be expected to produce unstable values. One would expect either no rehabilitations to satisfy the yield constraint, or so many to satisfy it that some other limit would have to be imposed on the model's desire to rehabilitate, convert, or merge projects. Differences ("Δ") can be quite explosive when modeled and used in this fashion. Let us continue the processing of Step Five.

In the model, upward "rent pressure" created by unsatisfied demand causes more of a given house type to be added until demand and pressure are reduced. Similarly, downward rent pressure, created by excess supply, causes prices to drop in an effort to make a housing type more competitive for existing demand. However, in the empirical context, the movement of price in response to fluctuations in demand is hard to summarize; it is neither instantaneous nor symmetrical. Representing these perversities in a model is an extremely difficult problem.

Borrowing an analogy from physics, ADL's model team decided that a function describing magnetic hysteresis, the "lagging of magnetization behind the magnetizing influence,"[46] was like these lagging and asymmetrical price fluctuations for housing demand. For the purpose of comparison the rent-pressure relationship from ADL's technical report is shown in Figure 11-2; Figure 11-3 shows some sample "B-H" or hystereses loops. The theoretical adequacy of the analogy will be considered in greater detail momentarily. For now it is sufficient to point out that rents are arbitrarily constrained to fluctuate a maximum of ($\pm$) 4 percent, no matter how great or deficient demand, and that the arrows in ADL's figure (reproduced exactly in 11-2) are backwards, as evidenced in ADL's verbalization of the process.

The meaning of the graph is as follows. If the space pressure is well above 1, this indicates that a larger number of households desire the particular housing type than there is stock available, and rents are caused to increase at a maximum rate. If pressures are well below 1, this indicates substantial vacancies, beyond the normal turnover. In the latter case, there would be a strong incentive for owners to reduce rents in order to increase the occupancy rate of their property. If pressures are only slightly lower than 1, the situation is ambiguous. The owner would like to reduce his rent slightly in order to fill the property; however, in doing so, he may also have to reduce the rent for those units that are currently occupied. Thus, he may gain more by keeping the rents fixed and tolerating the slight vacancy. Two different curves are used for rent as a function of pressure. The pressure at the time of the rental computation is compared with pressure one year ago. If the pressure is increasing, landlords will assume a basically more optimistic outlook than if the pressure is decreasing. Thus, the upper curve is used for rising pressure and the lower curve is used if pressure is decreasing; we have a rent-pressure, "hysteresis" effect. No matter how high the pressure on a given property, rents do not increase faster than 4 percent a year. Similarly, even with a very high vacancy rate, it is assumed that rents will not decrease more than 4 percent a year, due to natural inertia and the averaging effect of some properties feeling the pinch of vacancies more than others.

FIGURE 11-2

ADL's Rent Pressure Relationship

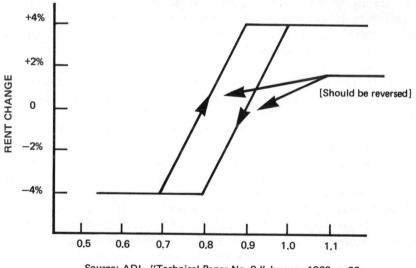

Source: ADL, "Technical Paper No. 8," January 1966, p. 26.

Pressures and new rental values are computed for every housing type in the total stock by the end of Step Five.

FIGURE 11-3

Hystereses Loops—Magnetics

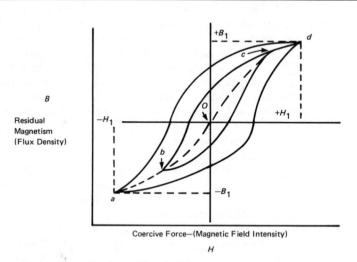

Source: C. E. Bennett, *Physics* (New York: Barnes and Noble, 1952), p. 101.

Step Six ranks likely private-market transitions on the basis of the values of pressures and yields just calculated.

Beginning with the most highly pressured house type, the program seeks for each house type whose rent pressure is greater than unity, a fract of that housing type that might be altered to reduce both pressure and demand. Yields for all likely transitions are computed, using either the new-construction or rehabilitation-yield relationships already discussed. If, for any possible transition, the transition yield exceeds the present yield, i.e. [*YIELD .GT.* 1.0], the fract associated with that transition is placed on a list of potential projects.

Step Seven orders the top 100 projects by descending value of yield and returns control of the program to Step Five, where the allocation process is repeated. This reiteration is intended to produce a better approximation of short-run supply and demand equilibrium. Besides the yield criterion, reallocation is subject to the constraints of zoning and single transition within a time period already discussed. The program cycles through the "Allocate-List-Execute" steps twice for each two-year time period; the choice of two cycles is arbitrary. Because iteration is designed to reduce rent pressure, thereby approximating a better reconciliation of supply and demand in the model, one might legitimately propose a technical test by asking the question: "How many cycles of the model through Steps Five, Six, and Seven are necessary before rent pressure is reduced and consequent transitions cease?" If these logical steps are working properly, one would expect convergence in several cycles, not necessarily two. Regardless, the test provides insight into the adequacy of the model's operation and simulated behavior.

Step Eight updates files and records excess demand and supply from the current period. The summary statistics recorded for each period include, among others, the current inventory of the entire housing stock by type, location, and condition; the level of rents for all types; the costs of transitions executed during Step Seven; the level of rent pressure; and the number and type of households that could not be successfully matched with the housing supply. The homeless residual is summarized and subsequently handled externally to the model by conventional analyses.

At this point, if the model has not processed all the intended analytical periods, control is transferred back to Step Two, a new set of inputs is read in, the stock is aged, and processing commences again. If the final period has been run through, control flows to Step Nine.

Step Nine accumulates and dumps all outputs onto a binary tape, which is subsequently processed by a set of output programs. The quantity of information generated by the model is prodigious, and little effort was expended to distill the outputs into an intelligible form. Analyzing the output from a production run of the model requires *at least one week* of mind-numbing devotion. There are no summary statistics, graphic displays, or critical indicators. This is a curious situation, to say the least, given the putative policy purposes of the enterprise.

A Thumbnail Sketch. The order of processing is depicted in nine overall, logical steps. At best, the model performs an accounting function. Indices and weights are calculated to set up demand preference orderings; housing supply elements are matched with these household demand orderings; and mismatches generate adjustments in the indices, weights, orderings, and levels of both supply and demand. The most critical facets of the model clearly are *population* estimates, *preference* orderings, *aging* procedures, and *rent pressure* calculations. Each of these provides a logical focus for theoretical assessment.

Theoretical Appraisal

Elements and their interrelationships and order of processing have been described in some detail. For each of the four important subroutines that have been identified, we may begin asking questions about theoretical origin, meaning, and plausibility.

THE CONTEXT

Population Estimates.[48] Determining what the total population of San Francisco would be in 1978, the terminal year of the forecast, was done on the basis of the assumption that the total population would increase in response to improving stocks of housing and expanding economic opportunities. A total population of 854,808 was forecast for 1978, an increase of 114,492 over the 1960 level.[49] When asked why their population estimate postulated a large increase, an ADL official explained:

> This prediction of a gain of one hundred thousand people was based on the assumption that the Community Renewal Program would in fact be implemented. I mention this because it comes up so frequently, people say, "You must have been crazy to say that population would grow, and everybody knows that there is no basis to say that the population would grow. The whole model must have been, therefore, haywire." Well, of couse, population was exogenous to the model. We used [name] over at Berkeley, the best man we could get. The assumption that we made about the future almost had to be that the CRP was going to be implemented; otherwise, there would have been no rationality.[50]

Rationality aside, the model depends delicately upon accurate demographic data and well-executed forecasts.[51]

Consider the problem of forecasting a total population level for a given area eighteen years hence and determining what that level will be at each of the consecutive two-year intervals. The problem is compounded by disaggregating the total population into 114 separate sectors and repeating the first two steps. As a demographer, you would be faced with the prodigious task of providing estimates for over 1,000 separate population parameters. Providing these data was exactly the task that confronted the ADL model team; the problem was hired out to a university-based demographer.

The mathematical model that he produced to make detailed estimates is much like the population-generating relationships developed in Part II. Total population at any period is a function of the prior period's population, the net increment or loss from migration, plus births, less deaths.

$$P_{t+1} = P_t + P_t(b + B_t) - P_t(d + D_t) + P_t(m + M_t) \qquad (11.6)$$

where,

P_t = total population at time t
b = birth rate
B_t = assumed annual rate of change of birth rate
d = death rate
D_t = assumed annual rate of change of death rate
m = net migration rate
M_t = assumed annual rate of change of net migration rate

This relationship was used to generate total populations for each of the intervening years between 1960 and the terminal year forecast, i.e. the 854,808 value. Obtaining values for the 1960 birth and death rates is straightforward; migration rates are usually a bit more problematical. However, a great deal rests on the assumptions and methods used to set rate of change parameters. In fact, with three "free parameters" (B_t, D_t, and M_t), almost *any* population time series could be produced by this relationship. Unfortunately, the available documentation does not clarify these matters, and one may only surmise what has been done to obtain the parameter values.

The population totals were partitioned into households in a similar manner. Total households at time t are assumed to be a simple proportion of population, modified by a rate of change parameter.

$$H_t = P_t(r + R_t) \tag{11.7}$$

where,

H_t = total households at time t
P_t = total population at time t
r = persons/household
R_t = assumed annual rate of change of r

Once the total number of households is known, it is partitioned into "I" groups according to their 1960 percentage distribution pattern, modified slightly by arbitrary assumptions about the changing character of the population. This partitioning is illustrated in Figure 11-4. The plausibility of what resulted from partitioning in this fashion is open to question.

If one assumes that the 20 percent sample census data are accurate, plus or minus 10 percent, then no less than thirty-one of the 114 "I" groups are populated by fewer households than the margin of data error. If one assumes plus or minus 20 percent inaccuracy (not unreasonable for highly disaggregated sample data), then forty-two out of the 114 "I" groups are within the margin of error. More than one-third of the model's fundamental units of population are indistinguishable from common measurement error. The ten largest "I" groups actually account for more than 40 percent of the total population; the residual 60 percent is of course distributed among the remaining 104 groups. The model's level of demographic detail errs significantly.

Given that these demographic estimates, the critical elements of demand, are implausible and probably erroneous, what the model produces cannot be taken too seriously.

Preference Lists. Two theoretical assumptions dominate the implementation of household preference lists—preferences do not change

FIGURE 11-4

Household—"I" Group Partitioning Scheme

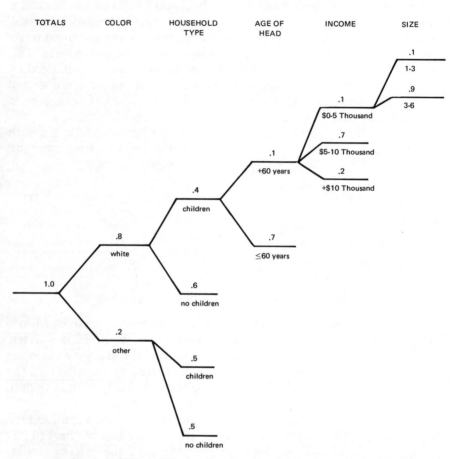

Source: R. P. O'Block, "The San Francisco Housing Simulation Model," p. 40.

over time, and 1960 preferences for housing are ultimate. Arbitrarily assigning "aspiration weights" (as ADL elected to do) fails to remove this severe static bias. These assumptions imply that the whole population's first preference for housing is for the most expensive type. With such a bias and a limited number of expensive units, it is a wonder that the model succeeds in allocating households at all.

No empirical work, for example, was done to substantiate the economic aspiration hypothesis. No effort was made to collect time series data that might have suggested trends and changes in locational preferences. The obvious point, that one does not compute flows or rates from a single, static source of data, partly obscures the more subtle issue that the model's structural specification effectively foreclosed necessary research.

Related to preference lists is the theoretical notion of rent-paying ability: the distribution of rental expenditures and their maximum and minimum for each household group. The notion of rent-paying ability is subject both to the same static bias that flaws preference orderings and to the measurement error problem of disaggregated household groupings. Not only is there little reason to believe in many of the household groups and their rent-paying abilities, but there is even less reason to believe that rent potential is normally distributed.

In the model we can handle any distribution. However, this would seem to place a significant burden on the data gathering efforts and, furthermore, it is probably unnecessary. I believe it will be easier to have a small set of standard distributions which can be easily specified by planners designing a computer run and which will be sufficiently flexible to approximate the kinds of distributions which are reasonable.[52]

It is one thing to will simple order on a context; it is quite another to observe, measure, and substantiate it.

Aging of the Housing Stock.[53] Data from a 1937-39 WPA real property survey were used to set the parameters in the aging subroutine of the model. These data are complete and of unusually high quality.[54] One major problem exists, however. A sharp contextual shift is related by one researcher:

... think of it as the basic data for constructing a standard mortality table for housing rather than people. It's like the insurance industry, you know? One problem, unfortunately, it missed completely. There was a major change in the housing stock as a result of World War II and immediately thereafter. This mortality table has a major discontinuity in it.[55]

The population of San Francisco in 1930 was 634,394; in 1940 it was 634,536; in 1945 it was estimated as 827,400; and in 1950 it was 775,357.[56] Approximately 200,000 additional people created a discontinuity in the context too severe to be ignored. Also ignored is the considerable out-migration to the suburbs of the 1950s, stimulated by improved transportation (the Golden Gate Bridge opened in 1937) and by low-cost government mortgage money. Estimating and applying decay rates from the prewar housing stock essentially ignores these discontinuities.[57] The process of deterioration does not occur in isolation.

"Technical Paper #2" reports that graphic plots of the WPA data produced

curves ... similar to those ... that are observed: 1. In chemical kinetics (single-stage irreversible reactions) and 2. In nuclear physics, where a radioactive parent element decays into a radioactive daughter product, which in turn decays into further radioactive daughter products.[58]

THE CONTEXT

Theoretically, how adequate is this physical analogy? Is the theory applicable to the problem of housing deterioration?

Markov processes operate with the following assumptions: Transitions depend only upon the present state of an entity. What state an entity came from, how it got there, and how long it has been in its present state are irrelevant. Thus, in the age of housing, transition is independent of an entity's age. All entities of a given class are homogenous. The assumptions of the Markov method should preclude the assumption that housing decay is cumulative, unrelenting, and irreversible—just "like nuclear decay" or "single-stage chemical kinetic" processes. The two assumptions are incompatible.

The particular Markov process used in the model can be decomposed into four transient states and one ergodic set. Conceivably, everything might pass downward in the chain until it attained steady state, i.e. until it was absorbed. This does not happen because quite apart from the aging routine, the model also creates and upgrades housing; steady state is never reached. Symbolically, ADL represents the process as follows:

$$C_1 \xrightarrow{k_1} C_2 \xrightarrow{k_2} C_3 \xrightarrow{k_3} C_4 \xrightarrow{k_4} C_5 \tag{11.8}$$

where, at any time t,

C_i = proportion or number of entities in various states
C_1 = proportion or number in sound condition
C_2 = proportion or number in need of minor repair
C_3 = proportion or number in deteriorated condition
C_4 = proportion or number in dilapidated condition
C_5 = proportion or number removed or absorbed
k_i = proportion of entity deteriorating to next lower class per unit of time

Relationship (11.8) may be generalized in the following form:

$$\frac{dC_i}{dt} = k_{i-1} C_{i-1} - k_i C_i \tag{11.9}$$

The relationship says that the rate of change of entities in condition C_i per unit time is a function of entities entering from the higher state, minus the entities leaving for a lesser state. This produces a set of differential equations comprised of i separate equations, which may be solved sequentially to give *levels* for C_i. For example, when $i = 1$,

$$C_1 = e^{-k_1 t} \tag{11.10}$$

The level or number of entities in condition state 1 (sound) is a simple exponential decay function of time, because $k_1t < 0$. Solutions for other condition states are of similar, but more complicated form. The point to be made by this brief exercise is that *time alone is explaining the deterioration of the housing stock.* The process flows toward a steady state; *ceteris paribus,* everything will be absorbed, given sufficient time. There are three other problems with the process.

Applying the aging routine to all housing of a given type, as is done, assumes homogeneity. That is to say, all houses of a type decay the same way regardless of any specific attributes. This seems implausible.

ADL makes a great point of noting that "there is a tendency for buildings to 'start falling apart' at around 18 years," with the result that "it [is] necessary to assign . . . different values [k_i] for buildings younger than 18 years of age, and older than 18 years."[59] This important empirical regularity and the treatment ADL recommends are made somewhat academic because the model lacks the capacity to account for the age of the housing stock. This seems erroneous.

And finally, aging is uniformly applied to *fracts,* units of analysis having neither empirical referent nor specific spatial location. Housing theory is at odds with physics on this point:

poor-quality dwellings will tend to be spatially concentrated and . . . an increase in the number of poor-quality units will tend to take place at the edges of existing concentrations rather than develop in new areas.[60]

This is an example of the well-known contagion phenomenon and is specifically excluded by the operation of the Markov process on fracts. This seems unreasonable.

Apparently what is needed is time series information relating actual housing conditions to variables thought to be contributing to decay. Allowing one's investment to deteriorate is indeed partly explained by the passage of time; however, far more important are the attitudinal, environmental, economic, and even political factors that operate. There is empirical information about these matters.

[A] basic problem in urban land use is the slowness with which the quantity and quality of housing and other urban improvements respond to changes in living standards, technology, location or urban activities, transportation facilities, and the host of other dynamic factors that influence land use. . . .

The removal of slums through the action of market forces alone appears to be related not so much to physical or economic depreciation as to alternative uses for the land, particularly the rate at which nonresidential can replace residential land use. This rate is dependent upon the rapidity and locational pattern of urban growth. . . .

Commonly accepted notions of the operation of the filtering-down process [conceptually akin to aging] are found to be ambiguous and inadequate when subjected to an empirical test, and a reformulation of the theory of filtering, which lends itself to verification, is suggested.[61]

Depending on the visceral appeal of a model's output as the criterion of acceptability is grossly inadequate. The physical analogy is of dubious utility at even the present pretheoretical level of crude approximation. The assumptions built into the aging routine are implausible and render it virtually useless as a replica of housing deterioration processes.[62]

Rent Pressure. Another analogy from physical science was relied on to describe the price response to fluctuations in demand. How plausible is the analogy?

Hysteresis, as we have noted, relates magnetic field intensity in a vacuum (H) and the flux or induction density of magnetic force in a real medium (B), according to the following relationship:

$$B = \mu H \tag{11.11}$$

where,

μ = magnetic permeability of the medium

Plotting B versus H, as was done in Figure 11-3, shows the variation of μ, i.e. its value decreases with increasing H until magnetic saturation is reached. The concept is derived from Coulomb's well-known law of magnetics.

$$F = \frac{mm'}{\mu r^2} \tag{11.12}$$

where,

F = force
mm' = mass units
r^2 = separation distance between m and m', squared

and,

$$H = \frac{F}{m'} = \frac{m}{\mu r^2} \tag{11.12a}$$

$$B = \frac{m}{r^2} \tag{11.12b}$$

B and H (modified by the parameter μ) are formally equivalent. Equivalency of "rent pressure" to "rent change" in the same sense is problematical. The concept of permeability has no theoretical or empirical equivalent in the housing concept either. In fact, a standard use of hysteresis in electrical engineering calls for the development of a normal magnetization curve, composed of plots of the tips of successive hystereses loops (dotted line segment *a,b,O,c,d* in Figure 11-3) to average out the effects of the phenomenon in its ascent and descent phases.[63] This would have been a far more persuasive use of the concept than saying, to put ADL's relationship into words: For all types, locations, and conditions of housing, rents will increase or decrease a fixed 4 percent per period, except for a range of difference between supply and demand in which rent changes become a linear function of the extent of difference. Why a linear function? Why a symmetrical function? Where are the data to support the hard relationship? Does common sense allow us to explain rent shifts solely as a function of pressure? All of this seems untenable.

There is empirical work to indicate that magnetic theory and housing theory differ in many respects. Sherman Maisel contends that changes in unoccupied dwellings are related to changes in the money market, particularly speculative money.[64] Rapkin, Winnick, and Blank have developed the important concept of "intended vacancy," the rational choice to hold vacant dwelling units.[65] And some systematic work has been done on the relationship between race and rent.[66]

If sufficient doubt were not already cast on the rent pressure relationship, consider that it is indiscriminately applied in the model to all housing types. This seems erroneous.

Depending upon the visceral appeal of a function's form as the criterion of its appropriateness for use in a model is unsatisfactory. In the absence of some empirical, supportive evidence, the physical analogy is not acceptable. The assumptions built into the rent pressure relationship are offensive to sense, common and otherwise. The yield relationships are equally offensive.

The value of the variable *YIELD* is the criterion for deciding when, how many, and what kind of houses will be built or rehabilitated. Relationship (11.2) for new construction says: If, after comparing present market value plus construction costs with the market value of a new land use, one perceives economic improvement in the new use, then list that property with all others that are potentially profitable, order them by descending yield, and execute the 100 most profitable. Housing construction is solely a function of market value and construction costs.

Some generally accessible evidence and theory suggests that this statement of the relationship is oversimplified to the point of uselessness.

Muth, writing in 1960 in a well-known article, links residential construction with *changes* in construction costs, *changes* in demographic characteristics (lagged several periods), *changes* in per capita income levels, and *changes* in interest rates charged for mortgage money.[67] On the question of estimating potential reuse values, Wallace F. Smith

141

comments, "Owners of property, in general, may have only vague notions of the re-use potential of their real estate, or the lack of such potential." As other determinants of new construction, Smith notes the importance of brokerage, the need for access to redevelopment financing, the need for contractor services, and the importance of particular income tax considerations, alternative investment opportunities, and judgments of the expected rate of increase of population.[68] Nowhere in this literature is there evidence that the elements configured in relationships (11.2) or (11.3) explain new construction or rehabilitation.[69]

Construction is subsumed into a single element (*COST*), which is initially read in and, although it could be, is never recalculated. It is used in the model as though construction costs were sufficiently stable to be considered constant. In fact, there are two well-known cycles in the highly volatile housing construction industry. Jack Guttentag, in characterizing the "short cycle," comments, "The demand for housing is extremely sensitive to the terms on which mortgage credit is available, . . . fluctuations in residential construction resulted from fluctuations in general economic activity."[70] And then, Arthur F. Burns's 1935 classic on the "long cycle"[71] has special relevance to an eighteen-year forecast: A cycle is not a single entity but a composite effect of many specific underlying factors, which combine to produce an overall regularity in the movement of some index. Of all cycles, perhaps one of the best known (an extensive literature predates World War II) is the construction cycle. It covers a space of fifteen to twenty years and is frequently called "the long cycle." Neither form of cycle is directly considered in the model. Furthermore, actual housing market activity was not considered either. Table 11-3 presents a crude idea of what an important segment of the construction industry in the Northern California region was actually doing in the 1950-60 decade. Incidentally, the model does not differentiate between house types with respect to the tendency to construction or rehabilitation, despite the contention of Rapkin, et al.:

. . . new construction of multiple dwellings is slower in getting started than single family construction, other things being equal. The larger scale investment requires more assurance that favorable market cost conditions will persist.[72]

Holding construction costs constant seems to be an unwarranted simplification. ADL was at least aware of this issue, as indicated in an internal memo on the relationship between construction and rent, dated May, 1964:

Construction in our model occurs in response to changes in yield, which result from changes in rent and changes in pressure. . . . the construction industry is not as rational and simple as we would like it to be. There are other factors entering the picture, and I think we have a lot of work ahead of us to pin these down.[73]

TABLE 11-3

Northern California—One-Family Housing Starts
1950-1960

YEAR	ONE-FAMILY HOUSE STARTS	PERCENT CHANGE FROM PRIOR YEAR
1950	49,800	—
1951	35,700	−28.5
1952	35,800	—
1953	33,800	−5.5
1954	50,300	+49.0
1955	57,800	+15.0
1956	38,600	−33.0
1957	31,500	−18.0
1958	36,227	+15.0
1959	46,663	+27.0
1960	35,766	−23.5

Source: John P. Herzog, *The Dynamics of Large-Scale House-building* (Berkeley: Center for Real Estate and Urban Economics, 1963), pp. 21, 44.

When one has a contractual and reputational obligation to build a model or to solve a problem by a specific date, details such as the volatile construction industry, money markets, general economic activity, specific tax constraints, and expected changes in housing demand all become less and less important. If a model-builder has never been sensitized to the details of a specific empirical context, one should not find fault with his great inferential leaps from decaying isotopes to decaying houses or from expanding and collapsing magnetic fields to expanding and collapsing rentals.

For whatever reasons, what resulted from the process of model specification and design in San Francisco is a model that is simultaneously quite *simple* and yet *complicated* beyond reason. This calls to mind a set of technical questions to which we now turn.

Technical Appraisal

Data, the analytical level of detail, the construction of the model, and its operating characteristics are four technical points of prime importance. Procedures for data identification, collection, and estimation are common concerns whose importance becomes crucial in data-dependent models. The San Francisco model has a voracious appetite because it is so disaggregated—because it operates at a "fine" level of detail. We shall review how this detail, the "significant relationships," and "determinants" divined by ADL's technicians were made into a working model.

Data. Data problems plagued the model-building effort from the start.

Because city data were unsuitable (or, equivalently, nonexistent), 1960 census data were relied on. Decennial censuses prior to 1960 were maintained at a level of aggregation unacceptable for the model and could not be used.

Discrepancies between what the census provided and what the model demanded were partially filled by ad hoc procedures. Exactitude yielded to expedience on more than one occasion.

As a portion of the city's in-kind contribution, firemen were asked to complete a housing condition questionnaire in the course of their routine fire safety inspections. This initially presented a problem, for according to one respondent, "The Fire Department wasn't about to collect this primary data over which they would have no control and which would conceivably totally destroy the image of the Fire Department in the City."[74] In time, however, the firemen did cooperate, but the raw data they assembled were never processed and for reasons that are unclear, did not find their way into the model-building activity.[75]

Only slightly more successful were ad hoc efforts to secure data on housing yields, a theoretical keystone of the model. ADL's report is indicative of the limitations of yield estimates:

> Data were gathered from listing sheets and sales folders at Coldwell-Banker [real estate brokers] for 305 properties. Age and condition information on these properties were taken from city files. . . . Each case was coded onto an IBM card to facilitate analysis.
>
> It is not obvious what is meant by "yield." Yield is a complex relationship between an owner with a particular tax status, financial status, and business judgment and a property with income possibilities which may vary according to his judgment.[76]

To satisfy the model, yield and rental data had to be supplied for each house type, in each location and in each condition.[77] (This is approximately $30 \times 14 \times 4 = 1,680$ bits of information.) A curious regularity of data values is discernible in the model's input deck.

As housing condition worsens, yield increases in orderly, stepwise progression. For example,[78] for JcL = 12,1,4—which is a family dwelling type of two to four members, rental, one room in sound condition, in a hilly, high-density, low-cost locale—rent is 1,000, yield is 7.9 percent; for the same J and L but in condition state 2—in need of minor repairs—rent is 492, yield is 8.2 percent; condition 3, *ceteris paribus*, rent is 440, yield 8.9 percent; and lastly, condition 4, rent is 300, yield is 9.2 percent. This example reflects another systematic bias: the large difference between sound and minor repair condition states. The input data rendition as of January-February, 1965, had rentals for condition 1 on the average double those for condition 2. No explanations and no empirical evidence are presented to justify this. Confronted with a fast-approaching contractual deadline, ADL replaced data collection by "manual reordering" and "inconsistency adjustments" as the procedural standard for data estimation. In April, 1965, the problem of "condition inversion" was noted:

It should be mentioned that the rents in both Models 10 and 11 were manually re-ordered to effect an ordinal array by condition. The rents in earlier runs had exhibited inversions such as condition 4 being higher priced than condition 3, etc. These inversions seem to suggest a reconsideration of census definitions ... At any rate, we should remember that the currently existing rents have been manually re-ordered ... [79]

By June, an expedient and efficient solution to the data problem had been worked out:

The rent differentials between condition 1 and condition 2 tend to be too large—there is a difference of about a factor of 2. ... In addition, many of the rents are inconsistent with one another; that is, we find the rent for C-3 less than the rent for C-4, or the rent for a larger number of rooms less than the rent for a smaller number of rooms. These arise in most instances from the lack of sufficient sample statistics in many JcL's.

To correct for these effects, I have reviewed all the rents and brought them more nearly into the ratio 1:.75:.5:.375, being the relative rents for conditions C-1, C-2, C-3, and C-4 (as determined from the very complete 1939 Housing Survey for the City).[80]

The professional problem is so glaring that one might lose sight of the fact that "slumlords" had just been "manually reordered" right out of the model by making it impossible for any housing in the worst possible condition (C-4) to return more rent than housing in superior states. At the very least, because they no longer correspond to any real phenomenon, these data had been rendered quite useless for any subsequent analysis.

As has already been noted, construction cost estimates are assumed to be constant for all periods in the model. It is unclear what connection exists between a very detailed special study on costs and the data actually used in the model.[81]

These and other general issues were suggested in an uninvited appraisal of the quality of the CRP data base by California Municipal Statistics, Inc., a San Francisco-based clearinghouse for financial and statistical data. In a long and specifically detailed letter to the City Planning Director, concerning ADL's "Final Report," it made severe professional assessments:

Tables of data and text discussion of matters falling within my fields of com-

145

petence, particularly municipal taxation, have been almost invariably erroneous. Indeed, I have noticed serious errors in tabulations of data for areas outside of my direct interests. . . . if those [data] I have not checked are no better than the ones I have, then I have very grave doubts about this entire study. . . .

It's not all so simple [reference to market value estimates]. I don't know if a proper analysis would even have the same conclusion, but certainly if such confused data is being given to the computer for the simulation model, then it's difficult to see how much reliance could be placed on its conclusions.[82]

If one does not have sufficient good, reliable data, and if the prospects for developing the data are not particularly encouraging, why construct a data-dependent model at an extremely fine level of detail? The answer is partly ideological and partly procedural.

Level of Detail. Planning, as a profession, exhibits a distinctly *manipulative* bias. The prevalent ideology demands that a diverse, fine-grained perspective be used to project the state of a specific context into the future. In terms of our caricature of orientations in Exhibit 2-1,[83] a planner's attitudes are contextual, intuitive, and extrapolative (chartist); his temporal perspectives are future-oriented, incrementally adjustive, and dynamic; and his perceptual preferences for analytical units and developmental possibilities are robust, but specifically defined and finely structured. This bias differs sharply from the one that occurs in what we have termed the *explanatory* mode. Differences are particularly severe with respect to the explanatory mode's prevalent static temporal perspective; generalized gross scale of analytical units; and limited interest in treating multiple-operational, useful alternatives.

As a matter of operating procedure, ADL gives primacy to a "group leader" in all matters related to a "case." The CRP case was led by a city planner. The interparticipant tension resulting from the clash of divergent attitudes and perspectives is remarkable for its persistence throughout the project and for the obvious derivative compromises built into the final model.

A senior ADL operations researcher makes the general case for the explanatory mode:

Between the planning people, in the City and ADL, and the model people in ADL, there was a continuing bitter dispute concerning the level of detail that was appropriate. . . .

The basic approach of the city planners is to divide the population groups and housing groups into certain arbitrary categories . . . this strikes you at first as being very logical, but when you start to make these distinctions, you characteristically find that some of the divisions are almost empty and some are over-full. . . .

The whole background, training, and temperament, as far as I can see, of city planners has been to be critically concerned with each population segment in a city and even to the detailed level of . . . say a small Mexican minority . . . wanting to know exactly where those people are going to live, what they will be doing, whether they will be split up by changes, exactly what you are going to do, etc. The model is not intended to answer those kinds of questions.[84]

Even though the model can't answer "those kinds of questions," it was decided to build in so much detail that those questions nonetheless appear to be asked. The best explanation for this is procedural:

The job was basically run by a city planner who happened to want this kind of information [pause] and we usually tend to give a lot of authority . . . to the man who is charged with the case. To an extent, we oozed into it.[85]

"Oozed" is an appropriate characterization. Specifically, according to another operations researcher, the original thirty population ("I") groups were as fine a disaggregation as the model could handle:

At one point [operations research team member] made the comment that, "I will stake my professional reputation on the fact that if you have more than thirty population groups, the thing won't fly." . . . So we started at the level of thirty. That lasted for about a week, and [name of planner] said, "Look, here is a four by eight [matrix], can't we have thirty-two?" I made the fatal mistake by saying, "OK, thirty-two is the same as thirty." The next time instead of four by eight it was five by eight. [pause] It was up to 120 by the time that we got on line.[86]

The divergent, *manipulative,* case is made by a planner: reality is perverse:

Because those guys [operations researchers], and I refer to them as "the guys at the other end of the hall," . . . were never involved in any urban problems, this was an education obviously for them. . . . They saw this in a very simplistic way in part because they really didn't understand the question. They *really* didn't understand! There was an interesting sort of anti-public bias. There was almost an ideological problem here.[87]

Apparently differences of orientation, initially termed ideological, manifest themselves in technical ways. The planner continues:

The area of the questions that [they] ought to be looking at, the OR guys weren't on the one hand interested in, and as a result of not being interested in them, they would tend always to be negative about the ability of the model to plug them in. . . .

What would happen was that once they understood your question, they would not agree with it, and they would resist it on technical grounds . . . implicitly because they did not think that it was important anyway. There is a kind of ideological opposition and then there is a technical opposition.[88]

Severe differences of orientation within ADL's own research group produced a model with extremely strenuous data requirements. This was unfortunate, because the data called for did not exist. A city planner was appointed project leader primarily because the consultant had contracted to produce both a model *and* many other more conventional planning studies. The choice had less than salutary effects, not the least of which was the considerable confusion as to who was the "master modeler."

Construction and Operation. During the interview phase of this inquiry, participants were asked, "Who would you call the master modeler?" The diversity of response is striking:

An operations researcher:

I was responsible for, let me put it this way, I had the responsibility for seeing that the model got developed.[89]

A second operations researcher:

Now that's going to be a little complicated to answer. Now I designed the general structure of the model. [Name "a"] and [name "b"] worked on segments of it; but towards the end, [name "c"], who had not been hired by us at the time of the start of the work, in the last half year . . . he did an enormous amount of the detailing in getting things to fit . . . . [Name "c"] probably knows more about the detail structure within the original framework than anyone else.[90]

A third operations researcher:

I don't think that there is anybody that you could say was the master modeler more than myself, and yet I never thought of myself as having total responsibility for the modeling effort. Titles and responsibilities changed throughout the project. . . . Nobody saw themselves as the master modeler.[91]

A fourth operations researcher: (None of the above)

I would say that [name "c"] ended up *the* person with the best understanding of the model. He understood what we were trying to do from a planning standpoint, but also could go in and—well not make programming changes—but he did know what would happen if you changed certain things . . . [92]

Not only was there no one man clearly designated as the author of the model, there is a lingering question about *who did* have control over model construction during the project! Without clear-cut authority, one should not expect the exercise of individual responsibility. In a large-scale model-building undertaking, lack of leadership is disastrous.

This is a model about housing economics. Not only did none of the conceptual work benefit from the insight of an economist—"You have to realize that there wasn't at that time [prior to February, 1965] a single economist on that group. There were no economists in the group. They were all planners and operations research types"[93]—but the model was coded under subcontract by a computer specialist whose exceptional technical skill in no way compensates for his shortcomings as an economic theorist. His reactions provide one good reason for having a single person execute the conceptual and program functions:

Mainly I was the programmer. In some cases I did change how the model operated. I did interact to the extent that I did change some of the conceptualization of the model because it was easier to do in a different way, and some of the things that they wanted to do weren't realistic in terms of the computer. . . . The basic model that they envisioned is still the same model that was done. But there were a lot of very interesting compromises—because this thing had to be managed—it had to go into a computer.[94]

Conceptual modifications were continuously transmitted to the programmer until he finally refused to accept them.[95] The almost casual attitude of several key respondents (mainly planners) toward programming belies the actual difficulty of the task. Besides getting the model to compile and run, the subcontractor had to suffer the vicissitudes of a local university computing center: "bugs" in the operating system that were triggered during data packing and unpacking routines, inadequate core storage (32K) to support the model, a "no-priority" turnaround policy, and a protracted—three-month—period of downtime caused by the installation of new hardware. That the model ran at all is a considerable achievement and attests to the skill and ingenuity of the programmer. It is, however, unfortunate that much of the model was written in idiosyncratic, albeit efficient, machine language. Most of this had eventually to be reprogrammed in FORTRAN for the MOD III version.

There is no documentation of the model in a form that would allow a qualified, technically skilled stranger to run the model. Pressures of time and money slipped documentation to successively lower priority levels.

When it came down to the actual documentation, in that stage of the model, by that time, the last thing that we were thinking about was documentation because we were fighting time and budget deadlines. The idea was to get the model going. I think by that time there just wasn't time for documentation. . . . To end up with so few people who really know it was a shame, but that was largely due to time and budget.[96]

The following exchange with the city's research agent and caretaker for the model illustrates the status of documentation in 1969 and some longer-range effects.

A: There is no documentation for this program. In other words, if you wanted a fresh programmer to come in here, it would take him at least two man-months of hard work just to learn it.

Q: A good programmer?

A: An *excellent* programmer. One who is able to lay that flow chart kind of thing out. One who is really astute.

Q: You mean to say that there are no flow charts?

A: No flow charts, no detailed charts for a computer programmer.

Q: You mean you have just a listing and nothing else?

A: Yes. Furthermore, the whole thing is on cards. You know you have eight or ten boxes . . .

Q: Just for the model?

A: Just for the model.

Q: My God, what is that, something on the order of 20,000 instructions?

A: We never were able to get a precise count, but we figure that it was between 20 and 25,000 instructions. . . . [Name of programmer] is the only guy who knows anything about the program—the only one. He is the only man who *still* knows anything about the programming.

Q: What would happen if he got hit by a truck?

A: [If he] did in fact get hit by a truck, and I hope to God that he doesn't. . . . somebody, sometime will have to go through the agony and labor of reconstructing it. It would be agony and labor and great cost—but that's the waste. One becomes inured watching the superfluous.[97]

One of the expensive lessons of this project is that no matter how thorough, documentation can never be overly rigorous, particularly if one is building a computer model for use by public officials. As one wiser official remarked: "Take plenty of time in developing and documenting every step, every single step. Just document the hell out of everything, so that you know what's in it and where you stand."[98] That seems like excellent advice.

In the face of an oppressive deadline, scientific and practical niceties, such as debugging logs, sensitivity tests, fine tuning, and efforts to validate, lost out to expediency. For example, in the book-length version of the project, ADL reports that debugging and final production runs were made simultaneously:

The program was completed [termination of the CRP contract] before the model became operational. When all the revisions were completed, the model-building team executed two nine-period (1960-1978) computer runs. Although these runs were executed primarily to "shake down" the model before turning it over to the city, they were also used to evaluate the approach suggested by the CRP. The results of this evaluation were gratifying to both the model-builders and their colleagues who had primary responsibility for this program.[99]

Besides raising the question of the wisdom of combining debugging and production runs, the report arouses one's curiosity. If the model was not operational, how *did* the CRP get produced?

One overriding objective explains most model construction activity during the final eight months of the project: Produce something that runs. It was a reasonable enough desire.

The objective is to deliver a workable model to the City of San Francisco on the 31st of July and to also develop and deliver a technical paper which characterizes and describes the model in terms of what it will and will not do.

It is my considered judgment [ADL executive] that the entire future of ADL in urban planning depends upon delivering a workable CRP model to the City. How we define the expression "Workable" is something that must be thrashed out by you and the project team.[100]

Making a "workable model" meant, in one instance, adjusting several free parameters to insure that generated total values were reasonable. For example, Subroutine *PRICE* (which reproduces the construction-cost data values from each major area or location table for use in critical *YIELD* calculations) has a curious sequence of instructions concerning one variable aptly labeled *FUDGE*. *FUDGE* may adjust *COST* input data by 15 percent or 20 percent, which in turn has direct effect on *YIELD* values. Cost calculations were also affected at one point by the employment of a so-called dangling vector, whose empirical referent remains a bit of a mystery.[101]

The version of the model presented to the city required approximately two hours and forty-five minutes of IBM 7040/7094 (Direct Couple System) computer time per run. Much of this time was expended packing and unpacking the data, which had been created by selecting a fine level of detail. The practical result of having such a long-running model was that few full runs were made. When given to the city, MOD II had been run fewer than twenty times. Even from those few runs, certain interesting behavior had already been noted by the model team.

Recall the theory that recycling through Steps Five, Six, and Seven would reduce the pressure and alleviate the model's propensity to construct and rehabilitate. Well, it doesn't. The rate index calculated for the rehabilitation value of *YIELD* is the most likely reason why it does not:[102]

> . . . project files have never, in any run, dropped below its full allowable component of 100 projects. At one time I tried a six cycle run all within the same period, and we did not exhaust the model's desire to build, and we are still doing a preponderance of rehabilitation with the yield indicating a desire to continue both rehabilitation and new building.[103]

The problem was noted in April, 1965. Rather than finding out why the model was not operating properly, ADL adopted the following expedient: "We [ADL] have taken the position that exogenous limitations (on the number of cycles during the period) can be justified on the basis of restrictions on the available supply of investable funds within a given area."[104] "Taking a position" does not debug a model. What is required are persistence, time, money, imagination, and good luck. The problem was corrected somewhat, after great effort, in the MOD III version.

Even though the model compiles and runs, testing and exploring its behavioral characteristics have not yet begun. Given its theoretical and informational shortcomings and the extent of basic developmental work that is yet to be undertaken, the city of San Francisco, for want of sufficient funds and skilled personnel, in 1968 elected to set the model aside:

> It is clear that neither existing funds, nor the staff available to pursue further development of this model are adequate to the scope of the task of bringing it to operational effectiveness. The current workload of the Department makes further

151

development infeasible, and one which cannot be accomplished without consider-able funding.[105]

A major contributing factor in this decision was the model's erratic behavior. Outputs were so at odds with the "common sense" of those knowledgeable about the context that little or no faith was engendered.

In an evaluation run of MOD III, the somewhat simplified, cheaper, and improved version of the model developed with city funds during 1968, it was determined that the number and magnitude of errors were unacceptable. For example, Table 11-4 reproduces one of the better runs compared to data from the 1960-66 period. Accuracy on point estimates is less important than attaining correspondence of trends and orders of magnitude. In this regard, the model's behavior is distressing. Note, for example, that the model "unloads" in one or a few location categories and produces nothing in the remainder. This would not be so serious except that there is no pattern to the error, probably signaling the presence of a structural flaw. Total values are malleable to the extent that a 3 percent error is obtained between generated and actual data; however, the component errors contributing to this overall excellent result are themselves exorbitant (as great as 1,600 percent!) and inconsistent over time. Even without comparisons to empirical data, the model's behavior is just not very convincing. It is incomprehensible how in 1969 any knowledgeable person could claim, as an ADL spokesman in fact did, that

The CRP was a massive effort to describe the system, and I think it was an excellent one. If you see that report [reference to *Status of the San Francisco Simulation Model*], in terms of reliable indicators of direction, what is frightening about it is its accuracy. We can run that model and gauge the impact of some of the major redevelopment moves.[106]

Perhaps this respondent had placed undue trust in ADL's earlier published version of the "Model Results" in "Technical Paper #8,"[107] where *total* construction is reported as the primary control for tuning the model. Table 11-5 is reproduced exactly from ADL's report, which also contained this self-appraisal:

This analysis of the two runs provides the basis for increased confidence in the effects of the Community Renewal Program and confirms the usefulness of a model in dealing with a complex system. In addition, it raises interesting questions about the real-world system that is simulated. *The apparent success of the model in simulating the complex decision-making activity, which we have termed the housing market, indicates that it is a valuable aid in gauging the impact of major plans and programs that may be considered by city planners and officials.*[108] (emphasis added)

As was indicated in Table 11-4, total control figures are relatively good, even excellent; however, the underlying subtotals are grossly unsatisfactory.

Ethical Appraisal

We shall consider the ethical biases of the model in terms of the information brought to bear in its formulation and its normative possibilities. We shall also consider how one solves a problem and sells an answer where there is little certainty about the analytical question.

Static Equilibrium. Though the model attempts to reconcile house supply and popular demand, no consideration has been given to the question of what is "normal" land use or how the norm is changing over time. In other words, it is assumed that contextual patterns from a single cross-section of time are not only indicative of a "normal" state but that these patterns are worthy of continuing replication. Hence we see popular preference orderings for housing based on the 1960 empirical case; we are told of the invariance of housing types, locational attributes, and condition definitions; and we are asked to accept 1937-39 rates of house decay and fixed construction costs for the eighteen-year forecast to 1978.

Better questions, obscured in the modeler's headlong rush to "get more data in there to get some good fits,"[109] might focus on the reasons for and rates of change of the items that this model considers final and immutable. Why do various population groups prefer various kinds of housing? How are these preference patterns changing through time? What policies could be devised to stimulate or retard these trends? Housing construction is volatile. What are the period and magnitude of the local and regional cycles? What are the effects of the cycles on preference orderings, levels, and rates of change? On migration levels and rates of change? The model's equilibrium bias pre-empts these matters and diverts limited attention to relatively uninteresting and unimportant questions.

Boundaries. As with classic utopian schemes, the model operates under the assumption that the system is physically closed, an unfortunate assumption. As one knowledgeable spectator opined, "[There are] few cases where ADL has recognized that San Francisco is not an isolated city with its own peculiar internally controlled economy, located in the middle of a vast prairie."[110] What becomes of a homeless residual? Do the homeless leave the city or crowd into inadequate shelter? What becomes of the "peopleless" residual of homes? Are migrants encouraged to fill them, or are they converted to alternative uses? Migration, the effects of a well-publicized transportation innovation (Bay Area Rapid Transit—BART), and the role of the city as a population reception center and dispersal point for the greater Bay Area region,[111] are excluded from the model and, consequently, given short shrift in other published CRP reports. Considering the city in isolation is at best a proposition of dubious value.[112]

TABLE 11-4

Sample Performance for New Construction of San Francisco Model

TYPE OF LOCA-TION	ACTUAL MARKET PERFORMANCE 1960-66 STRUCTURE TYPE				MODEL SIMULATION RESULTS PERIODS 1-3, 1960-66 STRUCTURE TYPE				PERCENT DEVIATION TOTAL UNITS MODEL FROM MARKET
	SINGLE FAMILY	2-4 UNITS	5+ UNITS	TOTAL UNITS	SINGLE FAMILY	2-4 UNITS	5+ UNITS	TOTAL UNITS	
Period 1 (1961-62)									
L1	755	336	962	2,053	684	800	320	1,804	−12
2	170	115	544	829	0	0	640	640	−23
3	17	0	20	37	0	0	0	0	0
4	16	73	229	318	0	450	0	450	+42
5	127	87	734	948	0	468	864	1,332	+40
6	13	76	812	901	56	0	1,650	1,706	+89
7	3	17	673	693	0	0	500	500	−28
8	2	2	60	64	0	0	1,092	1,092	+1600
Total	1,103	706	4,034	5,843	740	1,718	5,066	7,524	+29
Period 2 (1963-64)									
L1	782	379	1,033	2,194	684	720	960	2,364	+8
2	176	124	857	1,157	180	0	800	980	−15
3	14	2	0	16	48	0	0	48	+200
4	8	56	319	383	0	0	0	0	0
5	90	76	1,119	1,285	0	312	0	312	−76
6	27	84	2,020	2,131	0	0	3,025	3,025	+42
7	2	8	880	890	0	0	0	0	0
8	2	3	116	121	0	0	1,872	1,872	+1447
Total	1,101	732	6,344	8,177	912	1,032	6,657	8,601	+5

TABLE 11-4 (continued)

TYPE OF LOCATION	SINGLE FAMILY	2-4 UNITS	5+ UNITS	TOTAL UNITS	SINGLE FAMILY	2-4 UNITS	5+ UNITS	TOTAL UNITS	PERCENT DEVIATION TOTAL UNITS MODEL FROM MARKET
Period 3 (1965-66)									
L1	485	361	1,472	2,318	1,080	0	160	1,240	−46
2	134	127	328	589	240	0	0	240	−59
3	11	0	6	17	96	0	0	96	+570
4	9	33	354	396	0	0	0	0	0
5	9	93	535	637	136	0	216	352	−45
6	18	128	2,193	2,339	0	1,062	0	1,062	−55
7	4	24	840	868	0	0	500	500	−42
8	2	9	80	91	0	0	0	0	0
Total	672	775	5,808	7,255	1,552	1,062	876	3,490	−52
GRAND TOTAL	2,876	2,213	16,186	21,275	3,204	3,812	12,599	20,615	−3

Present Version of the Model
(Percent Variation of Actual Model Results from Market Data)

	STRUCTURE TYPE			
	SINGLE FAMILY	2-4 UNITS	5+ UNITS	TOTAL UNITS
Period 1	−33	143	26	29
Period 2	−17	41	5	5
Period 3	131	37	−85	−52
Total	11	72	−22	−3

Source: Department of City Planning, *Status of the San Francisco Simulation Model* (September 1968), pp. 22-23.

[155]

TABLE 11-5

Evidence Reported in Support of Model
New Construction Comparison of Investment
(Millions of Dollars)

	ACTUAL SAN FRANCISCO	SIMULATION RUNS	PERCENTAGE DIFFERENCE
Period 1 (1961-62)	$121.4	$121.7	+0.2
Period 2 (1963-64)	155.7	156.6	+0.5

COMPARISON OF NEW UNITS CONSTRUCTED

	ACTUAL SAN FRANCISCO*				SIMULATION RUNS				PERCENTAGE DIFFERENCE (Simulated vs. Actual)			
	SINGLE FAMILY	2-4 UNITS	5+ UNITS	TOTAL UNITS	SINGLE FAMILY	2-4 UNITS	5+ UNITS	TOTAL UNITS	SINGLE FAMILY	2-4 UNITS	5+ UNITS	TOTAL UNITS
Period 1 (1961-62)	1,415	756	5,891	8,062	428	828	6,886	8,142	−62.6	+9.5	+16.8	+0.9
Period 2 (1963-64)	855	790	8,240	9,885	798	560	7,830	9,188	−6.6	−29.1	−4.9	−7.0
Totals	2,270	1,546	14,131	17,947	1,226	1,388	14,716	17,330	−45.9	−10.2	+4.1	−3.4

Source: ADL, "Technical Paper No. 8," January 1966, pp. 37-38.
*Actual values differ slightly with those in Table 11-4 apparently because of differences in techniques and time of measurement.

Minimum Conflict; Maximum Pliability. The model ignores accessibility, the relationship of place of employment to house location. ADL assumes and argues that San Francisco's geographic compactness renders the concept insignificant.[113] If segments of the population were not packed into well-known ghettos—e.g. Orientals in Chinatown, Chicanos in the Mission, blacks in Fillmore and Hunter's Point—this oversight would be less objectionable. In point of fact, a black is paying a premium for the privilege of living in Hunter's Point if you consider the extent of his physical displacement from downtown places of employment. Assuming that locational factors either cancel out or are not important simply ignores the context.

In constructing preference orderings, it is assumed that current social rankings will continue for the full eighteen years of the model's forecast:

> Choose the user category best able to compete for space. This will depend on such factors as income, race, and children; the assumption being the higher income households, non-Negro races, and families without children are generally in a better position to compete for the type of housing they most desire.[114]

The model institutionalizes these socioeconomic disparities, a continuation of the status quo, by its order of processing. Socioeconomic ("I") groups are located by descending order of rent-paying ability, an income surrogate.[115] Furthermore, it is assumed that any household can and will change housing type during a period if its preferences and available housing can be made to correspond better. Maximum mobility of the population is guaranteed by the reallocation of housing at each period. In effect, all families must try to move to their highest preference type every two years. The highest preference type is defined as that held by the most affluent members of the same or closely related socioeconomic groups. Preference orderings have conservative biases. Population groups are excluded from locations in which none or few were living in 1960; economic mobility is retarded by holding all rent-paying abilities constant. The use of distinct income categories for whites, blacks, and others has already been noted. Population estimates, insofar as they assume a stabilized and increasing number of middle-class whites, also extend the status quo into the future.[116]

Rationality. It is assumed that property owners are perfectly informed and perfectly rational. How else would they know that rent pressure was sufficiently high to increase their rents or to change the use of their holdings? Financiers are likewise prescient and instantly make investment capital available for all profitable transitions;[117] no competing uses for scarce investment capital are considered or win out.[118] The well-known, pervasive, and chronic incidence of unsatisfied housing demand clearly contravenes these assumptions and derivative formalizations. It is simply too much to assume that each of the model's actors, participating in this maximally efficient allocation process, will have complete knowledge of the market and his respective place in it, and equal predisposition to move when rationality and economic self-interest dictate.

At the root of the problem is the recurring theme of differential orientations. One planner, a long-time resident and student of San Francisco, commented:

> It was with the OR guys that we had trouble. These were guys who had very little substantive knowledge of what a housing market does and what the peculiarities of it are. Unlike the security market or the commodity market, none of the principal actors in the housing market has adequate information upon which to base a decision. And so, everyone operates purely on their perceptions and lack of information. When someone looks for a house in the city, they don't have the whole array in front of them to choose from. They have tiny bits of information, tiny perceptions from here and there.[119]

Whether in the interest of efficiency or rationality, the model's treatment of rehabilitation and construction has unmistakable normative connotations. For instance, *only the 100 most profitable* projects are executed each period. Unless a project pays well, it does not get done. Also, "manually reordered" rental values had been rationalized into an orderly 1:.75:.5:.375 ratio for declining house-condition states, thereby eliminating "slumlords": i.e. distortions in market incentives to encourage exploitative behavior were effectively wiped out by the model team. By making these and other key assumptions in the model design and building process explicit, one can begin to see what the model can and cannot produce and what some of the implications are that follow from these assumptions.

Fudging Data. The model demands data that do not exist. When data were not discovered, someone had "to make use of the data that you have and to modify what is available . . . to skirt around with cute ways of getting around the data problems."[120] If data are not available, one should have enough integrity to admit it, enough courage to reassess his model and analytical question, and enough perseverance to gather the essential information. A consultant cannot afford these "luxuries" when solution competence and a contractual commitment are at stake. One who experienced the process comments:

> The problem is coming up with a report that does everything that you said you were going to do in the proposal for the amount of money that you got to do the job. Estimates were made long before knowing the extent of the problem or any of it really. That was one of ADL's problems with the data. The data weren't there, but they felt it wise to produce a working model.[121]

When a difficult or even insoluble problem is obscured or ignored by this kind of behavior, the extent of net harm done to the client, to the touted techniques, to an eventual mastery of the problem, and even to the consultant can only be imagined.

Selling the Locals. Selling has profound negative implications for all participants in the research process:

Look at Arthur D. Little's position. Had we in fact been able to make the fantastic breakthrough, you know developing the atom bomb for $600,000, my goodness, Arthur D. Little could have been in the make-every-city-in-the-country-rich-and-beautiful-for-$600,000-business forever. In other words, management was sold the same bill of goods that the city was, and they paid the price for it.[122]

As a result of ADL's sales pitch, some of the locals responded as if the consultant really did have a $600,000 urban A-bomb. An ADL researcher remarks:

I went in to see [name of planning director] to find out what he would like out of the model, you know, what kinds of outputs and so on. He said, "Christ, you tell me, you guys are supposed to be the experts." We really didn't get much help from those guys over there [in City Planning].[123]

A lawyer who was then on the ADL staff elaborates on several other effects of merchandising expertise:

One of the newspapers kept calling us the "Cambridge overthinkers." There was that kind of animosity. We were too "wiggy." We were foreigners, and we had to live with that too. It probably also prevented the client from really giving us any direction. I think that they really thought we were all too smart and that they were uncomfortable dealing with us.[124]

Selling, which contributed to the estrangement of the technically unsophisticated client, indirectly accounts for the model's limited focus on alternative future states. The consultant's operations researchers made these ethical choices by default:

You would want to get decisions, and nobody would give you decisions. So you made them yourself. Go ahead and ask, "What are the goals that the City is working for?" Nobody would tell you. So you had to go out and piece it together the best you could; because nobody was willing to take a stand. So the time keeps running away from you, and you have to have [these goals], so you piece them together. . . . That just isn't good enough.[125]

It plainly "isn't good enough," but that is the way it was done.

In the guise of maintaining and improving customer relations, selling persistently interfered with the ongoing research task. Management's corporate responsibility to "gain and hold attention . . . to hold hands with the weak sisters, baloney them along, coddle them along,"[126] had the effect of inflating expectations to even greater proportions.[127] A model-builder laments: "[the Board of Supervisors] didn't get it at all. Once in a while they would mouth something about 'modern techniques and this great big project that was going on.' They clearly didn't understand."[128] Besides other demands on their time and attention, they did not understand because they had contact with the project primarily through ADL's management, one of whom purportedly "was almost prepared to promise them that we would pick the right location for the extension of the Embarcadero [Freeway]. I finally had to grab him and say, 'Come on now!' "[129] These undesirable consequences were repeated on a larger scale when promotional activities expanded into the public arena. In April, 1965, one participating city official cited these outcomes:

> The consequences of the publicity [ADL management] had given the model . . . may be disastrous. There is a widespread belief that the model is "operational," that it has already produced valid results, that some of the CRP was tested. None of these beliefs are based on fact. . . . Already, people are asking whether or not it can be used to evaluate freeway routes. We really are not in a position to answer that. Yet assurance has been given by the consultant that this is possible. The use of the model is greatly over elaborated. . . . Too many people are expecting too much of it, and they are expecting immediate results with no real appreciation of the difficulty of obtaining those results.[130]

The public hearings following the project give some indication of one cost of promotional excess. The consultant's representatives made these presentations and reaped the harvest of public misinformation and mistrust. According to the project leader:

> Vicious? My God! It is as if they had been waiting for this, and they just came out of the walls. There was a group that would follow me from meeting to meeting. I would bring my wife along so that there would be one planted friend in the audience. . . . Oh, it was just awful. "Who the hell is Arthur D. Little? You guys came in from the East, what right have you got?"[131]

Selling the Feds. One federal official recalls that in the early promotional phase of the project, "ADL's guys described these models as operational and only in need of slight tuning. They hauled out two prestigious guys to make their case—it was really pretty impressive, their performances, the way that the public position was sold to the greatest possible limit."[132] If you were a federal bureaucrat charged with expending money to stimulate creative, innovative, comprehensive planning at the local level, and you were told by well-known, prestigious individuals that creative, innovative, and comprehensive devices existed that needed only to be tuned to the specific local context and that a reputable, established consulting firm would do the tuning, what would *you* expect and how would *you* spend your money?

In response to the question—"Do you have any notion of what ADL was trying to do, what did you expect out of the modeling portion of the project?"—the regional Renewal Area coordinator, the federal man on the scene, succinctly states his initial expectations and subsequent uneasiness:

160

What I expected to happen was that they would set up this computer system and that the City would then have an on-going system, an on-going system in one of its departments. But as time went on, we continually expressed concern in our meetings as I recall, they are a matter of record . . . But there wasn't a great deal that we could do, until the City had accepted it. . . . We had our technicians, [who] really didn't have the expertise in evaluating the model in detail, but they had general knowledge. [pause] I will just have to admit that we didn't have the time and the people who should have been following this thing through. We couldn't say, "No, stop it," because we weren't that far along, until it was finished, to see how the City reacted to it. Well it was finished, and the City still didn't do anything. They kept losing staff, and the people that were working with Little left. When it came down to the end, it was nothing, you see?[133]

When the payoffs are neither instantaneous nor decisive, the rational bureaucrat cuts his losses and begins to look for "new" solutions to his old problems.

In the spring of 1966, ADL attempted to reinterest George Belknap, then director of research and technology in HUD, in granting an additional $100,000 to the city for experimenting with the model and discovering how it works. It was claimed by ADL:

Our model is the first operational simulation model that is of sufficient detail and scope so that it can be used in housing analysis, renewal planning, and policy evaluation. The City of San Francisco has a trained group of specialists[134] in their Community Analysis and Research Section that operates with the model.[135]

In the Belknap letter, ADL also requested an additional $150,000 for "a one-year effort aimed at developing an improved, generalized version of the model. . . . to provide a pilot operation for the benefit of all future model users across the country."[136] In July, 1966, ADL tried to interest Charles Haar, then assistant secretary for metropolitan development in HUD. The price had increased since April, but then, so had the scope of the proposal. ADL first establishes its credentials and outlines the proposal:

. . . our experience indicates that a computer simulation of the complex urban housing market can provide a vitally needed framework for analyzing the impact of alternative programs as they interact with the crucial private sector of the urban environment.

Then it utters the appropriate, resonant symbols:

We believe that such a model can provide a basis for the type of cost effectiveness analysis that has demonstrated the usefulness of systems analysis to other Departments of the Federal Government.

One important use of the model will be to permit an evaluation of the comparative cost effectiveness of the alternative programs designed to improve the quality, quantity, or economic availability of housing.

Reestablishes its solution competency:

... the most direct use of the model [SF/CRP] is evaluating the impact of alternative programs, quality, quantity, price, and type of units available in the city's housing stock. The model was used to pre-test the effect of a code enforcement program, population increases, and a public housing program. It has been turned over to the San Francisco City Planning Commission and is being used as a planning tool.

The existing model provides a logical starting point for the development of a more powerful model.

And sets a price and date:

Our current estimate for the cost of the project [an expanded version of the SF/CRP] is $350,000 for professional services and expenses. We estimate that the entire project would be completed in 18 months after the starting date.[137]

ADL's request was denied, *which is in one important sense unfortunate.* They did have experience. They had learned some expensive, but invaluable lessons. They may very well have been ready to make some progress. Doubtless their promises and prices were as illusory in 1966 as they had been in 1963; but they were, relatively speaking, in a position to begin to make a contribution.

Fads change, and simulation had given way to other techniques: "bricks and mortar," action programs, and other

new gimmicks that will prove the other guys were completely on the wrong track, which of course they weren't. We know these things kind of move in fits and starts—and one flop is something that's discredited for years. And always *there is a tendency, everytime an experiment is conducted which is not satisfactory,* to regress to charlatanism.[138] (emphasis added)

Changeless, unfortunately, is the way the research game is played, "for glory and for profit . . . with the scientific aspects of the thing as the lowest priority items on the totem pole."[139] We shall later consider the effects of glory and profit incentives on attempts to master the complexity of urban decision.

Of what use is the San Francisco simulation model?

Pragmatic Appraisal

The model's utility for the practical applications of data manipulation, measurement, theory building, education, and policy-making will be assessed. The last application will receive detailed consideration.

Data Manipulation. The model appears to be well suited for data base management. Many of the routines are explicitly designed to move large quantities of data efficiently and accurately. Dimensions are consistent, and error-checking procedures have been liberally integrated into the program. To realize its potential as a data manipulator, better input and output routines are clearly required. For instance, it is ludicrous not to have executive control over the amount and format of outputs; there are few conceivable applications that consistently call for full output dumps after each run. Less critical, but highly desirable, would be the addition of a time-shared executive routine to control data input, edit, manipulation, and display routines. The model is a good first approximation of a data manipulation device.

Measurement. Little needs to be said after noting the absence of much of the necessary data and the low to marginal quality of what does exist. Data deficiencies plagued this project from start to finish. The model has no present and negligible prospective measurement utility.

Theory. Promotional activities aside, the model scarcely advances our theoretical understanding of the housing market, renewal processes, or urban decision-making. It contributes little because extant social theory has been supplanted by physical analogies of dubious appropriateness. An opportunity was missed, but data-impoverished environments need not go unexplored. Taking full advantage of whatever descriptive theory exists, one's understanding of structural processes may progress to relatively advanced levels with surprisingly little data. Indeed, a model may be used this way to indicate priorities for data collection.[140] This opportunity was foregone.

Education. The model has few intended educational uses. Because it is unwieldy and costly, it has only limited potential as an educational aid for officials or students. Because adequate documentation does not exist, transfer to other sites is effectively prohibited. The model lacks the imaginative interrelationship of elements and subroutines that characterizes better urban games; the theory upon which the model is structured is weak and consequently produces uninteresting and irrelevant behavioral results. And finally, the prodigious and nearly incomprehensible outputs are anything but fun to decipher. One simply cannot wait a week or two to appraise the effects of his decisions or plays.

The unintended educational uses of the model are legion. It is a negative paradigm for building policy models; elaboration of the paradigm is a major purpose of this inquiry so that the lessons learned by a few may be known more widely.

Policy-Making. The designer's emphasis on intended policy purposes requires us to assess their realized product primarily in those terms.

The model functioned as an unintended retardant to the development of the Community Renewal Program. This is explained best in terms of the time and attention expended on the tool as compared to that expended on the larger project. The role of "model as sedative" is described by a city official:

The model became a totem so that whenever you had a problem or an issue, you went to the totem with it.

Everybody talked about things in terms of the model . . . the model was the catchword. If you talked about changing the administration of the city . . . about changing zoning regulations . . . a great many decisions that had to be made in the course of time were deferred because of the possible development of the model.[141]

The model's novelty—its "sex appeal"—took a disproportionate amount of psychic energy—"because it was of great intellectual interest to the people on board the staff."[142] Nearing the end of the contract, the project leader "panicked" over the inability of the model to program anything or "to [be] a lick of help in designing a program and meeting the LPA [Local Public Authority] letter requirements on what a CRP ought to contain."[143] How these requirements were hastily approximated is a separate matter.

The policy function of descriptive clarification was not well executed. Adequate trend data did not exist to explicate the problem context or to make forecasts. How do you forecast from a single data point? It is difficult, but if you label it "testing alternative packages of policy," the logical fallacy is not so obvious, as illustrated in this exchange with a model-builder:

Q: Then you would characterize the model as an alternative testing device? Or as a projective device?
A: Merely an alternative testing device.
Q: But you ran it for twenty years.
A: Yes. But let's put it this way: It had the projective capacity of sorts. . . . But the basic purpose, at least as we always talked about it, was that it was a means of testing alternative packages of policy and not so much a question of forecasting . . .
Q: But you had only single point data.
A: Yes, that's right, there are no trends.
Q: I don't know how you could defend that, or do you bother?
A: Well, I don't know—I did know that at least we dealt with it. We thought more of it in terms of emphasis and direction, programs and policy. Projection was just a fallout.[144]

One does not derive rates of change for modeled variables from a single data point. The model as presently configured has negligible forecasting potential.

Norms or desired end states were specified only to the extent that the model-builders structured their preferences into the model. Decision-makers were curiously unwilling or unable to verbalize their preferred outcomes and defaulted to the technicians.

Of the possible *policy criteria* suggested in chapter 6 by our appraisal function, the initial clarification of the practical problem or "question" was an early casualty:

The whole thing rapidly tumbled headlong into enormous confusion, and the most confused thing of all was the model itself. The lack of clarity, the lack of a precise definition of what it was supposed to do. "What did we really want it to do for us?" No one really sat down and talked with us [city] about that.[145]

The present planning director flatly states, "To the extent that it *could* answer questions, they were questions that nobody was asking."[146] Not only was there confusion about the analytical question, there is a lingering question about who the proper client was. The following is a sampling of responses elicited by the "simple" question—"Who is the client for the model?"—asked of all model team members:

Anybody that would use it. . . . We worked with the Planning Department because that is the way the job was set up and organized. One of the most logical customers is the Tax Assessor.[147]

The major problem with the CRP . . . was that it was for the wrong client, and at the wrong time. . . . For this model there is only one client, one proper client, and that is HUD. There is only one purpose that I can see for it, that is to write a housing law.[148]

The problem, one of them, was that everybody was doing the project because he thought that somebody else wanted it done that way. I don't know of anyone who was doing the project because he wanted to do it this way. The City and we [ADL] were probably doing and responding to what we thought the Feds wanted. . . . It's hard to find out who wanted what. I don't know, maybe that's the problem.[149]

Besides raising fundamental questions about research management, these problems are so overpowering as to obviate more than a passing checkoff of other policy criteria.

The Department of City Planning controls very few programs. It is a weak institution, as compared to the Redevelopment Agency against which it competes in a four-way struggle with the Housing Department and the Mayor's Office. Insufficient attention was given to the planning cycle of the department. Planning prepares an annual program, and its recommendations are essentially irretrievable. "The model doesn't have to run very often . . . once we come up with a package of programs, how often do we need a model?—Every year, every two years, maybe."[150] The model-builders' insensitivity to the user's needs is further illustrated by the use of the analytical unit "fract." City Planning, of course, routinely operates with census tracts. However, machine limitations prevailed over the policy-maker's needs, and "all of a sudden, because their machine couldn't take all of the census tracts, they break into 'fracts,' or something like that. Something totally mad! It isn't even a piece of geography. It's nothing—but madness."[151] Thus, expediencies prompted by hardware limitations effectively obliterated the confidence and hence whatever utility the model might have had for one important policy-making agency—Planning. Insufficient attention was given its needs, partly because its policy-making potential was limited, partly because it did not feel compelled or know how to cooperate, and mainly because the researchers demonstrated precious little skill, interest, or sensitivity for understanding the policy-makers' problems.

If the research team had asked themselves the four questions suggested above in our discussion of the appraisal function as being appropriate before the fact,[152] their exercise would not have begun or, better, would have been executed very differently. Variables related to the question were neither accessible nor measurable at acceptable cost. Data did not exist, let alone in accessible, flexible formats. Some theory related to the question existed, although the researchers either were unaware or chose to ignore it. While theory may not have been good enough for building policy models, certainly existing theoretical possibilities should have been explored; e.g. many explanations for housing decay, alternative behavioral relationships and subroutines for housing demand, several population-housing interaction hypotheses. Of course, requisite data were not obtainable at acceptable costs in dollars or time.

Our ten ex post facto questions on appropriateness for policy-making are applied to the San Francisco model in Exhibit 11-1. The model has serious limitations as a policy-making or assisting device. Its most promising use seems to be as a data manipulator, but even here considerable additional work is required to develop better, more flexible input and output routines and some display capabilities. The general need for documentation and flow charting would have to be satisfied, no matter how the model is eventually used.[153]

EXHIBIT 11-1

Ten Questions: A Summary Appraisal of Policy Appropriateness

POLICY QUESTION	ASSESSMENT
1. DISTORTION between model and reference system?	EXCESSIVE: " . . . our evaluation of the model is that it is not, at present, a reliable device for simulation of the market. The range of variation . . . is simply too great to warrant faith in its long-term results."[a]
2. INPUT/OUTPUT familiar and intelligible?	UNINTELLIGIBLE; INCOMPREHENSIBLE: " . . . the complete output of a single run totals more than a six inches thick stack of paper completely covered with figures,"[b] and "the enormous quantities of information that the model was easily capable of producing was in large part meaningless, but at the same time could not be ignored."[c] Average analytical turnaround is two or three *weeks*.
3. COMMON SENSE?	OFFENSIVE: See Table 11-4 for extent of errors in the "best-fit" runs.

EXHIBIT 11-1 *(cont'd.)*

POLICY QUESTION	ASSESSMENT
4. "QUESTION" elements excluded in interest of precision or generalization?	YES: For example, location categories were artifacts created in the interest of precision and generalization. The effect of them on the policy-makers is noteworthy: "We got hung up on location categories. That was the thing that really blew his mind. [Policy-maker] just couldn't get it. He shook his head a couple of times, like a dog who has been hit by a car. We never talked about it again—I can't blame him. He is a busy guy, and he is not model-oriented."[d]
5. STATIC bias?	YES: Decidedly so with net detriment to project.
6. ALTER COMPONENTS?	WITH DIFFICULTY: And considerable cost.
7. Essential ELEMENTS of analytical question OMITTED?	NOT APPLICABLE: Because the analytical question was not defined and sensitivity testing was not done, one cannot make assessment.
8. PREDICTION of time series upon which formulated? PREDICTION of subsequent time series?	NOT APPLICABLE: The model was configured mainly from single point data. It has been unsuccessful in predicting more than gross detail of subsequent time series. See Table 11-4.
9. STRUCTURAL CHANGES in the context accounted for?	IGNORES; or ASSUMES CONSTANT: See section in text, "Theoretical Appraisal."
10. Consonance of the model with ETHICAL-MORAL standards of policy-makers? Populace? Profession?	NO; PROBABLY NOT; NO: See section in text, "Ethical Appraisal."

[a]*Status of the San Francisco Simulation Model*, p. 25.
[b]Internal Memo, ADL, HBW-24, May 7, 1965, Subject: "Status of the CRP Model," p. 3.
[c]Interview Document, July 17, 1969, p. 4.
[d]*Ibid.* p. 15.

Developing the CRP: Postscript. ADL management had agreed to present its recommendations as a public service on local television in June, 1965.[154] The problem was that "there had to be a report so that there would be something to talk about."[155] Recollections vary, but sometime around four to six months before the project was over, panic set in: "There [had to] be something to talk about," according to the project leader (planner), who assembled a separate team, but "no OR guys as such. We went into a room, and I said, 'We are not going to leave this room until we walk this thing through.' . . . The recommended Community Renewal Program was produced in this fashion."[156] This fashion meant "sitting down with the Census books [and] ... plotting enumeration district information ... [because] we really at that stage still didn't even know where the housing conditions were pretty bad." It meant occasionally leaving the room (the process took about two months) "to go out to do the quickest and dirtiest windshield surveys to confirm the '60 Census data." It meant that ADL at the last moment "flew some writers out from Cambridge ... to polish [the report] up. It was kind of a round-the-clock operation such that one of the guys who flew out ... died of a heart attack about a week later. It was really that bad."[157] And it meant finding out "that it [the CRP] could have been done ... without going through the agony of the model."[158]

On a post-interview questionnaire, responding to the question—"What do you think the City got from the project?"—fourteen of the eighteen principal respondents replied "nothing," "very little," or "negligible benefits." One particularly cynical respondent offered this extreme assessment, "The City got about 3¢ on the dollar."

Summary

The San Francisco Community Renewal Program provides some valuable lessons about current difficulties and longer-term prospects for the integration of the computer into the urban decision process. If the experience is indeed representative:

1. The magnitude of the problem is far in excess of common expectations. A million dollars in a one-shot project is wholly insufficient.
2. The extent of the gaps between the orientations and expectations of key participants in the process is in excess of what might a priori be estimated. The gaps are so great as to debilitate research.
3. The state of readily accessible data and adequate theory to configure these data has been tested and found wanting.
4. Procedures, institutions, and systems of incentive and motivation to cope effectively with the problem are sorely deficient.
5. The extent of the "appraisal gap" is excessive if the disparity between this assessment and all earlier published reports is indicative.

Let us apply the criteria developed as components of our "Appraisal Function" to the case of Pittsburgh.

12

Pittsburgh

Pittsburgh's Department of City Planning, with the University of Pittsburgh as the prime contractor, asked CONSAD to help in developing for use a digital computer simulation model to test the economic, social, and locational consequences of various hypotheses of new investment and urban change. The model describes the entire urban area of the City of Pittsburgh and forecasts the impact of proposed land-use policies.
"The Challenge of Decision-Making,"
CONSAD Research Corporation

Pittsburgh is a political town. The research and model-building processes of the Community Renewal Program were prematurely terminated for elementary political reasons.

We shall trace the decision to model, the initial scope and purpose of the project, and the strengths and weaknesses of the three major submodels that were produced. We conclude the Pittsburgh case with a discussion of one university's limitations as a research agent and some observations on doing research in a politically inhospitable environment.

As with the San Francisco case, the remarkable candor and thorough cooperation of those who participated in the Pittsburgh effort truly made this inquiry possible. On the technical side, special thanks are due Steve Putman, J. P. Crecine, and I. S. Lowry, who explained and detailed important characteristics of the models for me. Calvin Hamilton, John Mauro, Neil Douglas, Aldo Colautti, and Michael Scott-Morton provided much valuable information about planning and politics in the city of Pittsburgh. Charles Leven, Benjamin Chinitz, and Wilbur Steger gave generously of their time and recalled in detail many of the challenges and frustrations of attempting to advance the urban problem-solving process.

Decision to Model

As an integral component of Pittsburgh's on-going restoration in the late fifties and early sixties, a nationally prominent city planner was hired to execute its Community Renewal Program. The decision to use sophisticated analytical techniques to develop the CRP just "happened" as a result of several chance events involving this new director of City Planning, the Center for Regional Economic Studies at the University of Pittsburgh, the CONSAD Research Corporation, federal renewal officials, and the local "establishment."

Publics: Local. The city's interest in modeling can be linked to the separate considerations of *reputation, money, politics,* and *naiveté.*

The Allegheny Conference on Community Development, a nonprofit organization representing the corporate interests resident in Pittsburgh and generally acknowledged to be a major motive force behind Pittsburgh's postwar renaissance, had hired an outside consultant to recommend changes in the functioning of the moribund City Planning Department. The consultant recommended that the department be increased in size and that new, vigorous, and nationally prominent leadership be instituted. The consultant's report was little more than an ex post facto validation of the Allegheny Conference's preferences. According to an observer close to the mayor:

> The Conference Director came in to talk to us and said, "Here's a demonstrated need to up-grade and professionalize the Planning Department." The Mayor agreed somewhat, and we started sort of tentatively agreeing that what we need is a new Planning Director. So a committee was established to do some recruiting across the country, which for Pittsburgh was a very unusual step.[1]

After its search, the committee unanimously selected Calvin Hamilton for the newly created executive directorship of the Planning Department. In the process the mayor incurred several political costs. "Persuading the City Council to hire a foreigner . . . ; to pay him a salary higher than anyone had been previously paid in a function like that; and to grant him a residency waiver,"[2] were all extraordinary measures that did little to engender local political support for the interloper.

The mayor's expectations for the CRP were fairly straightforward:

> Regardless of what the output would turn out to be in terms of a CRP, here was a backdoor way of improving the City Planning staff, *developing the kind of raw data that we knew we didn't have,* and getting the kind of overall inputs that were just missing.[3] (emphasis added)

In the final analysis, "fake credit" and federal dollars proved to be the key selling points to an "unpersuaded and somewhat skeptical, cynical, and critical" City Council.[4] The mayor's man at Council "would usually wind up these meetings [with Hamilton] by saying, 'In any case, it is not going to cost us any money—Federal funds will underwrite this program. Our one-third share will be made up by in-kind services, and we really don't have anything to lose.' "[5]

From these inauspicious beginnings of merely trying to collect data

170

to do some better conventional planning, the CRP became increasingly ambitious. To meet the well-known data deficiencies, a graduate student from the University of Pittsburgh was hired as the city's director of data processing.[6] The job was formidable. Existing city data that were collected were inconsistently coded; different departments were using different kinds and definitions of data and were uninterested in sharing what little they had; and the computer system was a simply configured IBM Model 1401 that "belonged" to the city controller, who cooperated by allowing the director of data processing to use the machine after midnight. Nevertheless, the ideas of management science techniques and computers had a certain attractiveness, particularly for a new executive director who was expected to innovate. The general level of experience, however, left a great deal to be desired. In the words of the new director of data processing, "I was the only one who understood, who had built models, and who had run them, and in that sense understood the kinds of things that were going to be problems."[7]

Hamilton is brutally candid about his own limitations. "I had no knowledge of data processing at all. I had no knowledge of econometrics, or operations research, or simulation."[8] In his supplementary role as an adjunct professor of planning at Pitt, Hamilton inquired of his academic colleagues how best to solve his problems.

I talked with [Herbert] Simon at Carnegie and Don Stone and Ed Hoover, and guys in various parts of the country. They said that the best way ... was to mathematically model to be able to test alternative strategies and locational patterns of renewal and then be able to test to see what the different applications were. You had to create a series of mathematical models—and this was simulation—create a simulation model. Well, I didn't know anything about simulation, but they gave me a lot of things to read. We came to that conclusion [to build a simulation model].[9]

Armed with the well-intentioned advice and best wishes of his academic colleagues, Hamilton broached the subject of simulation models with the City Council. It became clear that the Council had little to offer in these matters. As one observer recalls:

The reaction of one of the intellectual giants on the Council when this was first presented ... when the term "simulation model" first came out [is indicative]. He sat back in his chair, and he looked, and then said in all seriousness, "Is that anything like artificial insemination?" They didn't even know what the term or the concept, any of it was. We were bridging a big gap—a lot bigger than the generation gap.[10]

Apparently federal renewal officials were only slightly better informed.
Publics: Federal. According to HHFA's regional project monitor:

As I look back on that exercise I have shivers, because what I thought I understood at that point, I frankly did not understand. ... We were just saying things with no comprehension of the full meaning and implications and with only two established facts, tangible, palpable facts: One, it meant money and two, with that money we could get some capable people there to maybe produce something.[11]

It is essential to note that as of 1962, the Community Renewal Program had not, nationwide, lived up to the hopes of its proponents. At stake were several reputations and a program that had been thoroughly advertised,[12] when

down the pike came Cal Hamilton's proposal . . . a really sexy kind of proposal—a "far-out" kind of proposal. A proposal which began to receive some nationwide publicity because Cal was talking about this in all of his speeches throughout the country. . . . So there was a swell of support for Cal at this point that combined with the interest on [Community Development Branch's (in HHFA)] part to invest in something that was different and promising that they could begin to point to as some example of what a CRP should be,[13] I think contributed largely to the fact that he got everything he wanted—he got the whole grant. Alright, then the real fun begins at this point—now do it![14]

Confronted with the task of "doing it," and feeling the enormity of that task to be outside his capabilities, Hamilton enlisted the assistance of experts from the University of Pittsburgh and a California-based consulting firm.

Technics: Center for Regional Economic Studies (CRES). External *institutional* and *professional* considerations best account for CRES's willingness to participate in the Pittsburgh CRP. After its major project, the Pittsburgh Regional Economic Study, had terminated, CRES's continuing institutional viability depended upon securing new contracts and new money. As a federal official recalls:

Now I think the University of Pittsburgh's interest in this thing at the outset really was not commensurate with the interests of Cal or the City. They were in it for what they could get out of it. They had a great chance to bring together some people for some research purposes within the center over there that would be interesting and stimulating and to help [names] expand their own programs.[15]

CRES had no one on its staff with simulation or model-building skills. Its staff consisted of skilled regional economists, none of whom had practical experience in computer simulation or large-scale mathematical modeling. That CRES was staffed by regional economists is not surprising—why they should be so willing to undertake a large-scale urban simulation and model-building project is important.

While in Santa Monica one summer, Benjamin Chinitz, CRES's associate director, became familiar with CONSAD of California, a new firm composed of former Rand, Hughes, Lockheed, and Douglas Corporation researchers under the leadership of R. S. Snoyer and Wilbur Steger. In one participant's view, the initial connection between CRES and CONSAD was

totally serendipitous. Ben [Chinitz] had known Wil Steger at Graduate School at

172

Harvard. . . . And they were talking about the kinds of things they were interested in doing, and Ben said, "Gee, you know I have been talking to people down at City Planning [Pittsburgh] about doing some modeling about urban renewal. Why don't you come and talk to them? Maybe we can get into this together?"[16]

Technics: CONSAD. CONSAD's concern with its viability as an institution clearly accounts for its eagerness to participate in the project. Selling a contract was apparently more important than working within the company's substantive limitations. A former CRES staff member remarks:

I personally feel that the CONSAD people, for a variety of reasons, maybe naiveté, perhaps because of their very real commercial interests, tended to exaggerate the capacity of simulation models. Their acquaintance with urban problems, with any urban research, was extremely limited.[17] They were good computer people, they knew what computers could do in training pilots, gaming and that sort of thing. But in terms of hard research results and in terms of policy-making, I think they had the naive notion that because simulation, computer simulation, could do these other things it also could make policy and could produce research findings of very advanced types.[18]

This personal appraisal is supported by an examination of CONSAD's 1962 composite bibliography for citations related to urban, housing, or renewal subject matters. Of the eight men listed, Steger most nearly fit the bill, but his expertise was in income tax, particularly at the federal level. To summarize CONSAD's substantive credentials once more: "CONSAD had very good computer people and people with experience in simulation. They had no real social scientists outside of Wil Steger who did his work in public finance. Pitt [CRES] had a good collection of social scientists, primarily economists."[19] Convinced of the transferability to the urban field of computer skills acquired in the military sector, CONSAD representatives began making proposals to local and federal officials. A local official recalls:

Their president [R. S. Snoyer] came by first and had some discussions with the Mayor and the City Planning people, you know—[and] with the Feds. Then CONSAD began the hard sell approach about why we ought to have this project. They began to put together memos to sell the urban renewal people on why this would be a good idea. The documents that CONSAD put together sort of sold the project.[20]

The process of "selling the project" culminated in May, 1962, when the final, formal proposal was made. "It was an impressive team that was going to do an impressive job."[21]

Unfortunately, at about the same time, CONSAD experienced internal managerial difficulties. CONSAD of California was dissolved, and Steger moved to Pittsburgh, where CONSAD was reincorporated. Selling the CRP contract now acquired a new importance for CONSAD. Institutional survival accounts for the decision to participate for both the university and the consultant. CRES was at the end of a large-scale project and needed new money. CONSAD was an embryonic firm that simply needed business.

Initial Design.[22] It is remarkable how little attention was devoted to what the simulation was to be and to accomplish. Figure 12-1, reproduced from the proposal, reports the status of the model at that time:

Figure [12-1] demonstrates the basic features of the proposed simulation model. The model's basic concepts are by no means new, *having been exercised* in several other simulation models and *presently being used* in efforts such as simulation of the U.S. economy.

The flow diagram represents a one-glance portrayal of all the elements of *the model constructed to date.*[23] (emphasis added)

The consultant's optimism for the general technique was persuasive; the tripartite administrative arrangement with the University of Pittsburgh, CONSAD, and the city seemed well suited for the task; federal renewal officials saw an interesting, sophisticated, and apparently tried and tested approach to solve their problem of a flagging national program; Executive Director Hamilton saw a means to innovate—his immediate objective—and a way "to show that the planners were capable of doing . . . modeling and data processing, that which they should have been doing for a long time and [so] not to lose the whole kit and caboodle to the transportation guys,"[24]—his long-term objective; and the city's politicians knew that they had nothing to lose: "Cost: None to City—Feds all excited—will pay."[25]

The computer models that resulted are reported in several sources, none of which provides more than sketchy documentation. The information on which my appraisal is based was gleaned not only from the published accounts, but also from interviews and from tedious dissections of model listings, unpublished technical reports, and computer printouts.[26]

Scope and Purpose

The original expectations for Pittsburgh's CRP have been recounted in detail elsewhere.[27] While these public reports consistently reflect an ambitious and optimistic scope, the ultimate reality test of meeting a contractual deadline and making final reports (the test that had cut short dreams in San Francisco) was effectively avoided in Pittsburgh. This is not to say that a multitude of familiar problems were also avoided; they were not. It is to say that unexpected events in Pittsburgh gave the technicians a reprieve. The purpose, to build policy-making, forecasting devices, remained constant throughout.

FIGURE 12-1

*An Example of a Flow Diagram for Simulation of Pittsburgh's
Urban Renewal Planning Process*

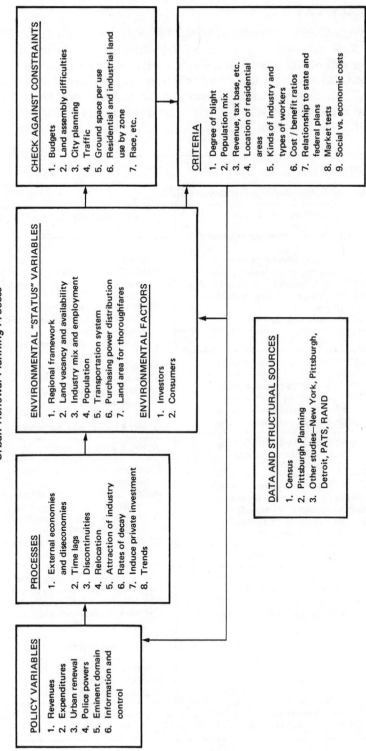

POLICY VARIABLES

1. Revenues
2. Expenditures
3. Urban renewal
4. Police powers
5. Eminent domain
6. Information and control

PROCESSES

1. External economies and diseconomies
2. Time lags
3. Discontinuities
4. Relocation
5. Attraction of industry
6. Rates of decay
7. Induce private investment
8. Trends

ENVIRONMENTAL "STATUS" VARIABLES

1. Regional framework
2. Land vacancy and availability
3. Industry mix and employment
4. Population
5. Transportation system
6. Purchasing power distribution
7. Land area for thoroughfares

ENVIRONMENTAL FACTORS

1. Investors
2. Consumers

CHECK AGAINST CONSTRAINTS

1. Budgets
2. Land assembly difficulties
3. City planning
4. Traffic
5. Ground space per use
6. Residential and industrial land use by zone
7. Race, etc.

CRITERIA

1. Degree of blight
2. Population mix
3. Revenue, tax base, etc.
4. Location of residential areas
5. Kinds of industry and types of workers
6. Cost / benefit ratios
7. Relationship to state and federal plans
8. Market tests
9. Social vs. economic costs

DATA AND STRUCTURAL SOURCES

1. Census
2. Pittsburgh Planning
3. Other studies—New York, Pittsburgh, Detroit, PATS, RAND

Source: W. A. Steger, "A Proposed Use of Simulation Experimentation Techniques in the Pittsburgh Urban Renewal Process" (Santa Monica: CONSAD, TP 62-110, May 1962).

THE CONTEXT

Scope. In an elaborate discussion, "Simulation Model," *CRP Progress Report Number 5,*[28] the relationships between the various component subroutines listed in Exhibit 12-1 were presented in a flow chart entitled, "Overview—Urban Systems Simulation Flow Chart—December, 1963," which is shown in abbreviated form in Figure 12-2. The scope of the project as it was publicized in 1963 was truly Brobdingnagian; according to one public document, it had changed little as late as 1967.

EXHIBIT 12-1

Proposed Subroutines in Pittsburgh CRP

EXOGENOUS INPUTS	CONNECTION OF PLANS TO OTHER SUBMODELS
NMPLNS—Nonmunicipal governmental plans URPLNS—Urban renewal plans CIPLNS—Capital improvement plans EXOPOP—Population (through cohort/ratio method and independent density estimates) BASEMP—Basic employment	PLNTIM—Timing of specific events implied by plans NCLCON—Matching attributes of plans to make efficient use of noncash credits RESRHB—Residential rehabilitation "direct" impact (upon households' actions) of plans LNDIMP—Land (and structures) "direct" impact of plans ACCIMP—Access impact RELIMP—Relocation impact POCIMP—Project-oriented capital improvements POCOST—Project-oriented costs POEMP—Project-oriented employment
DATA SOURCES	
IODAT—Input/output interindustry model INDDAT—Industrial-oriented data CFDAT—Community facilities data COMDAT—Commercial-oriented data RESDAT—Residential-oriented data	
DATA ANALYSIS RESULTS (coefficients and structural equations)	**SUPPLY AND DEMAND SUBMODELS**
DISANA—Distance-gradients analysis COMANA—Commercial data analysis RESANA—Residential data analysis INDANA—Industrial data analysis FACANA—Factor analysis	*IOIIM*—Input/output interindustry model *INIMP*—Industrial spatial allocation model *TOMM*—Time-oriented (residential and commercial) metropolitan GOVPRO—Governmental revenues and expenditure projections STANDA—Governmental expenditure projections based upon standards PROPRI—Project-oriented priorities SOCIND—Social index projection DECANA—Governmental decision analysis
RECONCILIATIONS	
REcon 1—Total employment, income, labor force and population REcon 2—Commercial employment REcon 3—Population spatial distribution	
	BLIGHT INDICES
	COMBLI—Commercial blight INDBLI—Industrial blight RESBLI—Residential blight

Source: "Simulation Model," *CRP Technical Report Number 5* (Pittsburgh: CONSAD and Department of City Planning, January, 1964), pp. 8-9.

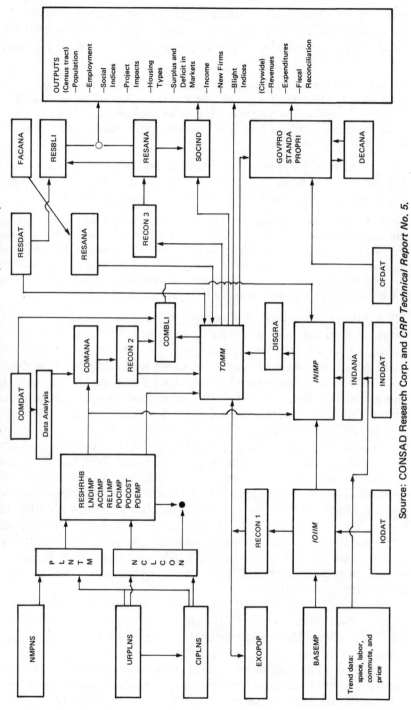

FIGURE 12-2

Overview—Urban Systems Simulation Flow Chart, December, 1963

Source: CONSAD Research Corp. and *CRP Technical Report No. 5.*

While most participants were too ignorant or uninterested to question the consultant on this point, several people who had some of the appropriate skills sensed the impending problems but remained silent. A senior researcher in CRES:

My personal view on the project at that time [October, 1963] was that it was a good idea. I think that I believed that it was possible to develop models of that kind. I was suspicious of Steger in terms of his over-optimism; he seemed to be able to do anything. I thought that he was grossly underbudget, but *I was not directly involved.*[29] (emphasis added)

For less than a quarter of a million dollars, and within two years' time, a great deal had been promised. In terms of data collection and processing *alone,* the task was formidable. Calvin Hamilton on data:

We had enormous problems. . . . The City Controller wasn't a bit interested in innovation, he was more interested in how he did his operation. We had to do all our work at night after midnight on his 1401. . . . We had to do it every kind of ingenious way, always around end runs to get the kinds of data that we needed. Because the Mayor never issued the kind of order that would allow us to get the kinds of data that we knew we needed. He just wouldn't do it.[30]

He wouldn't do it probably because he saw few possible payoffs. The political quid pro quo was never established. The data problem was so pressing that a hiatus "to catch up on data" because "the problem was waiting for the data to come in; there was really nothing for us to do,"[31] was openly discussed between CRES and the city at the eighteen-month mark. But, according to the federal monitor, it was decided instead to apply for an extension of time and for more money. More will be said about this at the conclusion of the chapter.

To cope with technical problems, CONSAD hired two graduate students, one in industrial organization at Carnegie Tech[32] and the other in operations research from Pitt,[33] to build two key submodels in the system: TOMM—Time-Oriented (Residential and Commercial) Metropolitan Model and INIMP—Industrial Spatial Allocation Model, respectively. The student-researchers were to translate proposal promises into theoretical models and computer code for the purpose of making public policy. The third key submodel, IOIIM—Input/Output, Inter-Industry Model—was produced at CRES, "as a truncated version of the Pittsburgh Regional Study."[34]

Who builds models and the quality or absence of data are relatively unimportant issues for nearly all possible purposes *except* policy-making, where the most stringent criteria and standards *ought* to obtain.

Purposes. The purpose was clear: construct a family of independent, nearly decomposed, but conceptually interrelated submodels for use in unconditional and normative forecasts of policy alternatives. The May,

1962, proposal summarized all the ways in which the model would be used:

Specifically, in terms of the stated goals of the Pittsburgh Community Renewal Program, the following goals are likely to be more fully implemented through the analysis of the simulation model:

1. The determination of the total public fiscal requirements necessary to meet the future governmental needs of the City of Pittsburgh and the effects on the tax base of meeting these needs.
2. The testing of the alternative uses of specific geographical areas to determine preferred ways to satisfy the needs of these areas but always within the context of the overall economic ability of the City to carry out renewal to accomplish these alternatives.
3. The examination of the short-run and long-run costs and benefits, priorities, and advantages for alternative methods (complete or partial redevelopment, rehabilitation, or minor public and private action and expenditure) of accomplishing CRP goals.
4. The determination of how residential and commercial areas shall be handled in the light of the fiscal ability of the City to effect total or partial redevelopment.[35]

The distinct policy purpose was reiterated in the January, 1964, *CRP Progress Report Number 5.* "We are constructing a decision model, i.e. one intended to produce information against which municipal decision makers must apply their own choice set of (subjective) values."[36] And finally, the projective and policy purposes are flatly articulated in the often cited *Journal of the American Institute of Planners* report in May, 1965. "This report summarizes the current status of the digital computer simulation model for urban renewal decision-making purposes, . . . [it is] designed to test long range alternative urban renewal plans, and is therefore a simulation of the 'conditional prediction' variety."[37] And in a separate article in that same journal, it was claimed, "In the Pittsburgh Community Renewal Program it is now possible to measure the cumulative effects of certain program decisions over a period of time."[38]

Such clarity of purpose demands that the models be carefully appraised with respect to that purpose.

The Models

From Figure 12-2, we recall the logical order of processing of the models: IOIIM precedes INIMP, which precedes TOMM. In other words, levels of various types of industrial employment produced by the input/output matrix provide essential raw inputs to the industry location submodel. Once these industries and associated employees are located in space, TOMM's residential and commercial entities may then be located. For purposes of appraisal, we shall consider each as a separate model, recycling through the various criteria from the order of processing through the pragmatic appraisal.

IOIIM—INPUT/OUTPUT INTER-INDUSTRY MODEL

The input/output submodel is designed to produce employment levels by industrial class for the six-county Pittsburgh region, Allegheny County, and the city of Pittsburgh. Data and projected economic activities for the region already existed in the Pittsburgh Regional Economic Study.

Order of Processing. IOIIM accounts for the transactions between thirty standard industrial categories in each of the three spatial disaggregations—region, county, and city—the final demand for households generated by these industries by area, and the amount of external demand generated by each of the industries. Figure 12-3 reproduces

FIGURE 12-3

IOIIM—Input/Output Inter-Industry Accounts

Inter-Industry Matrices				Final Demand Households				Export		Total Employment
T_{11}	T_{12}	T_{13}		C_{11}	C_{12}	C_{13}		E_1		X_1
T_{21}	T_{22}	T_{23}		C_{21}	C_{22}	C_{23}		E_2		X_2
T_{31}	T_{32}	T_{33}		C_{31}	C_{32}	C_{33}		E_3		X_3

Source: *CRP Progress Report No. 4*, p. 8.
1 = City
2 = Allegheny County-City
3 = Region-(County and City)
T_{ij} = employment in region i producing for industries in region j (each T_{ij} has n rows and columns for n industries, i.e. 9 — 30 x 30 matrices)
C_{ij} = employment in region i producing for households in region j
E_i = employment in region i producing for export
X_i = employment in region i

these outputs. This submodel differs from usual input/output accounting or bookkeeping procedures in that employment levels have been substituted for the sales levels usually calculated. A second deviation from the norm is the replacement of technological coefficients—the proportion of a given input needed to produce a unit of output for another industry—by trade coefficients—the proportion of employees needed to produce inputs for a single unit of output in another industry.[39] These accounts describe a region's economic structure with respect to employment levels for a single base year, which for Pittsburgh was 1963.

Theoretical Appraisal. IOIIM, like any input/output system, is statically biased and relies on additional, external estimates for its forecasts. That is to say, there is no theory in the basic scheme capable of deducing behavioral time series for system variables. Projections were obtained from diverse sources.

The Pittsburgh Regional Economic Study made an estimate of regional industrial demand for the target year 1985. Biennial estimates were obtained simply by interpolating the 1985 estimates back to the 1963 base year. Labor force participation rates for Pittsburgh were assumed to "change in the figure in accordance with the same trend indicated for the nation as a whole in the Department of Commerce projections."[40] It is an expedient, but questionable assumption, given Pittsburgh's own distinctive labor force composition. Productivity estimates from the well-known National Planning Association decennial projections for the nation were used in a similar manner. It was assumed "that wages will rise in proportion to productivity . . ."[41] While the assumption is probably acceptable for the gross detail of a truly regional accounting scheme, one must begin raising some serious questions of contextual adequacy when attention shifts to the finer detail of individual industrial categories within a single city.

Technical Appraisal. The level of detail of the earlier regional effort was twenty industrial categories; ten more categories were added "on an ad hoc basis with consultation from Professor Edgar Hoover, the Director of the Regional Economic Study."[42] Since Hoover disavows *any* participation in the CRP, it is unclear how these important disaggregations were in fact made.[43] There is a hint in one source about these procedures. The expedient by which regional estimates of industrial demand were disaggregated is described as the "assign[ment] of increments to demand according to the present distribution among the three areas of each industry."[44] In other words, assume nothing will change with respect to relative demand at the city, county, and regional levels for the full period of the analysis.

The major problem, of course, was data deficiency. If one must develop some numbers to satisfy the input demands of other finely structured models and there are only regional and national data, one uses those data and fills in empty cells in the data matrix as best he can. Why there were no data is the issue. According to the author of IOIIM:

Mainly it was simply institutional malfunction. Due to the reliance on one or more departments that just didn't deliver because they had a lot of low-skilled, underpaid people with a high turnover that didn't give one damn about this thing. They made lots of mistakes. They got the forms wrong all the time. The other thing is that it was very, very counterproductive for this model to be built within the context of the CRP, within a fixed time interval. . . .

There were just no data to run it on. So there it sits. It was a good experience for me. I mainly learned about administration; I didn't learn much economics from it.[45]

One can scarcely fault the use of the well-developed input/output technique. Indeed, the measure of control one gains over masses of disorderly data commends the technique. The fundamental problem was that there were no masses of data to manage.

Ethical Appraisal. A key city decision-maker recalls how employment and population estimates for the city were eventually made in the final moments of the project:

I remember sitting in a conference room, and they [researchers] had a map of the City. They started asking, "Where do you think people are likely to move or what do you think the patterns have been?" I know I spent the next hour rather accurately describing how people had moved and how they were likely to move in terms of racial patterns and so forth. My point in bringing this up [is that] they were making some dots on the map on the results of one hour's conversation. I got the impression that the result of that conversation wound up that they adapted all of the work that they had done [because] they finally realized that it was inconclusive and perhaps inaccurate. I think they revised all the work and wound up reflecting the judgment of one or two people as to how people were going to move. . . . It was a consensus. I think they made up their model and their data to fit the consensus.[46]

The well-known pressures of time, a contractual obligation, and lack of data forced researchers to adopt expedients. Credibility and user trust were sacrificed in the process.

Pragmatic Appraisal. A policy-maker remembers thinking, "I don't know what techniques they've been using, but if their conclusions don't correspond to what happened or what I think is going to happen—I got the feeling that . . . that exercise [employment and population projections for the city] had been developed in a pretty shoddy manner."[47]

IOIIM may have some utility as a data management device, but no more so than other input/output accounting schemes. The essential point is that the basic information generated in IOIIM and subsequently processed by the other submodels is of questionable validity. At the very least, policy-making pretensions are forfeited.

INIMP—INDUSTRIAL SPATIAL ALLOCATION MODEL

INIMP is simple.[48] Primarily it serves as a link between the input/output and residential-commercial models. It allocates the former's projected industry employment to the census tracts of the city for subsequent processing by the latter (TOMM). Secondarily, INIMP accounts for the city's industrial plants by type, number, and location. Employment changes are distributed among existing facilities until full-capacity or shutdown thresholds are passed, at which point new industries are created and located or deleted.

Order of Processing. The process is logically represented by the flow chart in Figure 12-4. Let us consider the elements and relationships. The underlying assumption of the allocation relationships, i.e. the "heart" of the model, is that industries will continue to do what they are at present doing—more (or less) of the same, in the same locations. Symbolically,

$$\Delta E_{i,t}^k = \Delta E_{T,t}^k \, (E_{i,t-1}^k \, / \sum_{k=1}^{k} E_{i,t-1}^k)$$

(12.1)

and verbally,

The change in employment for an SIC (Standard Industrial Classification) type (k) by census tract (i) at time (t) is equal to the total (T) change in employment citywide for that SIC type times the proportion of total employment represented by the SIC in the prior period $(t-1)$ in the given tract.[49]

If, for example, all primary metal facilities within the city were to change by 5 percent in a given year, then SIC type 20—Primary Metal Industries—would also change by 5 percent in that year.

When employment in an industry is predicted to decrease, the forecasted percentage decrease is compared with "shutdown" percentages, the maximum per annum decrease a firm of a given absolute size can absorb before it is forced to close (subroutine PAOED). Seven sizes of firms were selected, and shutdown percentages "were developed by trial and error based on alternate runs of the model."[50] The numbers used in a recent version of INIMP are illustrated in Table 12-1. If decreases do not exceed shutdown percentages, the allocation algorithm in relationship (12.1) is used to distribute the total decrement. If shutdown percentages are reached, a random number is generated to indicate which facility of a given class size must be deleted, its number of employees is deducted from the needed citywide employment decrease, and allocation continues for the remainder of the year (subroutine CTCHG).

Increases are handled differently (subroutine PAOEI). If, after application of the allocation algorithm, full-capacity thresholds have been attained for given facilities, the program takes a separate branch to generate and locate new facilities for that SIC.

For each tract in which the SIC exists, facilities of the SIC are characterized by a distribution of the ratios of employees to square feet of plant, a capacity constraint. A random number is generated to pick a density ratio greater than or equal to that existing in the tract being processed (subroutine DENSE). This represents a maximum employee density for that industry in that tract at that time. Any surplus, i.e. employment above this maximum density constraint, is set aside for generating new facilities. However, if that constraint has not been

183

FIGURE 12-4

Flow Chart of INIMP Subsections for Processing Individuals SIC's

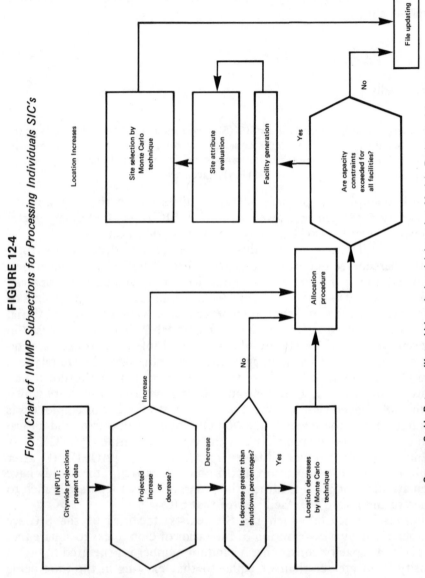

Source: S. H. Putman, "Intra-Urban Industrial Location Model: Design and Implementation," p. 23 (paper, manuscript version).

TABLE 12-1

Example Shutdown Percentages and
Firm Class Sizes: INIMP, Subroutine PAOED

CLASS	AVERAGE SIZE (Number of Employees)	SHUTDOWN PERCENTAGE	NUMBER OF FIRMS REPORTED*
1	10.0	.10	483
2	35.0	.15	214
3	75.0	.20	87
4	175.0	.25	62
5	375.0	.30	37
6	750.0	.40	13
7	1700.0	.50	7

Source: Listing of model.
*Putnam, "Intra-Urban Industrial Location Model," p. 9.

reached, the system absorbs employment increases into existing facilities. After the "slack" in existing facilities has been filled, excess or unlocated employees of the SIC type are totaled, and this value is compared with a distribution of average firm sizes for firms of that type. A random number is generated to pick a size class of firms smaller than or equal to the unlocated employee total; a new facility of that SIC type and size is generated. If the new facility does not absorb all the unlocated employees, the process is repeated.

As possible sites for the new facility, individual census tracts are evaluated on four attributes and one constraint: *assessed value*—a weighted mean of per unit assessed value of industrial site area (or buildings) in tracts where the given SIC type has located in the past; *available land*—whether the amount of vacant industrial land in a tract satisfies the needs of locating facility; *structural density*—a weighted index of industrial building area to total industrial land area in a tract; *industrial clustering*—a weighted mean of the proportion of industrial area to total area in the immediately adjacent tracts; and the *policy default* or *constraint*—a flag which indicates an excluded tract, e.g. airport land, river front property, railroad yards, or improperly zoned areas. The constraint has logical precedence over the four attributes, i.e. a site can be perfectly matched with a new facility and still not be selected if the policy default is operating (subroutines CLUST, MISC, ASSES).

Attribute evaluation proceeds in two logical steps, approximating the coarse and fine screening and matching of sites and new facilities. Generally, location of an SIC type is made in tracts already having a high concentration of the type. In the first step, simple binary choices are made based on existing facilities locations within a given SIC. Do a new facility and potential site agree within some (±) percentage range of

185

each attribute criterion? Yes or no? From this reduced set of possible locations, arbitrary weights are applied to the four attributes "to produce a measure of total attribute desirability for each census tract."[51] The tract with "highest attribute desirability" is selected for the new facility, or, in case of ties, a random number is generated to choose among tracts. Files are updated after all adjustments are made, and control switches back to the input for the next year.

INIMP is a "persistence" model. Based on information about existing conditions—in this case, locational distribution patterns of SIC types, changes in status are approximated. It is persistent in that one assumes there will be "more of the same." Reasons why the firms located in the past or might locate in the future, i.e. decision-making concerns, are implicitly ignored; only spatial location patterns of the existing industrial stock are analytically treated.

Theoretical Appraisal. When one is uncertain about the structural or theoretical properties of a process, random selections, or Monte Carlo techniques, are often used to represent the process.

There is in fact some theoretical literature on how firms choose their locations,[52] but it tends to be quite abstract and becomes less applicable as the fineness of spatial detail increases. The Pittsburgh modelers chose to ignore this theoretical leverage, substituting random processes for theory in the questionable interest of forecasting census-tract level of detail. Thus, INIMP is best termed a heuristic device. It is, nevertheless, a well-constructed, consistent model capable of producing plausible gross behavior.

Assuming that industrial location patterns remain the same may be acceptable in the short run, but as the time frame increases, the assumption loses its plausibility. INIMP illustrates John Kain and John Meyer's general contention that "little effort has been made to explain the existing pattern of industry location. Even less attention has been devoted to explaining changes in this pattern."[53] Insufficient attention to changing trends in structural patterns of industrial location and excessive reliance on statically biased employment projections, such as those provided by IOIIM, insure a conservatively biased model. New industry locates near old; old industrial areas become more densely populated; areas known to be developing are underestimated; changes in industrial type within a tract are overlooked although overall employment levels for the tract are approximated by the model; and so on. What we need are data describing *changes* in industrial location by size and type, and continuous field surveys and interviews to investigate the company decision-making processes that bring those changes about. Models like INIMP, which have attained qualified success in surmounting data and theory deficiencies, divert attention from the research and data collection efforts that are so urgently needed.

Technical Appraisal. INIMP's author succinctly summarizes the major technical issue—data:

> You are left in the unenviable situation of saying, "OK, which do I vitiate? Do I change my construct to match the data? Or, do I say, 'The data are an approximation of what's needed; we'll keep the construct but use the wrong data'?" Neither of those is a completely satisfactory solution. *Or,* another kind of thing, someone knows in advance what the data look like, and they try to build a model around it. . . . That's the situation we face now . . . ten [*sic*] years later, and we are still faced with the same problem of not having the data to match what would be a good theoretical construct.[54]

The design of any model is to a large extent constrained by available data. In INIMP's allocation algorithm, for example, shutdown percentages were not observed; they were convenient estimates that allowed the model to produce plausible behavior. Originally, weights on site-attribute evaluations were to be set by surveying local land brokers and business executives; but time and money ran out, and weights were "guesstimated." The density constraints on maximum facility size had to be set by random processes after a crude questionnaire produced a few uneven responses.

The model itself is well constructed, easy to follow, and consists of less than 900 instructions. While no system manual per se is available, the author's written accounts and a program listing are sufficiently detailed to allow a moderately skilled stranger to run it.[55] One inexplicable idiosyncrasy of the model is its sensitivity to minor adjustments in shutdown percentages—i.e. the model produces wild and unreasonable results for only slight (±) changes in these rates in a period of declining population. Another problem seems to be its inability to handle large—(±) 50 percent—population shocks. Again, erratic behavior in subsequent periods results. This derives in large part from the lack of adequate feedback loops in the structure. Minor changes create large, uncorrected behavioral outputs. If one does not have any theory about adjustment mechanisms in the context, there is no reason to expect feedback loops in a model. It should be noted that these mildly negative observations are based on the version of the model that I used, which was reduced in size and employed synthetic, albeit "plausible" data.[56] These three points plus the prior observation on persistence of locational preference patterns are particular areas requiring attention. Nonetheless, INIMP is able to "produce projections of employment by many classes, by small areal units" that are correct as to order of magnitude and trend.[57]

Ethical Appraisal. The model exhibits several of the classic utopian biases mentioned in chapter 7. It is *static* with respect to its data inputs and range of locational preferences.[58] It is constrained by the *boundaries* of Pittsburgh; however, as in the San Francisco case, this is mainly attributable to rigidities inherent in the Community Renewal Program. *Rationality* and *efficiency* considerations abound. For example, increases or decreases in the employed population are rationally distributed citywide throughout SICs of a given type. Shutdown percentages increase in orderly, stepwise fashion for each size class of firm, regardless of type or location. Size classes are differentiated without regard to differences that may or may not exist between types. Does a firm employing an average of seventy-five people act differently from one having 175? Perhaps, but we need some data. Are there observable differences between size types? Obviously there are, but we have to find out what these observed differences are, and what they have to do with the classification scheme actually used. There is no reason to expect, a priori, that the scheme used and that which might be observed will correspond. All we know is that the breakdowns actually used were convenient, handy, and efficient for the model-builder. The racial composition of the population is ignored in a context where race is a prime issue.[59] The modelers' preferences for site selection attributes may be acceptable for some purposes, but there is no reason to believe that politicians or businessmen share the same preferences. Indeed, arguments and examples of other attributes come readily to mind; e.g. access to transportation links, preferential taxing policies, readily tapped labor pools, etc. Unfortunately, data on these alternatives are even less accessible than those already used in INIMP.

Pragmatic Appraisal. INIMP conforms best to our characterization of an educational model.[60] It is a heuristic device that subsumes a quantity of information into an efficient and inexpensive program. It is limited in scope and operates with a small and, in many senses, non-existent data base. Its predictive accuracy is low by even the most optimistic assessments.

The theoretical use of the model is promising in that it so vividly identifies areas needing additional conceptual and measurement effort. One not only has a demonstrated need to do field work on various segments of INIMP, but this new research may be related to a more comprehensive whole. The functions of model qua data indicator and hypothesis generator are not to be underestimated at our current levels of understanding. What data there are inform the theoretical processes and hypotheses formalized in the model; the model supports or refutes to some extent the putative patterns in the data. The process iterates as model outputs and observed data converge through the improvement of relationships and the addition of variables. The model offers us the opportunity to understand the context better by considering a logically complete set of behavioral relationships, by measuring the elements in the model that are important, and by experimenting with the model to appraise and adjust it continually.

Measurement and data management applications of this model, as now configured, are nil.

This key segment of the highly touted "digital computer simulation model for urban renewal decision-making purposes,"[61] must be carefully appraised for its *utility for policy-making.*

Model development functioned as a retardant to the achievement of the more generalized goals of the Community Renewal Program. One official reports the tranquilizing effect of working with the consultants:

> Hiring the consultants became some kind of a cureall, probably sedative is a better word. The people who are supposed to do the work sleep, you know. They wait for the consultant to turn in his report and so they bide their time. What happens in the process is the consultant, without day-to-day supervision and a responsible guy supervising, goes floundering off in twenty directions. You wind up saying, "What the hell, that wasn't what we started out to study," when he turns in his report.[62]

A key politician saw it in much the same way. "I got the impression on the research side that they became so enamored with getting this model off of the ground, and the payoffs looked so great . . . that most of the other parts of the CRP were just put aside."[63]

A corollary to this unintended function is the problem of errors caused by hasty assembly of data to support the models. On this role of model qua obfuscator and error generator, Pittsburgh's recent deputy director of planning for research and data processing in 1969 was questioned:

> Q: How was the data bank when you took over? You have alluded to the fact that because the simulation effort was central, the data bank was in bad shape. How is that?
>
> A: It was done by a guy who just wasn't a competent professional and who was so busy with the models that he really—as a matter of fact, he wasn't really busy with the models; he was on the fringes since that wasn't his real function. He was trying to learn about the modeling, and then he had this other job. As a result, controls just weren't set up properly to handle the input data.[64]

As a result of being diverted, of "looking so far ahead" and not "bother[ing] to clean up the details very much," the city "wound up with a host of information that was almost unusable because of a high percentage of errors."[65] While these deficiencies are not totally attributable to the one model, INIMP, they are symptomatic.

The policy function of descriptive clarification was not attained because of time, money, personnel, and data limitations. Needed interviews, surveys, and questionnaires either were not done or were so hastily done as to be useless; hence the dependence on Monte Carlo techniques, projections that continued the status quo, and other expedients. The forecasting function, if carried out at all, is seriously limited by the questionable employment estimates generated by the input/output submodel. The model was specified mainly by a technician's preferences. Decision-makers were "unpersuaded and somewhat skeptical, cynical, and critical"[66] and did not participate in the model building, defaulting to a graduate student in operations research who had to meet a contract deadline. The result was predictable.

Because it was in a relatively advanced state of development, INIMP was demonstrated to officials to support the contractors' request for an extension of funds and time. A key policy-maker reportedly rejected the results on the grounds, "Well, this model is no good. I know a company who can open a foundry in this census tract; it doesn't show any foundry there. What good is it?"[67] Besides illustrating the extent of difference between the needs and sophistication of policy-makers and researchers, this example points to the importance of the *policy criterion* of the analytic question.

Because a model compiles and runs is no reason to assume that it is an acceptable policy-making device, or, as one politician puts it:

I think, subject to certain refinements, some of the models are "working" models. But the real question is: Do they relate to anything that anybody wants to know and in any particular situation? That's where the problem comes up.[68]

Lack of concern for the analytic question stemmed from a gross underestimation of the difficulty of the problem and from the often hostile indifference of the supposed users. One participant summarizes the situation:

Because there were no objectives at the beginning, there could not have been success at the end. . . . [It was really nobody's fault.] It was in these social systems simulation models that you really didn't know what the hell you were doing in the first place. It was one of the new ones, a first-time kind of thing, and so it was probably unreasonable to expect it to be very well-defined. We didn't know enough about it.[69]

Lacking agreement on a question, or worse, lacking any questions for the model to answer, our four ex ante queries of policy relevance are unanswerable. The ten ex post facto questions of policy appropriateness from our "Appraisal Function" are applied to INIMP in Exhibit 12-2. The model is unacceptable as a policy-making or assisting device. However, this is not to underrate its promising educational and theory-building applications. In fact, INIMP's builder, Putnam, indicated that he would use it in this fashion in his teaching/research assignment at the University of Pennsylvania.

TOMM—TIME-ORIENTED (RESIDENTIAL AND COMMERCIAL) METROPOLITAN MODEL

The residential and commercial submodel is a direct descendant of Ira S. Lowry's *Model of Metropolis,*[70] probably the most serious and

EXHIBIT 12-2

*Ten Questions: A Summary Appraisal of Policy Appropriateness—*INIMP

POLICY QUESTION	ASSESSMENT
1. DISTORTION between model and reference system?	EXCESSIVE: "In making a sheer mechanical projection . . . the conclusions were wrong and faulty. . . . I'm not quarreling with the use of intricate mathematical formulas to arrive at a conclusion. Don't make the devices the showpiece of the study. It's the accuracy of the thing that elected officials are interested in."[a]
2. INPUT/OUTPUT familiar and intelligible?	UNINTELLIGIBLE; INCOMPREHENSIBLE: "When I called [name] over and asked, 'What does this mean and what does that mean?' he could no better translate [it] to me than the person who prepared it."[b]
3. COMMON SENSE?	OFFENSIVE (to policy-makers); OK—GOOD (technicians).
4. "QUESTION" elements excluded in the interest of precision or generalization?	NOT APPLICABLE: "Question" was never asked.
5. STATIC bias?	YES.
6. ALTER COMPONENTS?	YES: The model is simply configured and alternative subroutines or individual relationships could easily be introduced.
7. Essential ELEMENTS of the analytical question OMITTED?	NOT APPLICABLE.
8. PREDICTION of time series upon which formulated? PREDICTION of subsequent time series?	NOT APPLICABLE IN GROSS DETAIL: The model did not benefit from time series information. Preliminary validation attempts made several years after termination of the CRP produced some "reasonable" approximations to subsequent events.[c]
9. STRUCTURAL CHANGES in the context accounted for?	ASSUMES CONSTANT, PERSISTENT state. Cf., "Theoretical Appraisal" in text.
10. Consonance of the model with ETHICAL-MORAL standards of policy-makers? Populace? Profession?	INDETERMINATE: PROBABLY NOT; YES.[d] Cf., "Ethical Appraisal" in text.

[a]Interview Document, October 23, 1969, p. 9 (politician).

[b]*Ibid.,* p. 15 (planner).

[c]S. H. Putman, "Intra-Urban Industrial Location Model," pp. 22-29.

[d]*Ibid.* Putman has been scrupulously and refreshingly candid about the model's limitations.

careful descriptive work on metropolitan structure extant. Lowry produced his model under the aegis of the Pittsburgh Regional Planning Association[71] and graciously made it available for further development.

THE CONTEXT

TOMM is essentially the Lowry model with marginal modifications.[72] However, Lowry's original caveat about his model pertains to its altered progeny as well:

I should make it quite clear that I do not consider the Pittsburgh Model a finished product, which is usable at this point for any serious practical purpose. It is at best a prototype with a promising future. Its present value lies mainly in the guide-lines it offers for further research.[73]

To understand and appraise TOMM, one must begin by understanding the essential characteristics and weaknesses of *A Model of Metropolis.*

The Lowry Model Characterized. The interested reader is encouraged to read the important source document, *A Model of Metropolis,* for a more thorough and careful exposition of the basic model. However, to better understand the general character and overall logic of the model, we present this summary description. The information flows of the model are represented in Figure 12-5. The model's spatial units are one-mile-square tracts; each tract is characterized by industrial ("basic" in Lowry's parlance) employment disaggregated by type of industrial classification and number of employees, or size of firm. From these data the model determines the amount of retail ("service") employment and the residential population dependent on basic employment, and assigns these to spatial units.

The theoretical basis for these allocations is the "gravity" principle that the probability of interaction between people and places varies directly with their relative attractiveness or size (mass) and inversely with their distance or separation.[74] Each employment site attracts households and (indirectly) retail establishments as an inverse monotonic function of distance. The quality of an activity located within a tract is limited by a maximum density constraint (Z_j^H), the value for which is provided as input data. This constraint prevents the model from lumping residences too close to the sites of employment attracting them.

Residential Population. The total number of households in the region is a function of total employment, symbolically,

$$N = f \sum_{j=1}^{n} E_j \tag{12.2}$$

where,

N = total number of households
E_j = total employment of tract j

and,

$E_j = E^b + E^r$
(basic) (retail)
$E_j = f(E^b)$

192

FIGURE 12-5 *Lowry Model Logic*

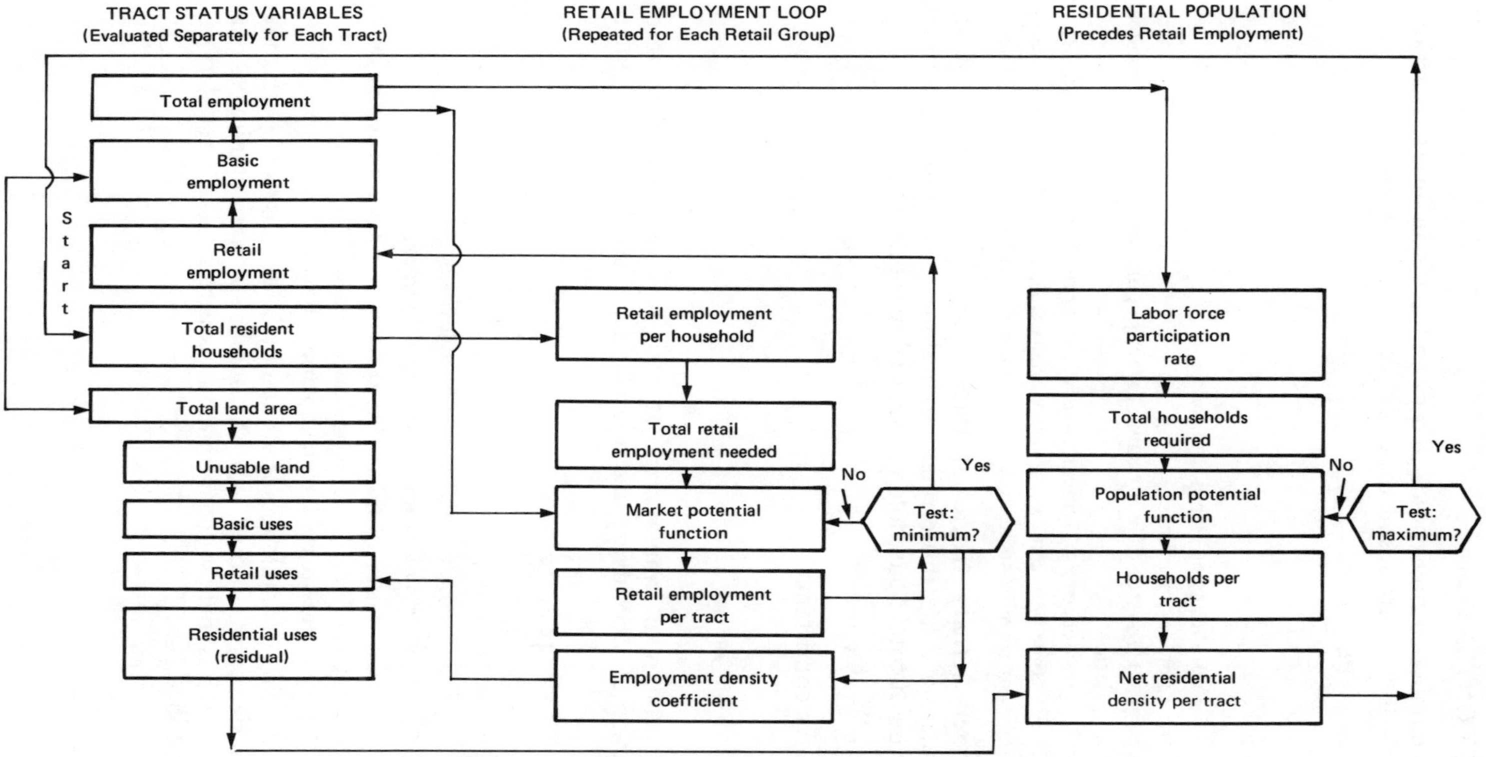

Source: I. S. Lowry, *Model of Metropolis* (Santa Monica: The Rand Corporation, RM A 4035-RC, August 1964), p. 5.

THE CONTEXT

The number of households in a given tract is an inverse function of the tract's distance from sources of employment:

$$N_j = g \sum_{i=1}^{n} \frac{E_i}{T_{ij}} \tag{12.3}$$

where,

> N_j = number of households in tract j
>
> E_i = population of tract i. $i \neq j$
>
> g = scale factor to insure sum of tract population equals total regional population
>
> T_{ij} = residence-employment, *trip distribution index*, a measurement of distance between two separate tracts (i,j), e.g. airline distance, travel time, or travel costs between two points. (Lowry used airline distance.)

Retail Activity. There are three types of retail employment. Total population using those retail establishments of type k is a simple proportion of total household (residential) population:

$$E^K = a^K N \tag{12.4}$$

and, for consistency,

$$E^K = \sum_{j=1}^{n} E_j^k \tag{12.5}$$

The total retail employment of each type is allocated to tracts as a function of accessibility and household and employment populations.

$$E_j^K = b^K \left[\sum_{i=1}^{n} \left(\frac{c^K N_i}{T_{ij}^k} \right) + d^K E_j \right] \tag{12.6}$$

where,

> K = superscript for type of retail employment
>
> E_j^K = total employment of retail type K in tract j
>
> b^K = scale factor to insure that the sum of retail employment in the tracts equals totals for the region calculated in (12.4)
>
> T_{ij}^K = residence to retail trade trip distribution index for retail type K

The location of employees is limited by both density (Z_j^H) and minimum retail size constraints (Z^K). If the number of retail employees demanded in a tract is below the minimum constraint, that retail type is not established.

$$E_j^K \geq Z^K \tag{12.7}$$

otherwise,

$$E_j^K = 0$$

Each sector uses land, subject to the identity:[75]

$$A_j = A_j^U + A_j^B + A_j^R + A_j^H \tag{12.8}$$

where,

A_j = total area in spatial tract j

and the superscripts,

U = unusable land for tract j (given as data)
B = basic sector (industrial data read as data)
R = retail sector (determined by model)
H = household sector (determined as a residual)
$A_j^H = A_j - (A_j^U + A_j^B + A_j^R)$.

The amount of land used in retail trade is determined as a function of retail employment and an exogenous retail employment density constraint—e^K.

$$A_j^R = \sum_{k=1}^{n} e^K E_j^K \tag{12.9}$$

Retail land use is logically limited by a constraint that prevents it from going negative.

$$A_j^R \geq \left[A_j - A_j^U - A_j^B \right] \tag{12.10}$$

Convergence. Because the model is static, equilibrium between the distribution of household population and retail employment is approximated by an iterative procedure. To Lowry's credit, the behavioral process being replicated provided the basis for approximating a non-unique, but empirically persuasive, "solution."

To recapitulate: Given number, type, and location of basic industrial activity in a region, determine the number and location of residential population induced by that activity; determine the number, type, and location of retail activity induced by that residential population; and determine, by successive approximation, the convergence of residential and retail activities for individual tracts with respect to several logical consistency constraints. The model consists of five behavioral relationships, four accounting identities, and three constraints. It is a very simple model, complicated only by the fact that it operates with a large number of disaggregated tracts.

The Lowry Model Appraised. The Lowry model is not a policy model. *A Model of Metropolis* is an explanatory device in the senses described in chapter 2. Its variables are limited (partial) and well defined. The temporal perspective is static, single point in time (Lowry

195

used 1958 Pittsburgh data, ignored time series, trends, etc.). Its context and units of analysis are both general and gross (households are undifferentiated, retail activities are crudely differentiated into three categories). And by attempting to achieve a unique solution, a single path was approximated as the development possibility. Lowry eschews *all* policy pretenses:

> I tried to see if using limited information as the input, I could come out with a full description of the region. I was just successful enough so that the thing was interesting—to other people. I don't think that I was successful enough to make it a useful tool for any practical purpose.[76]

Accepting Lowry at his word, let us briefly consider the model's limitations as an explanatory device.

Gravity models have a long history in social science,[77] and while their general properties are known,[78] model-builders tend to overlook some of their critical limitations.[79] The operating assumption in the model is that social *interaction decreases with increasing distance*. Empirically this assumption is viable; however, a behavioral-theoretical reason *why* this should be is hard to articulate. A serious limitation of gravity models is that they depend upon very gross levels of population data. "The gravity model is designed to account for the behavior of large groups of people. It rests on the assumption that group behavior is predictable on the basis of mathematical probability . . . "[80] Hence Lowry treats all households as indistinguishable, relies on only three gross retail activities disaggregated according to market-spatial (not functional) characteristics, and considers the full region as the logical analytic context.

The level of spatial detail is a limitation to the extent that one's interest is in units smaller than one square mile. Lowry clearly and concisely states:

> The Pittsburgh Model has a structural capacity for generating output detail for territorial units as small as a square mile. In experimental work to date, I judge the *minimum grain of usable output to be at least four times as large.*[81] (emphasis added)

A third major limitation is the omission of time, although Lowry recommends ways in which the model might be adapted to account for this, as well as several other shortcomings.

In general, it was a modest, remarkably honest, and path-breaking early effort to capture the grossest spatial character of a large region at a single cross-section of time. *A Model of Metropolis* is not a policy model. TOMM is not a policy model, either.

Order of Processing: TOMM.[82] Besides adding time subscripts to create a marginal, time-dependent, nonequilibrium version of the Lowry model, TOMM also modifies the household relationship (12.4), disaggregates the household sector by income types, redefines the retail employment relationship (12.5), and finally reduces the analytic context to the limits of the city of Pittsburgh. The overall logic generally remains the same. Elements of the exogenous employment sector interact asymmetrically with a partially decomposed system containing elements of the household and retail sectors.[83]

Theoretical Appraisal. Households are a function of the basic industrial employment for each time t generated (ostensibly) by INIMP; but, unlike Lowry's version, here the number of households is modified by total available land. Relationship (12.4) becomes,[84]

$$N_{j,t}^{H*} = g \sum_{i=1}^{n} \left[\frac{E_{i,t}}{T_{ij}} \right] A_{j,t}^{H*} \tag{12.11}$$

where, the new term

$A_{j,t}^{H*}$ = total amount of land available for residential (household) location in tract j at time t

  * = cumulative total or stock; absence of asterisk implies the variable as a flow or difference between t and $t-1$

$E_{i,t}$ = increment of basic, industrial employees being employed in tract i at time t

T_{ij} = household-employment trip distribution index

and verbally,

The total stock of households in census tract j at time t equals the increase in a one-year period of basic employment to tract i modified by an index of current accessibility of tract i to tract j, times the total stock of available residential land, all modified by a scale factor g to reconcile generated total tracts with given total populations. Or, residential population is directly related to basic employment population and available land is inversely related to the distance from that source of employment.

If one shifts the $(A_{j,t}^{H*})$ term to the left side of the equation, relationship (12.11) is revealed to be a density measure, as opposed to Lowry's more straightforward determination of population level. No beneficial effects are apparent, and the substantive interpretation has obviously been weakened.

Disaggregation of the household relationship by income types is an apparently minor adjustment that has serious theoretical and practical implications for the model. The initial disaggregation is accounted in relationship (12.12).[85]

$$N_{j,t}^{HI*} = N_{j,t}^{HI} + N_{j,t-1}^{HI*} \tag{12.12}$$

where,

197

$N_{j,t}^{HI*}$ = total stock of households of income type l in tract j at time t.

$N_{j,t}^{HI}$ = increment of households of type l locating in tract j at time t.

This relocated annual increment is determined in another new relationship, whose substantive interpretation is at best questionable.[86]

$$N_{j,t}^{HI} = r_j \left[p_1 N_{j,t-1}^{HI*} + w_1 \sum_{i=1}^{n} \left(\frac{E_{i,t}}{T_{ij}} \right) \right] \qquad (12.13)$$

where,

p_1, w_1 = constants (elasticities) for each household type 1

r_j = scale factor to insure that sum of residential population disaggregated by household type equals total residential population

and verbally,

The increase in households of type l located in tract j at time t is equal to a proportion of the total stock of households of that type in the previous period $t - 1$, plus some proportion of the annual increment of new basic employees, modified by an accessibility measure.

Think about that in simple terms. All households are relocated in each time period by this relationship. If a household is already located, why would one want to relocate it in the same place in the subsequent year? The *Technical Paper* indicates that "households tend to cluster around other households of the same type,"[87] which may or may not be the case; however, the newly located increment is surely not solely a function of existing stocks, and the symbolic form actually used in the model has nothing to do with clustering. Logically ($N_{j,t}^{HI}$) might be a function of households switching from one l type to another in a given year, i.e. economic mobility. It could be a function of intraregional migration of household types for reasons other than employment shifts, the phenomenon subsumed into the last term of the relationship. In either of these cases, the complexity of calculation and specification increases rapidly. Relationship (12.13) will return a number, but it is a number whose meaning is derived from a logical imponderable.

The practical implication of disaggregating the household relationship is driven home by its impact on the original retail employment relationship (12.5). Besides the addition of the time subscript, the only change is in the old (N_i) term, which is transformed into ($N_{i,t}^{HI}$). In words, the new relationship says that various household types l create different types of markets; e.g. richer classes frequent different types and numbers of retail establishments than poorer classes. If one is going to make that plausible assumption, based on the earlier disaggregation of households by income, then for the sake of consistency, one must be prepared to collect data for new indices of accessibility (T_{ij}) for each of the $n(n - l)$ census tract pairs in the analytical context for all retail types k and household types l. Is the accessibility to a given retail type the same for a rich household as for a poor household? Probably not. Or, is the accessibility of a given household type to a variety of retail establishments constant? (In more homely terms, is a poor family as willing to travel a given distance to an exotic boutique as to a discount department store?) Probably not. *One simple disaggregation* has generated a need for about *one-half million additional pieces of data.*[88] Apparently this logical demand was overlooked or ignored, and a single accessibility measure was imposed on differentiated elements in the model. This is a fairly serious shortcoming.

Another serious problem is the effect of using the basic employment inputs forecasted by INIMP, as indicated in the "Overview—Urban Systems Simulation Flow Chart," Figure 12-2. TOMM's simple theoretical structure is predicated on the availability of data on the number, size, type, and location of basic industrial employment. The Lowry model effectively asked this question: "If *we know exactly* where all types and sizes of basic industry are located, then where will homes and retail activities locate with respect to that employment?" Given the "lumpiness" and multiplier effects of different primary activities, it makes a great deal of difference, in fact as well as in TOMM's operation, whether a plant employing 10,000 people is located at point x rather than at point y; it makes a great deal of difference whether that plant employs one or 10,000.[89] Small area forecasts of large, lumpy capital investment may not be a very productive expenditure of research attention and resources; it is an inherently unpredictable kind of activity.[90] This point is forcefully made, for example, in an extensive Department of Commerce survey on industrial location: an overwhelming number of locational decisions are made quite subjectively, without benefit of data or analysis, by one or a few participants.[91] The point is that INIMP's forecasts are simply inadequate.

Recently, the theoretical adequacy of accessibility has been questioned on the grounds that "it tells us very little about the locational *decision process* of housing consumers," tending to "reflect the existing pattern of residential development [rather] than the process by which housing consumers move about within that fixed pattern."[92] Since the data used in the design and calibration of *A Model of Metropolis* and subsequently TOMM were primarily from the Pittsburgh Area Transportation Study, the use of trip—origin-destination—data is understandable. It may have diverted attention, however, from the need to gain insight into residential decision processes. Alternative, albeit immature, lines of thought on these matters have been articulated by Richard Meier and, distinctly, by Karl W. Deutsch in terms of cohesive communities defined by "their ability to receive and transmit information,"[93] and more recently by F. Stuart Chapin, Jr., in terms of clusterings of differential activity patterns.[94] Perhaps now it is time to reconsider the utility of accessibility in terms of some evidence[95] and alternative theoretical images. To the extent that accessibility is inadequate, so, too, is TOMM.

From all of this there are two concluding considerations that are worth making: (1) Small area models, like TOMM, that depend upon quantities of highly speculative input data and exclude important structural characteristics of a context may not be worth large expenditures of time and research resources to build and operate. (2) It may be inefficient and ineffective to graft and transplant an existing model to accomplish purposes for which the original formulation was neither intended nor designed.

Technical Appraisal. There was not enough data to run the model.

In June of 1966, a graduate student regional planner from Cornell was hired by City Planning to make TOMM operational, "with the hope that some part of the project could be salvaged and used."[96] Despite his intensive efforts and subsequent work by CONSAD, the technical problems were worse than one might have expected:

- Original data from the 1958 Pittsburgh Area Transportation Study had to be reaggregated from the one-quarter-square-mile blocks.
- Employment data were available for mile squares only.
- 1960 census population data had to be specially reaggregated and tediously keypunched.
- Even at that, it was impossible to obtain compatible spatial units of analysis.

"In no case did data fall out naturally from a source or from processing other data; it was always necessary to force the data into a new form, making compromises with compromises."[97]

In addition, TOMM was written in FORTRAN II, an unwieldy and dated language, and the documentation left with the city by the consultant is poor to nonexistent:[98] no system manual, no debugging and technical modification logs, no detailed flow charts, etc.

The model has two particularly curious operational idiosyncrasies. Small variations in the accessibility measure, for example, produce inexplicably large variations in output. The structure of the model is such that this is not unexpected; however, the structure falsely indicates an extraordinary sensitivity to small variations in distance that probably does not empirically exist. A second persistent problem, in all permutations of the Lowry model, is the tendency toward somewhat unrealistic dispersion of the population. For instance, Lowry notes that "for other parts of the central city . . . the model projects population losses, with commensurate gains for the low density fringe."[99] This phenomenon was also evidenced in the city's version of TOMM, which CONSAD ran once in 1967.[100] A city planning technician noted in correspondence: "Generally I find the output disappointing since the results seem so unreasonable. Apparently the model has an area bias that should be corrected in future runs."[101] The full model has been run once using Allegheny County as the analytical context; however, the county has nearly 500 census tracts, and "the model as presently constructed will only handle 200 areal units. In addition, computer time for model execution increases by the square of the number of areal units."[102] To accommodate machine limitations, a special-purpose spatial measure was derived. Using 177 "super tracts" and inputs from the 1960 census, the 1958 Pittsburgh Area Transportation Study, and an ad hoc approximation of accessibility (T_{ij}) determined solely as the airline distance between centroids of supertracts,[103] TOMM produced the results summarized in Table 12-2. Approximately 87 percent of the

TABLE 12-2

Sample Performance of Pittsburgh Model—TOMM

NUMBER OF SUPERTRACTS	1960-70 PERCENTAGE CHANGE	NUMBER OF 1960 HOUSEHOLDS
3	$X \geq -30.0\%$	5,901
5	$-5.0\% \leq X < -30.0\%$	9,664
160	$+5.0\% \leq X < -5.0\%$	45,959
156*	$-2.0\% \leq X \leq -2.5\%$	42,240
1	$+5.0\% < X \leq +30.0\%$	1,909
2	$+30.0\% < X \leq 100.0\%$	1,115
1	$100.0\% < X \leq 200.0\%$	745
1	$200.0\% < X \leq 300.0\%$	860
3	$300.0\% < X \leq 500.0\%$	1,488
1	$X > 500.0\%$	111
Totals: 177		67,752

Source: CONSAD Research Corporation for the Pittsburgh Department of City Planning, "Impact on Allegheny County Due to the Relocation of Residential and Commercial Activity in the East Street Valley" (Pittsburgh: DCP, March 8, 1967), pp. 16-20.

*Subset of (±) 5 percent Set.

supertracts lost 2.0 to 2.5 percent of their population in the decade 1960 to 1970; this accounts for more than 62 percent of the total number of 1960 households. Eight tracts had declines greater than 5 percent; nine had gains greater than 5 percent. In general, TOMM was siphoning off a small, fixed percentage from the majority of tracts and dumping this total into fewer than nine tracts out of 177. Furthermore, these nine receiving tracts lie on the fringes of the analytical context. If this is the *best* performance obtainable from TOMM (and we assume that this is at least partly true because CONSAD was using the results to attempt to rekindle city interest), it seems unnecessary to operate at levels of disaggregation even as fine as a "supertract." The model's behavior is just not very convincing. With these outputs and performance, it is inconceivable how any knowledgeable person could claim, as a CONSAD spokesman in fact did, that

the Pittsburgh CRP effort has been one of the leaders in the utilization of both computer-based urban information system and modeling techniques to determine the consequences of alternative renewal actions, it is only now [December 12, 1967]—five years since its inception—that there is substantial utility in ongoing decision processes.[104]

Ethical Appraisal. The model's biases are much like those already noted for INIMP. It is *static*—despite claims to the contrary—with respect to its data inputs, structure, and locational preferences. It is *bounded* by Pittsburgh's city limits, even though its one operational trial was made for the region.

Is it reasonable to assume, as TOMM does, that high- and low-income groups place the same value on accessibility to various retail locations? To places of employment? If, as Stegman notes, accessibility is "such a valued good, only the fortunate and the affluent should gain command of inlying residential land while the poor are pushed outward into the fringe."[105] TOMM's assumption seems a bit implausible, upon reflection. But if making these distinctions implies the collection of 500,000 more bits of data, and those data don't exist, the modeler finds it necessary to rationalize the distinction away . . . with obvious consequent harm to the analysis. Ethnic differences, amenities of individual residential locations and areas, access to transportation networks, zoning and other observed land-use characteristics and contextual restrictions are not accounted for.

The advisability of using airline distance as a measure of accessibility is open to question, given the discontinuous nature of Pittsburgh's topography; it is not the unobstructed plane implied by the location procedures in TOMM. Ignoring the geographic context reinforces the model's tendency to produce symmetrical outputs.[106]

Alice laughed. "There's no use trying," she said: "one *can't* believe impossible things."

"I daresay you haven't had much practice," said the Queen. "When I was your age, I always did it for half-an-hour a day. Why, sometimes I've believed as many as six impossible things before breakfast."[107]

Apparently credibility was put to the test in Pittsburgh, too. Of what use is TOMM?

Pragmatic Appraisal. Given its crude and cumbersome input and output routines and its relatively inefficient computer language, the model has negligible utility for data base management. Likewise, measurement applications are few. Data deficiencies of a most fundamental sort are the hallmark of the Pittsburgh CRP; but then, it was to collect simple raw data, among other reasons, that the politicians agreed to do the project in the first place.

TOMM's contribution to our theoretical understanding of urban spatial location is two-edged. Because it attempts, however limited its success, to describe an existing *static* spatial pattern, one may easily make the erroneous assumption that TOMM has explained how the pattern came into being, and when and where changes in that pattern will occur. TOMM's theoretical contribution is negative insofar as it falsely obscures alternative explanations of the process of urban location decisions. The more critical issues of change, the collection of more time series information on fewer, less detailed variables, and efforts to understand the behavioral processes underlying static patterns in both the data and the context are all overwhelmed by the data requirements of an elaborate and finely detailed cross-sectional model. We ought not waste resources satisfying the data needs of a statically biased configuration, when what is needed are explanations of processes and data on rates of structural change.[108]

The model has a distinct educational application; it has already fulfilled this function to some extent for the project's participants. In answer to the question, "What do you think CONSAD got out of all this?" one city official replied, "Money, experience, and I think they learned that there were things that you couldn't do."[109] One of the graduate student model-builders termed the CRP, "The best no-cost professional experience one could have ever had."[110] In much revised form, the model has demonstrated its broader educational potential as a constituent submodel of Richard D. Duke's METRO urban game at the University of Michigan.[111] TOMM conforms to our educational characterization: it is minimally predictive, limited in scope, gross in theoretical detail (although microscopic in spatial detail), and works with an outdated data base. On the other hand, in its revised form, it is reasonably manageable, flexible, and economical to operate. For educational purposes, TOMM is reportedly satisfactory.[112] Its *policy-making* utility is another matter.

TOMM is as guilty as INIMP of performing the unintended functions of project retardation and error generation; in these aspects the models cannot be distinguished from one another. A politician describes his own pragmatic reality test:

> In making the pitch for simulation models, [they] stressed the fact to me for developing a data bank. . . . [I]t developed that when people went to use some of the data that had been collected, much of it was inaccurate. . . . I would call up and say, "I would like to know how many vacant lots we have in the 15th Ward that might be suitable sites for housing" [raw information within TOMM's domain]. Hamilton would say, "I'll get this back to you; you ought to get it in an hour." Four days later I would call back and say, "I wanted to know how many—." All they had was a very elaborate reason why they couldn't get it. From the computer I got one of two things, either nothing and an excuse, or an answer that turned out later to be wrong.[113]

There is an even subtler unintended function evident in the Pitts-burgh case. It is difficult to describe, but is related to communications problems between modelers, salesmen, and users. It seems that the inherent analytical difficulties of the task—the problems of intention, specification, control, and validation noted in chapters 8 and 9—may be misconstrued by policy-makers. One politician describes the issue as "the lack of guts to make a decision, you know, going in to do one endless study. That's the place they wound up in the CRP exercise."[114] Misrepresenting how difficult and time consuming are model specifica-tion and data collection and management is, in the long haul, self-defeating and counter-productive; it should be avoided or alleviated if at all possible.

Descriptive clarification was accomplished insofar as the Pittsburgh region was described by several variables for a large number of spatial units at one point in time, 1958. The problem, from the policy perspec-tive, is that no one cares very much about a ten-year-old context, least of all the decision-makers.

> I'll tell you one of the greatest tragedies here, as far as I'm concerned, with data, is the tremendous rapidity of change going on in the City today. Changes brought about by social unrest, criminal attacks, sales of property because the Blacks are moving in. We are still sitting here with 1960 Census data [1969 interview date] . . . . Analyzing what happens in a neighborhood becomes very simple, if you find out the area's lost 30 percent of the population in five years and you see a lot of "For Sale" signs up. For that you don't need a computer.[115]

TOMM's forecasting potential is constrained by its original design purpose and by the unavailability of trend data from which structural modifications and rate-of-change parameters might be derived. The normative limitations, as noted, are severe enough to render the model of dubious value for policy assistance.

Once again we encounter a divergence in orientation. The politician works at the margin of time with a large number of variables. The model-builder prefers to work where he can find a body of data, regard-less of its timeliness, scope, or utility. "What the professional model-builder wants is to be left alone to do his thing, which is model-build-ing. The price he has to pay for that is thinking up something to tell the client."[116] That is to say, scientific and policy *criteria* differ as to the fundamental analytical questions being asked. Lowry's parting words in *A Model of Metropolis* are both prophetic and ironic: "In the develop-ment of public policy, as in scientific research, the proper formulation of a question is the most important step in reaching an effective answer."[117] Any overlap between the rather well-defined scientific ques-tions Lowry posed and the ill-defined questions one expects from a policy-maker is fortuitous. In short, if TOMM answers any question at all, it is some variant of Lowry's earlier scientific question, but not a policy question.

Without clear specification of the analytical question, we must again bypass our four ex ante queries on policy relevance. The model's policy appropriateness is summarized in Exhibit 12-3. As presently configured, the model has very limited policy utility. Its career as an educational device seems assured and reasonably well deserved.

Despite generous publicity, none of the three basic submodels from the Pittsburgh CRP has much utility as a policy device. The effects of selling the model-building scheme were more debilitating in Pittsburgh than in San Francisco—if this is possible.

Selling

Caveat emptor is an ill-suited bromide for technically unsophisticated public officials when the disease is a sophisticated problem solution, for a price. Selling seriously impeded the Pittsburgh project; the phenomenon warrants fuller consideration so that its incidence and ill-effects may be limited in the future.

As in the San Francisco case, commercialism had the effects of further repressing skeptical clients and causing responsibility for model-building to be forfeited to technicians. Unlike San Francisco, in Pittsburgh efforts to promote the model tended to inflate the expectations mainly of curious nonparticipants and have not yet resulted in adverse public reaction or a "bad press."

User Estrangement. A politician describes the distrust of consultants that grew from his experience in the CRP:

> In the first place, I am skeptical of consultants generally. I don't think that any outfit coming into town can really get an appreciation of a project in six months, or a problem in six months to a year. What they wind up doing, generally, is going around picking everybody's brains, and then they watch to see which way the wind is going to blow, and then they write your report. Then they walk away from it with all kinds of irresponsible conclusions. . . . There has been a misuse and abuse of consultants. When I want to hire a consultant now, I want to give him a very specific and narrow task to do.[118]

Emphasis on sophisticated techniques, coupled with the problem of divergent orientations, encouraged noncommunication between researcher and user. One user's opinion was that "we were kind of looked upon as some clods out of the country that did not understand this."[119] From a technical point of view the city's representatives were just as described in this statement, but how or why should it have been otherwise?

EXHIBIT 12-3

Ten Questions: A Summary Appraisal of Policy Appropriateness—TOMM

POLICY QUESTION	ASSESSMENT
1. DISTORTION between model and reference system?	EXCESSIVE: In the 1967 East Street Valley test: "It just so happened that the run that predicted the distribution of population seemed to me so unreal that I haven't published it at all"[a] [city planning technician].
2. INPUT/OUTPUT familiar and intelligible?	UNINTELLIGIBLE; INTIMIDATING: Inputs were scarcely intelligible to the model-builders. [Cf. above, "Technical Appraisal."] In describing outputs, a politician claims, "We always got the x, y, z mumbo-jumbo from the firm's consultants and the staff that understood it."[b]
3. COMMON SENSE?	OFFENSIVE: "Generally I find the output disappointing since the results seem so unreasonable. . . . [They] seem to fly in the face of both past relocation patterns and local preferences which link displacees to areas closely adjoining their former homes."[c]
4. "QUESTION" elements excluded in the interest of precision or generalization?	NOT APPLICABLE.
5. STATIC bias?	DECIDEDLY YES: Net detriment for policy purposes.
6. ALTER COMPONENTS?	YES: Alternative relationships or subroutines could be introduced. At the University of Michigan, for example, TOMM has been altered a great deal without incurring outrageous costs.
7. Essential ELEMENTS of the analytical question OMITTED?	NOT APPLICABLE.
8. PREDICTION of time series upon which formulated? PREDICTION of subsequent time series?	NOT APPLICABLE; NO.
9. STRUCTURAL CHANGES in the context accounted for?	ASSUMES CONSTANT.
10. Consonance of the model with ETHICAL-MORAL standards of policy-makers? Populace? Profession?	INDETERMINATE; PROBABLY NOT; TO SOME EXTENT.

[a] Interview Document, October 21, 1969, pp. 5-6 (user).
[b] Interview Document, October 22, 1969, p. 2 (user).
[c] Correspondence (city official), March 17, 1967.

A researcher describes one of the elaborate attempts that were made "to win" the officials over. The approach has very little to commend it.

We tried it on two different occasions, in terms of inviting city officials from City Hall. Bob Pease of the Redevelopment Authority, the Executive Director from the Allegheny Conference, some of the senior staff from the County Redevelopment Agency, the Housing Authority guy, we had a whole bunch of these guys assembled at the University of Pittsburgh for an entire day. We had the Washington officials there, to give it a touch of legitimacy, attempting to explain and to win them over. It didn't work. *We failed. We didn't communicate. I think that the animosity, the lack of trust between the agencies was stifling.*[120] (emphasis added)

Selling, communication problems, hostility, mistrust—these are basic ingredients in the Pittsburgh Community Renewal Program.

Confusing the Issue; Misplaced Relevance. Another kind of commercialism also operated in Pittsburgh: the marketing of innovative ideas.

One phase of the process involves dissemination of ideas in learned articles, speeches, and by word of mouth. Hamilton, in keeping with his philosophy "of trying to provide part of this link [so that] large planning organizations along with universities can be consistently moving the state of the art forward,"[121] began touring the country, making speeches about the Pittsburgh CRP. One effect was immediate, and limited to the project; another was more far-reaching.

One participant's view is that, "having launched this noble experiment, Hamilton proceeded to pay too little attention to it. He was running around the country making speeches. He delegated the thing to others in a way that it was just bound to get out of control."[122] It was "bound to get out of control" for another reason noted by a federal participant: "The City Planning Department did not have anybody with enough technical expertise to evaluate what was being done . . . to evaluate it, and be able to contribute."[123]

One widespread effect of selling is the inflation of nonparticipant expectations. A city politician reports on his experiences at an IBM symposium for local urban officials:

I heard reference to the use of the computer and developing of simulation models for Pittsburgh, We were using IBM equipment, that accounts for it [his attendance]. I kidded the IBM officials that asked me to go there, because I clearly thought the whole experiment was being exaggerated in terms of what to expect. I was surprised to hear that the experiment was being treated as a successful one—or reported as such.[124]

Such experiences cannot in any way facilitate the immediate research enterprise. Imagine a politician's reaction when he is exposed in this manner. It would not be surprising if he became irritated and embittered enough to threaten, "If anybody calls me up and wants to find out what really happened, and they repeat that CONSAD oversold them [on a subsequent project], I'm going to disenchant them God-damned fast."[125] Indeed, in the long run, this may be the more injurious form of selling. Distorted accounts proliferate; there are no realistic assessments of the actual state of the art; and, consequently, badly needed research is not undertaken or is misdirected.

> You know, the thing is not working, but I don't think the profession as a whole is aware of this, let alone the outside world. The articles which appear in the *AIP Journal* [*Journal of the American Institute of Planners*], for example, suggest that everything is coming up roses. The *Journal* has had whole issues devoted to models ... Steger had an article [in one]; it was very glowing and there was no hint of the fact that we've got something here that hasn't produced very much.[126]

This brings us to the role of the university (CRES) in the project and to an assessment of what seemed to be some substantial limitations.

University Participation: Research and Responsibility

Participation of the Center for Regional Economic Studies in the Community Renewal Program illustrates two apparent weaknesses of university-based, policy-oriented research. Universities may lack sufficient control over their human, fiscal, and moral resources to deliver on concerted activities. For many university researchers, discipline-relevant sources of reward and deprivation take clear precedence over questions of immediate public policy.

CRES's performance in the Pittsburgh Community Renewal Program must be rated mediocre to poor.

Inadequate Control. CRES contracted responsibility to execute a number of tasks for the CRP;[127] its actions do little to dispel doubts about the university's ability to play a productive role in policy-oriented research.

By July of 1963, the associate director of CRES, whose initial participation included helping to sell the contract and assembling research talent, had taken on new responsibilities as an administrator and researcher for the President's Appalachian Regional Economic Commission.[128] So it had been necessary, after the signing of the contract in March of that year, to recruit an additional CRES staff-faculty member. He joined CRES from the University of Pennsylvania. In his words:

> I was an associate professor in the Department [Economics] and was affiliated with CRES in some way. In November, a deal was made with me. The deal was: I'll be made associate director [of CRES]. I'll be given a big salary increase, and I have to take over the CRP model project that I had never conceived—I did it—OK?[129]

Changing project leadership had deleterious effects. One can understand the new project leader's position and subsequent behavior by realizing that he had acquired a mixed collection of people, a limited quantity of resources, and a multitude of problems over which he had little direct control. Selling intruded into the process once again:

I inherited a staff which was not very viable. . . . There definitely were some problems at home base! The problems were mainly limitations on my own time, the fact that I didn't have much resources to work with—it was grossly underbudgeted—coupled with [CONSAD's] willingness to run with any ball . . . , got me into a situation where I felt I just wasn't able to control it. They would just unilaterally talk about what was going to be done without checking with me. The point was I couldn't really say, "Look, you must check with me on everything," because I didn't have the capacity to review all these things.[130]

Partly this feeling of limited capacity stemmed from the lack of support by several of his colleagues at CRES. One colleague offered this explanation of how he resolved the problem of competing demands on his time and attention:

[The new project leader] more or less moved in after it became clear that my own inclinations and skills were not going to contribute a great deal to the ultimate model. . . . I'm not sure that was a conscious motive. Oh, there were several things. One of the most important of which was that I was trying to split my time between teaching and research; and these are two very different kinds of activity, as I discovered to my sorrow . . . I found that because I had to meet my courses every other day, I spent at least 85 to 90 percent of my time preparing courses and working on them, and the remaining time, as I found it, went into research.[131]

The problem appears to lie in engendering and sustaining an academic's interest in a given project. In these matters, external or authoritative controls do not exist in the university environment. The same staffer reflects on this: "I think I would have have done more had there appeared to be a real challenge, and were I involved in a project where I knew I could contribute something. . . . It was that lack of incentive [and] a very full schedule."[132] The collective effect of this individually rational academic behavior on other participants in the decision context is bluntly and perhaps unfairly stated by a politician: "They have a lot of people out there who overload themselves with consulting and who do a half-assed job, who do as little as they can get away with. Unless, once in a while they get really intrigued with something, only then do they put more into it than what they are compensated for."[133] With respect to CRES, one former city planner states simply, "They walked out on us; they took the job saying they would do it, and then they didn't."[134]

This behavior appears in part to be deeply rooted in contempt for the policy-makers. One of the early academic promoters of the project, a former Pitt faculty member who is noteworthy for his limited participation once the contract was signed, had these depressing, but insightful, personal opinions on the matter:

Bums running the system, then you get bums turned out. That's my whole point. (You can talk about that if you want to, I don't care.) Cities on the whole are run by low-level bums. In terms of the kind of problems they talk about—I have no faith [that] it is necessarily going to get better. I believe the development of technology would take place independently of the administration of the city, although they cast up problems which make it interesting for us to work. The incompetence level is the real problem there.[135]

These personal observations may be correct; that, however, is not at issue. What is at issue is the fact that an agency of the University of Pittsburgh entered into a contract with the city of Pittsburgh and the federal government to produce certain items. It did not exactly fail to deliver; rather, it shifted the burden of responsibility to CONSAD, the consulting organization, which was eager "to run with any ball they had a chance to." CRES's replacement project leader outlines the sequence of events:

I made this strategic decision to shift the responsibility to CONSAD. . . . The subcontract to them got increased [and so on] . . . . I successfully created a situation where the City Planning Department viewed [CONSAD and CRES] as jointly responsible. It did not view me as responsible for them, which was a great mercy. It was one of my more skillful administrative achievements. I thought there was a bomb there. I thought you really couldn't deliver for the kind of money and time what was promised. I really didn't believe it was possible; and CONSAD kept believing it was possible.[136]

Hamilton, the executive director of City Planning, did not quite see the matter in the same terms:

Q: Did you have the feeling that the temporal constraints in the contract were really the overriding consideration, particularly as the project neared completion? Maybe that's not a fair question?
A: No, that is a very fair question. I never felt that way about Wil Steger [CONSAD]. Wil Steger is one of the finest men that I have ever known. [However], I am not so sure that I feel that way about the rest of the group at the University of Pittsburgh. I think that at the end of the time, they began to think that they just had to produce something.[137]

These opinions may or may not be widely shared; however, the pronounced lack of responsiveness to the policy-makers and the project, and the university's reluctance or inability to control its various resources are commonly acknowledged. One explanation for this is perhaps a general preoccupation with discipline-relevant rather than policy-relevant questions.[138]

Inadequate Responsiveness. The initial question of "Research for whom?" was answered by the academic participants in such a way as to make most policy outcomes anticlimactic. An early intellectual promoter's recollections indicate this clear academic bias:

But the beautiful thing about the Pittsburgh simulation . . . , and simulation in general was, we were going to be able to deal at a level of complexity with social institutions that we hitherto were not . . . able to deal, had been able to deal with. So that I was able to deal with a whole new range of problems. Now to do this, I not only had to reperceive the universe, but [also] get a technological instrument that would make the problem manageable.[139]

Reperceiving the universe may be a proper academic pastime, but it is a far cry from planning renewal in Pittsburgh. The marketing of innovative ideas, divorced from tangible results, may be symptomatic of a misplaced responsiveness to the policy-maker's needs. A former colleague from the Pitt days notes about this same intellectual promoter:

He is a person who has great confidence in rational analysis, computer-type analysis and simulation. I don't think he has ever done any simulation, but he talks well about it and was a very persuasive salesman of the whole idea. He was instrumental, I think, in persuading the HUD people . . . that this made sense and that there was a real potential here.[140]

Marketing innovative ideas has other enervating effects on policy-relevant research. One of the model-builders puts his finger squarely on a problem. "You have to publish something at a relatively consistent rate, and if you want to make a really good journal, then you've got to have something really new and innovative and great to publish."[141] With respect to publication in learned journals, disciplinary imperatives and policy imperatives do not necessarily coincide, to the detriment of the latter. Based on his experience with CRES, Planning Director Hamilton supports this contention: "They did it solely to be able to get their name on a publication, on a new piece of research to be able to do better academically."[142] One cannot fault those who produce and disseminate new knowledge; good, fresh ideas will always be among the world's scarcer commodities. The problem comes when "in-principle" arguments for advanced scientific and management skills and techniques are sold as if they were "in-practice" facts. In Pittsburgh, at least, a forward-looking and creative planner, who as an act of faith trusted certain of his academic colleagues to supply technical expertise he did not have, paid dearly for not realizing the difference between "principle" and "practice."[143] A recent deputy director of planning put it in these frank terms:

There are a hell of a lot of people who are charlatans of the first water, and they have exhibited it in this kind of undertaking. They have gone out and grabbed contracts, didn't know what the hell they were doing, and learned at the expense of the client. . . . In the case of Wil Steger [CONSAD], as is the problem with most consultants that don't perform, their problem was the client. With the academic people, . . . even under good supervision, I don't think some of them are capable of doing some of the jobs. They were cutting themselves so damned thin and were putting a lot less energy per dollar of compensation than in my opinion they should have into the project.[144]

To these stinging indictments add this sad commentary by a policy-maker on the university's responsiveness:

At lease some of the academic types, who had no real exposure to the real world problems, were largely responsible, I think, for getting Hamilton carried away with what he might be able to do. They had no comprehension of what the problems were.[145]

One of the greatest and most obvious problems was the political environment in which the CRP was cast. Misperceiving this context had several severe consequences. Pittsburgh is a political town.

Misperceiving the Complexity of Urban Decision

By ignoring and occasionally showing outright contempt for the local rules of the political game, Hamilton, his staff, and consultants earned the enmity of the established bureaucracy and politicians. In time, they so threatened the entrenched interests that Hamilton was fired, and the project was terminated.

Operating Rules. Pittsburgh has for years been run on one level by a very close-knit political organization; this is a well-known fact. At another level, and less well-known, is the fact that much of the city's day-to-day activity and nearly all its impetus for change derive from several strategically located operators. As one highly placed politician summarizes it:

Hamilton, I'm sure, never got the flavor and the essence of Pittsburgh. . . . This is going to sound a little hokey, but Pittsburgh in the last decade gained the reputation in the country for having a handful of people who, despite the politically flavored atmosphere, have the conscientiousness, brains, and commitment to do a fairly good job of holding one big city temporarily together. The City is not really run by R. K. Mellon [October, 1969] ; the people think it's a company town, but it isn't in this sense. It was a handful of technicians who with their ideas and their commitments and convictions kept things going. Cal never understood this, never was close to any of these four or five people I have in mind.

Personal and political survival apparently hinges on one's relations with these few technicians. It was at this point that the rules of the local game began breaking down. The politician continues:

Cal never could develop a strong commitment or feeling about any one place. His eyes were not on the sparrow; they were always huddled on some other illusive goal. He just didn't understand us. . . . He used to say to me, "I don't see how you could work with all these political considerations." Then he said, "That would defeat me." The point was that was all part of Pittsburgh—*that* was the closeness. The trick is how to work within that framework to change things if you can. He just never understood that.[146]

Hamilton was at least aware of all of this; however, for what appear to be very complex reasons, he never was able to "get close" to that critical "handful of technicians." His own assessment indicates the problem and sets the stage for consequent events:

> My greatest opposition was within City Hall itself. The Redevelopment Authority was interested, but not very helpful. The City's housing guy was skeptical, but didn't fight it. The head of the Industrial Development . . . was openly in opposition to it. The man who was the head of the Housing Authority, a strong member of the team—thought it was a bunch of foolishness. Ed McGee, who was the head of the *Allegheny Conference on Community Development, didn't care as long as we produced something.* As long as we produced other things, he was willing to cooperate. . . . I always had a good relationship with Bill Barr [the mayor] , but not very close.[147] (emphasis added)

The effects on the project were mostly negative.

Indicators of mistrust and noncooperation have already been noted. The controller provided neither cooperation nor data, and only grudgingly allowed after-hours access to "his" computer. Similar experiences can be recounted for other data-producing agencies of the local bureaucracy.

On the day-to-day personal level, the situation quickly polarized. A researcher's view was that "we existed in Pittsburgh every day under the rules of 'Here are the good guys and there are the bad guys.' There were some powerful stereotypes operating here."[148] Hamilton had "warned us specifically to stay out of messing around with the politicians, because he thought we would do more harm than good, which I think was certainly right, as it later turned out."[149]

Failing to reach acceptable arrangements within the city and "failing to communicate, to earn the trust of the agencies,"[150] members of Hamilton's staff increasingly turned to the real source of succor, federal renewal officials, further exacerbating an already deteriorating situation. "One-upping" the locals is in the long run an unhealthy tactic. According to one of Hamilton's staff members, "City Hall was always quite skeptical. But we always one-upped them because we were always able to establish real rapport and gain the respect of people in Washington. We didn't need the Mayor's Office."[151]

The political context, in broad outline, was neither ready nor willing to accept an innovator like Hamilton, an outsider, a man variously described as a "wild man,"[152] "colorful, imaginative, flamboyant,"[153] and "charismatic" by supporters and detractors alike. What should one expect when such a person intrudes on a "close-knit" town, gives his staff protection and a free rein to innovate, attracts considerable sums of federal money and widespread public attention, involves the local university in a local project to an unheard of extent, and finally enlists the support of other outside experts with advanced scientific and management skills? This question is answered by a former planner in terms of threat:

They [City Hall and others] didn't understand what the hell was going on. They thought that we were dealing with a lot more than we were dealing with. They thought that we were in the process of actually getting in and taking over, and coercing, and so forth. Believe me, nothing could have been farther from our minds.[154]

Perceptions of Threat. It was on the minds of the politicians though. In describing the threat of increasing public participation, one politician comments:

We really had some conflicts when the planners got out into the neighborhoods and started inciting the people and criticizing the administration. The Council got angered with that whole operation. . . . One of the biggest things that I saw coming out over the organization of the neighborhoods was that you were out there raising expectations, promising things that you didn't have a snowball's chance in hell of delivering. This is not only tough politically, it is tough on the neighborhoods.[155]

A federal official saw the threat in slightly different terms, which scarcely matters given the eventual outcome.

A whole new dimension of citizen involvement in government was beginning to impress [us] to an absolutely enormous degree; and frankly the politicians were afraid that these communities would begin to develop expectations and aspirations that [they] weren't able politically to follow through on. . . . [So they] began to put the squeeze on.[156]

Because Hamilton was the obvious center of the threat, "he got busted, he got the meat grinder."[157]

Terminate with All Due Prejudice. "Getting the meat grinder" meant, according to Hamilton, being "brought before the City Council," being accused "of doing all sorts of things with the secretaries, of wasting public money."[158] Ultimately it meant that "they fired me, and I was the only one who could really see it [the CRP] through."[159]

For the staff that Hamilton had assembled, it was all over. The new planning director, a long-time Pittsburgher, "went out to re-staff this department. I got rid of quite a few people: social theoreticians, theoretical people and looked for guys who not only wanted to plan but wanted some of it built."[160] Which meant, according to one spectator, that "the Planning Department was decimated in terms of anybody who had participated in the CRP, . . . as an expression of the mounting hostility to Cal and to the project in general."[161]

For the research and modeling enterprise it meant, according to one model-builder, "completely throwing out 96 percent of the analytical work that had been done."[162]

For the consultants it meant having to present and justify a barely running model (INIMP) to the new planning director in order to get his approval for a six months' extension and an additional $50,000 that federal officials had already authorized. When INIMP didn't locate a foundry the new director knew about,[163] it meant that "the local government turned Federal money down that was already coming in."[164]

Mostly it meant a return to the status quo ante. The new planning director recites the epitaph:

I scrapped the whole thing. You know this was costing our office an awful lot of money [sic]. They had runs costing seventy or a hundred thousand dollars [sic]. They weren't getting anything out. So frankly, I went back to the old approach, that is, what this agency should do is address itself to the physical planning problems.[165]

And so ends the story of decision-assisting computer models in the city of Pittsburgh.

Summary

The Pittsburgh Community Renewal Program reinforces all of the lessons learned in the San Francisco experience and provides us with insight into several other difficult problem areas. If the experience is even partially representative, the long-term prospects for the integration of the computer into the urban decision process are dismal indeed. The five summary assessments from the San Francisco case as to (1) the magnitude of the problem, (2) the extent of gaps in orientations and expectations, (3) the status and adequacy of theory and data, (4) the structure of incentive and motivation, and (5) the extent of the "appraisal gap," *all* hold for Pittsburgh with only minor shadings of emphasis. In addition we might conclude that (6) selling poor, high-risk, or speculative research is counter-productive; (7) the university's lack of control over its various resources and the systems of incentive and motivation pertinent to its personnel reduce its effectiveness for purposes of integrating the computer into the urban decision process; and (8) at current levels of ignorance, the hostility and potential virulence of a given political context for social science research should not be underestimated. We turn our attention to a fuller examination of these and several related topics associated with the problem-solving process.

13

The Problem-Solving Process

*The rise of modern technology and the growth
in the complexity of the knowledge structure
of the society is perhaps the dominant force in
the political process of modern times.*

Kenneth Boulding
The Image[1]

Three distinct aspects of the problem-solving process are obvious and
need attention: the people, the sequence of interactions in which they
participated, and the products they produced. The two cases are similar
enough in these aspects to permit joint consideration. Differences will
be shown where appropriate.

Participants

After we recount some administrative details connected with the data-
gathering efforts, we will describe the participants with respect to their
demographic characteristics; their expectations and assessments of
realized outcomes; their distinctive verbal preoccupation in the interviews; and the dimension and degree of difference in orientation among
them.

Administrative Details. While more than 100 people were consulted
in the course of this project, coincidentally in each case eighteen individuals were judged to be so directly involved that they required more
detailed interrogation efforts. These efforts included interviews ranging
in length from forty-five minutes to over eight hours, spread over several days. The average formal interview lasted 110 minutes, was tape-
recorded, and was structured to include several general areas of interest;
emphases and specific information, of course, varied greatly.[2] My pursuit of any general line of inquiry depended upon the respondent's
knowledge, interest, and willingness to talk. At the end of his interview,
each of the thirty-six respondents was given a brief questionnaire to
complete and return at his leisure. The questionnaire served as a check

216

on the more unstructured interview and freed the face-to-face segment of data collection from some menial but necessary intrusions. The rate of response for questionnaires was a gratifying 93 percent, and many respondents volunteered additional insightful information that had not been initially offered. In general, interviews and questionnaires were executed in a surprisingly candid, constructive, and thorough manner. All interviews were reproduced verbatim (over 2,000 pages of typed transcription), reviewed for fidelity of transcription, coded by means of the scheme listed in Appendix B, and analyzed for verbal content using a version of the "Lasswell Value Dictionary."[3]

Demographic Characteristics. To begin understanding these data, a preliminary stage of the analysis involved the generation of simple contingency tables for pairs of coded variables. The methodology is inelegant, but the advantage one obtains in terms of broad understanding and occasional valuable insights makes the exercise worthwhile.

The sample is strikingly well-educated; thirty-two of thirty-six respondents hold advanced degrees, of which seventeen are Ph.D.s. However, only six people claimed to have "excellent" skill in the use of any one computer language; nineteen persons, or more than half of the sample, had *no* facility with *any* computer language at all. A mere eleven respondents could write a flow chart, code, and run the simplest process, such as the example used in chapter 3. Mathematical skill was in similarly short supply. One explanation seems to be that professionals (planners, lawyers, businessmen) and social scientists, who respectively make up 47.2 percent and 33.3 percent, or 80.5 percent of the sample, have not had training in these skills. Indeed, sixteen out of the seventeen professionals and seven of the twelve trained in the social sciences indicated their inability to write a program (X^2 significant at .01 level).

Most of the respondents were in their forties; but four of the six persons reporting excellent computer and mathematical skills were in their twenties at the time of the project. In fact, they were at that time graduate students. The other two highly skilled participants are physicists manqués.

At the beginning of the project, eleven were earning less than $10,000 per year; at the present time twenty-four are earning more than $20,000. In the space of five or six years, respondents have in general been quite upwardly mobile economically. Twenty-seven have increased their earnings, there was no economic change in five cases, and four participants are earning less—mostly a result of movement from the private to the lower-paying academic and public sectors. Although others have also done well, social scientists have fared the best in terms of wages: ten of the twelve are at present earning more than $20,000 per year ($X^2$ at .01).

Pittsburgh's major demographic distinction is that the technically skilled participants were both younger and worse paid than the others interviewed. Of six Pittsburgh respondents under forty years of age, five were earning less than \$10,000 per year at the project's start (X^2 at .05). The point is that those bearing the major responsibility for model building were young and poorly paid, as compared with others in the process.

We will use these demographic features of the sample to sort out expectational and assessment variables.

Expectations. Most of the participants, twenty-five of thirty-six, or 69.9 percent, expected that the primary use of the models would be for policy-making. For San Francisco, thirteen of the eighteen expected this outcome; in Pittsburgh twelve of the eighteen. Data manipulation and experimentation are distant second choices in each. Of the nineteen who listed absolutely no computer skills, fourteen expected the model primarily to aid policy-making and secondarily to aid in projection studies (X^2 at .05). There is no question, given contracts and written and spoken documentation, that the participants generally understood and expected that the models would be useful to policy-makers.

Assessments. Final assessments vary considerably from the initial expectations. Cross-tabulating primary initial purposes with the primary final purpose indicates the extent of unintended outcomes and nonperformance. After all was said and done, only three out of thirty-six described the models as policy-making devices. Assessments are evenly divided between experimentation and education as final model purposes.

The major problem cited is not data deficiency, as we might have expected. Instead, it is a set of professional, personal, and philosophical factors that we have labeled "differential orientations." Data and technico-theoretical considerations are of considerably less importance for most of the sample.

Selling ($\frac{15}{36}$ or 41.9 percent) and politics ($\frac{10}{36}$ or 27.8 percent) were the factors cited most often as impeding the project's development. "Communication" or immediate human management problems are seen as far from trivial and warrant serious consideration in future undertakings.

Most respondents see no improvement in the operations of either city and no particular payoffs accruing to either the cities ("No" = $\frac{31}{36}$) or the politicians ("No" = $\frac{29}{36}$) as a result of these projects. The few exceptions are people with current vested interests in data systems and files that originated with the CRP. But quid pro quo—the political staff of life—is the name of the game. One does not stay in the policy-assisting, problem-solving business for long without providing some political or prestige benefits or payoffs to the client. What could be more inimical to the interests of innovation than threatening technically deficient, but otherwise extremely sophisticated, politicians with computers and consultants while simultaneously offering them no tangible, immediate payoffs? Those respondents who believe that the models are acceptable for policy-making simultaneously indicate that politicians were the major impediment in the project! However, those who think the models are primarily useful as educational devices strongly indicate that selling and consultants were the major project impediments (X^2 at .001 level).

Significant negative assessment, bordering on outright rejection of the project, is concentrated in the nonskilled, professional, decision-making segment of the sample. Model-builders and researchers are more temperate in their judgments. Of the twenty-five who cannot write and execute a simple computer program, twenty-two think the cities got nothing or only negligible benefits; on the other hand, seven of eleven with computer skills think the cities got some or considerable benefits—usually cited are the beginnings of a data system or a graphic realization of the scope of their analytic deficiencies (X^2 at .05). This pattern repeats for the less stringent skill variable, COMSKL, any degree of proficiency with any computer language; eighteen of nineteen non-skilled respondents answer that they believe payoffs were "maximally negative," i.e. simultaneously, no operational impact, no benefits to the city, and no political benefits as indicated in PRBSCL, a summary index. However, four of six having the highest computer skills think that there were moderate payoffs (X^2 at .001). The pattern repeats for the variable MTHSKL, any degree of proficiency with any college-level mathematical techniques; sixteen of eighteen nonskilled respondents are maximally negative about payoffs or benefits, but four of six highly mathematically skilled respondents indicate that a moderate level of benefits was obtained (X^2 at .05). Considering that the nonskilled respondents are predominantly professional and that these same professionals overwhelmingly had the highest expectations for the undertakings, it is safe to conclude that *these participating decision-makers had experienced a "rejection of the foreign model."* If one accepts the well-known institutional innovational sequence of (1) initial rejection of foreign models, (2) attempted total incorporation of foreign symbols and techniques, and (3) partial rejection to account for the individual needs of specific contexts,[4] present efforts to develop appraisal criteria seem particularly appropriate. We may be in a period of consolidation prior to more widespread and wholehearted attempts at incorporation of these sophisticated techniques.

The problems and impediments that various subsets of the sample frequently note give some indication of why these projects were finally rejected. In terms of major impediments, ten of seventeen professionally trained respondents cite "selling" or the "consultant," and six of seventeen feel that "politicians" were most obstructive. Most of those trained in the natural sciences, mathematics, or engineering hold technical problems, particularly data deficiency, to be the major impediments. Skilled respondents either choose to ignore or simply value less the pedestrian political and selling impediments; at the same time, professionals are clearly not interested in the technical issues (X^2 at .05). Asked whether educational, theoretical, personal, or technical problems predominated in the projects, eleven of nineteen non-computer skilled respondents reply that interpersonal problems were most salient; none of the skilled respondents think so; they split their votes between technical and educational issues (X^2 at .05).

Verbal Behavior. To differentiate the respondents along another dimension, all interviews were coded for verbal content. The total number of column-inches each respondent devoted to *power, enlightenment, wealth,* or *skill* topics was measured. Fully describing the method is beyond the scope of this report and has been done elsewhere.[5] However, discussions of profits or costs in the consulting business are clearly wealth-related; university-centered topics relate to enlightenment; politics and political processes are within the power domain; and, models, data bases, computers, etc. are skill-related. These choices were easily made, given the gross column-inch unit of measure. Percentages devoted to each value category were computed and summarized in variable *VALMAX,* the category receiving the greatest proportion of a respondent's verbal attention. (Sum of *P, E, W, S,* equals 100 percent; other values and miscellaneous discourse are ignored.) Power is the dominant preoccupation for one-third (twelve) of the sample; skill is second with eleven; enlightenment is third with eight; and wealth is fourth, or least salient, with five respondents. In the role of interviewer, my own verbal ordering for the aggregate of all interviews is slightly different. Skill topics at 52 percent are first; power, at 28 percent, second; enlightenment, at 13 percent, third; and wealth, at 7 percent, fourth.

The people who talked most about power also expected the overall enterprise to produce policy models ($\frac{8}{12}$). They are also the most pessimistic or negative about realized outcomes. All twelve who verbalized most about power are also "maximally negative" about outcomes (X^2 at .01). Those most concerned with enlightenment (mainly social scientists) have more moderate assessments of the projects.

In general, verbal behavior provides an alternative, supplementary dimension for the analysis. A larger, more detailed content analysis might be worth executing at some future date to pursue these issues further.

Differential Orientations. The problem of differential orientations intruded into virtually all aspects of these undertakings. We have cited evidences of it in the appraisal of the models. We have touched on parts of it again, with slightly more precision, in our discussion of participants' characteristics, expectations, and assessments. However, the concept and the problem seem important enough to warrant an attempt to summarize our partial insights and hunches in one or a few easy-to-understand measures.

Multidimensional scaling, a technique more widely known to psychologists than to political scientists, offers some interesting possibilities.[6] Generally, the technique is directed to the problem of interrelating objects—i.e. people, events, observations, etc.—according to several measured characteristics. More than just identifying similar (or dissimilar) objects, the technique spatially locates them according to aggregate, underlying structural features or *dimensions* contained in the data.

Interpreting what these dimensions mean is largely a matter of judgment. Determining how many dimensions constitute a "solution" is facilitated by the calculation of a "goodness of fit" statistic called "stress" (a fuller discussion of which is contained in Appendix C).

The variables measured in the present analysis were, with two exceptions, coded ordinally. For example, COMSKL (variable #10 in the appended code book—see Appendix B) was either, "none," "poor," "OK," or "excellent," in that order. Project purposes variables, (PRPSI1-3 and PRPSF1-3) were ordered according to stringency of demands on the model with respect to stated application purpose: "none," "education," "data management," "theory development," "experimentation," "projection," "operations or policy-making," in that order, according to our discussion in chapter 6, "Pragmatic Appraisal."[7] Discipline and occupational variables were ordered according to assumed levels of technical (mathematical and computer-oriented) training. For example, variable DISCPL, the general area of disciplinary training, was respectively coded as "humanities," "professional," "social science," and "natural science."

All variables were transformed into unit normal form, and a "distance matrix," the simple geometric distance between pairs of all variables, was generated and used as input for the multidimensional scaling analysis.

In this case, six dimensions provide a stress value of 5.3 percent, which is considered to be good; improvements in fit caused by adding more dimensions thereafter were not large. What six dimensions may be operating is extremely difficult to say. Interpretation of structure beyond three dimensions pressed the limits of my time, patience, and imagination; however, three- and two-dimensional configurations presented relatively straightforward interpretive tasks. The two-dimensional configuration is represented in Figure 13-1. Coordinate axes and absolute values are of less importance than the relative location of points. Indeed, axes may be rotated as long as the relative configuration is not disturbed. Several of the participants are singled out to illustrate the dimensions, which are conveniently labeled "Technician—Non-

Technician" and "Whigs–Tories,"[8] corresponding approximately to degree of technical skill or competency to build models and to one's optimism or pessimism about the experience. A third dimension was clearly entrepreneurial. All salesmen were aligned in a knot at the one

FIGURE 13-1

Configuration in Two Dimensions

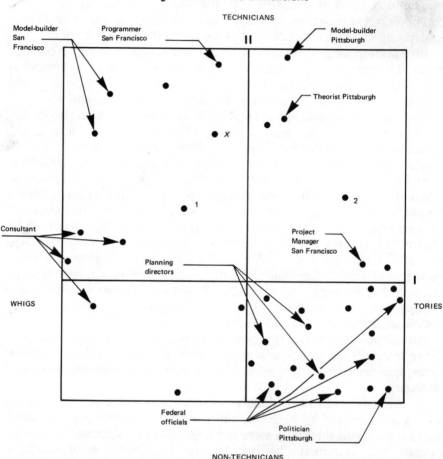

extreme, and the local officials were located at the other; other participants were scattered between.

Using interview and questionnaire data and taking seriously Abelson and Tukey's notion that rank-order knowledge of a set of interpoint distances is nearly as good as direct measurement,[9] an approximation of the extent of differentiation in the respondent sample was developed.

These measurements are persuasive at an intuitive level and provide three easily labeled dimensions along which dissimilarities tended to coalesce.

One final note on procedure: In the spirit of bringing to consciousness the interaction of "self" with "others" in the context, data on the author of this report were coded, and the entire procedure was repeated.[10] While the addition of one more observation discomposed each configuration, differences at the second dimension were mostly incremental.[11] The character X in Figure 13-1 approximates "my" location with respect to "other" participants. A personal aside is in order. Interviews with those closest in the configuration were lengthier and more convivial. With these respondents I felt that information was communicated most efficiently. The same cannot be reported for several respondents who are more distant in the configuration.

One is prompted to ask what might be done to alleviate the orientation problem. Education is the easiest palliative, but it is unsatisfactory on several accounts. Mainly, it is time consuming, expensive, and perhaps wasteful of scarce resources. Rather than approach the problem in "scattershot" fashion, an argument can be made to concentrate on those few individuals who are located in-between technicians and non-technicians, Whigs and Tories, and salesmen and non-salesmen.

Policy Envoys. The role of translator and envoy between inimical groups is suggested by the functions actually performed by respondents numbered 1 and 2 in Figure 13-1. Number 1 is a mathematically oriented business economist currently employed as a consultant; however, his career has been marked by many shifts between public- and private-sector participation. Number 2 is a young, mathematically trained planner, whose career is distinguished also by several shifts—from private, for-profit consultant, to nonprofit consultant, to large public agency. His interview contains several self-references (overlooked by the author until the multidimensional scaling analysis brought the issue into focus) to this envoy-translator function. Yehezkel Dror and others have precisely defined this role theoretically;[12] it seems that we have crudely sketched it out empirically:

> We are not interested in putting out fires, we are interested in making changes if we can, if needed, finding out if something is really needed and then finding out if you can do it. . . . You have to begin by discovering what is going on and really understanding which decisions have to be made, have to be made when, with relation to what, and then bring more and better analysis to bear on those questions. That's step one. There is a great audience for analysis like that. . . . the biggest jump is from getting a bunch of guys who know the whole problem and who talk about it over lunch or at a meeting, where [for example] "Charlie," who really knows the mortgage market, tells you what will happen. The next step is to get "Charlie" to write it down or to write down what "Charlie" and fourteen other

"Charlies" have to say, then begin to apply some very simple analytical techniques to that. Bring other data to bear . . . reach out carefully from the immediate, biting off a little more each time.[13]

Procedures

Analysis of the decision sequence generally employed in both cases provides many insights into that process. By describing the interaction of participants in the sequence, we hope to direct the attention of those participants and others toward improving the process.[14]

Initiation: Intelligence. The earliest phase of the sequence is dominated by (usually) distinguished academics performing for society "the function that fantasies and imaginings play in the lives of individuals."[15] The "in-principle" myth is writ large by them, for instance in learned journals, but it goes mostly unnoticed except for the occasional internecine intellectual debate. At some point in time, particular societal needs are felt to require expert assistance. In our two cases, this meant that several federal administrators began casting about for problem solutions of a sophisticated sort. Perhaps they were responding to diffuse stimulation from one or a few federal politicians; perhaps not. The initial events are not clear. But the new interest *was* clear to entrepreneurs of these problem solutions, who quickly entered the sequence to make the connection between academic "patricians" and federal policymakers.

Promotion. The promotional phase of the process involves academic patricians and federal administrators in various conferences, symposia, and private discussions. Orchestration of promotional activities is the special function of the entrepreneur.

One local official graphically characterized academic participation in this phase as "mountaineering," where

guys come out of the university, give you the word from the mountain, and then get out before they have to get any of the consequences of what they are going to do—what they have proposed to do. . . . And then they write another book or an article on [our] idiocy which increases their academic standing, which also happens to give them a higher hourly or daily rate the next time that they go out to consult. There is a kind of madness in that. It is what I call "mountaineering."[16]

Discounting the bitterness of the charge, we find some accuracy in that description for our two cases.

Entrepreneurial activity begins in earnest during the promotional phase, although it pervades nearly the entire sequence in varying guises and to varying degrees. "Advertise the System" and "Sell the System" are slogans well known in the military sector; however, one suspects that they are more widely applicable:

Military systems in particular may be sold before the design even begins. Sometimes the results are less than spectacular: the system simply cannot be designed, built, and made to work satisfactorily.... Once produced and sold, the advertising of military systems is usually done on only a modest scale to help create a favorable image of the producer in the minds of engineers who might be recruited and in the minds of the general public.[17]

Our two cases demonstrate many of these peculiar characteristics. Especially with increasing numbers of displaced aerospace and military problem-solvers finding employment in the public, urban sector,[18] these are trends to be conscious of and to discourage.

Prescription. Local officials actively enter the sequence and expand the arena during the prescriptive phase. Contracts are negotiated; local politicians are "sold" on the low-risk, high "in-principle" payoffs of the system; and the timing of specific parts of the project is worked out. During this phase readily accessible and preferably distinguished academics are brought in as consultants by the entrepreneurs, to assuage fears, to validate the specific proposal, and to attest to the wisdom of the undertaking.

Execution: Invocation and Application. The principal participants during project execution are local administrative officials, entrepreneurs, and a new group of undistinguished academic "plebeians." Local officials are occupied with myriad specific fiscal and administrative details that seem to be both ubiquitous and indispensable. Entrepreneurs are occupied with the complex but necessary task of securing the next contract: "ginning up" proposals, advertising in diverse locations by many media, and in general working diligently to "keep the contractual pipeline full." Plebeian academics come in several stripes. They may be graduate students hired out of a local university by the usually higher paying consultant, or in some instances by the local public agency itself. They may be "staffers" of the consulting firm: faceless, multipurpose, hardworking, and compliant producers of the attractively packaged report and the flashy "dog and pony shows" complete with slides, Vu-graphs, and flip charts. Or, to a lesser extent, they may be very junior academics who simply need the additional money and may incidentally have some substantive interest in the content of the problem. Two curious aspects of the execution phase are that the patrician academics do not take an active role, except to validate the proceedings by means of infrequent consultation, and that politicians of all persuasions are largely uninterested as long as researchers do not incite local citizens or otherwise disrupt the political status quo. Federal participation is limited to one or a few low- to mid-range program managers, whose major responsibilities are fiscal and administrative.

Appraisal. Who does *not* appraise? As long as a project produces innocuous, irrelevant, or neutral results and recommendations, and as long as the simulators do not perturb the real-world environment, politicians have very little incentive to appraise. This matters little, because few politicians have the technical skills to comment on either the content of "scientific" models or the model design and development procedures. When a project does get political attention, the motive for the appraisal is often vindictive. Trying to fix blame, to finger a whipping boy, as it were, is no substitute for decent appraisal. Bureaucrats typically lack the appropriate skills and necessary incentives and resources (in terms of time, money, or contacts) to go outside for help. Curiously, distinguished academic patricians are not much help either. Academics interested in these activities are few and far between, though well known to one another, and they generally have little incentive to "rock the boat" by evaluating a colleague's work or setting tough professional standards.

Who then *does* appraise? Entrepreneurs sometimes appraise competitors' work unconstructively by word of mouth or through innuendo in hopes of gaining relative economic advantage. Local administrators who are not "inured watching the superfluous,"[19] and who have more than average technical competence, infrequently produce uneven evaluations in internal memos or working papers. These efforts tend to be of low quality and are narrowly distributed. Such activities are "irrational" in a strict bureaucratic sense because they break with accepted procedural patterns; hence, one cannot depend on this source of appraisal. Academic plebeians occasionally do appraisals of a very tightly defined and limited variety. Their readership is even more circumscribed than that of the local official. None of these activities is carried out "with comprehensiveness, competence, reliability, independence, promptitude, and economy,"[20] the preferred standards for our "Appraisal Function."

Termination. Participants most concerned with terminal activities include local administrators, who must account for funds, write reports, and prepare presentations for public hearings; local politicians, who make public appearances and speak on behalf of the project (if the project results contain affirmative or neutral pronouncements and recommendations for ongoing procedures and activities—otherwise the politicians will probably not participate); federal administrators, who have to clear the books and collect the reports to attest to their own productivity; and entrepreneurs, who must kindle the interest of other potential clients.

The interaction of various participants through the phases of the decision sequence is summarized in Figure 13-2. The size of individual blocks varies to suggest in a crude way variations in the amount, frequency, or intensity of participant interaction. More precise, substantiating data could be collected, but that is a task for another time.

Individual Differences. The decision sequence just described fails to capture several important specific details in each of the two contexts. In Pittsburgh, as we have noted, local politicians were drawn into the

FIGURE 13-2

Interaction and Flow of the Problem-Solving Process

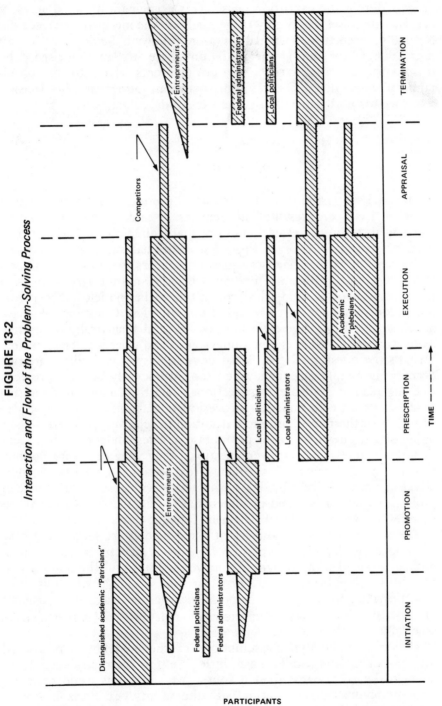

process during the execution phase. This participation forced an early negative appraisal based only tangentially on the merits of the research. Naturally, premature termination soon followed. Selling was a very noticeable factor during the initiation phase in San Francisco. The reasons for this appear to be extraneous events related to the consultant's planned diversification and expansion. Otherwise, the decision sequence for both generally fits the pattern described.

Products

A detailed exposition of the model "products" of this decision sequence has been presented in chapters 11 and 12 in terms of their theoretical, technical, ethical, and pragmatic dimensions. These distinctions are also useful in organizing a few additional, summary comments.

Inattention to the analytical question appears to be the basic underlying theoretical problem. There must be some mutual agreement as to what portion of the empirical context is to be modeled. *Everything* hinges on obtaining a clear definition of "The Question." Success depends to a large degree on how clearly and realistically *all* participants understand what is being undertaken and what is to be expected. "What's the question?" and "What does an answer look like?" are two deceptively simple questions asked too infrequently in these projects.

Using readily available cross-sectional data to produce an operating model does little to enhance theoretical understanding of urban processes. It furthermore misdirects attention to relatively uninteresting or unimportant questions, or to paraphrase one respondent, to the extent that the models *could* answer questions, they were questions nobody was asking. Relying on inadequate cross-sectional data has the dual effect of conservatively biasing formulations with respect to change or projections over time, and of unnecessarily complicating formulations with respect to spatial detail. The need for time series data is urgent.

The severe ethical weaknesses of these models are several and have been noted in detail. As important an issue as race, for instance, ought not be assumed away or ignored, however distasteful the implications for the local political client. It is difficult to judge which is more objectionable, to overlook race or to incorporate it and then to make "acceptably" innocuous assumptions about its effects. Neither tactic is especially desirable.

The initial, underlying assumptions of the model-builders assured that policy-makers would have little use for their products. What policy-maker is interested in a four-, five-, or ten-year-old context? What policy-maker is operating with the twenty-year horizon used in the forecasts? What policy-maker cares about spatial detail as fine as a

census tract, unless the tract has extraordinary political or social significance? On the one hand, what policy-maker cares about a metropolitan
region, the analytical context the Pittsburgh model eventually ended up
using; and, on the other hand, how can a policy-maker be made to
believe a model constrained to his constituency and failing to account
for the surrounding region, as in San Francisco? The weak to nonexistent policy utility of these models does not mean they are devoid of
use. Quite the contrary, their educational applications are very important. Data management, measurement, experimentation, projection,
and theory-building uses are more doubtful.

Ultimately, the issue arising from these contexts is one of trust. It is
asking too much of any policy-maker to conform to the model-builder's
discipline and ethic; rather, those who wish to realize the "in-principle"
myth must make their own tools conform to the policy-maker's needs.
A policy-maker must be able to say, "You tell me what I want and
what I can get," and have some expectation of receiving an honest and
useful reply.

Addenda

Whether the model-building community will reconsider either these particular cases, or, more importantly, the problem-solving process that
underlies them both, is an open question. If we have brought some
insight to these matters, we will have fulfilled a major part of our
purpose.

In the interest of self-appraisal, it must be noted that the various
criteria and questions developed in Part I, "The Appraisal Function,"
were *adequate* as a first approximation. Generally the standards were
too high, the demands placed on the models were too stringent, and the
number and detail of the criteria were too great. Considering the inherent difficulty of these undertakings, our appraisal may be too harsh.
But then, it may seem harsh only because there are few alternative
assessments for comparison.

This is not the place to offer extensive comments on the Community
Renewal Program, the instrument for these model-building cases. However, the time appears to be right for a full-scale assessment; hopefully,
others will assume responsibility. The following impressions of the San
Francisco and Pittsburgh experiences are offered to these unknown
appraisers:

- There are insufficient payoffs structured into the CRP. Once the comprehensive plan is drawn up there is no reason to expect a city council to enact it.
- The expert advisers who assist in plan development are not retained to exe-

cute the plan. In fact, the on-the-job training these outsiders give a local planning staff may result in the loss of upwardly mobile local talent, i.e. a net local human-resource deficit.

- A twenty-year time frame for present-day policy-makers is questionable. What decision-maker has a twenty-year horizon? A two- to five-year time perspective seems more in tune with the realities of the two cases that we have examined. For other purposes, twenty years is obviously insufficient; but for the CRP, as presently configured, it may be excessive.

- The CRP places too great a reliance on social science theory that is either weak or nonexistent. A more productive alternative to the hiring of high-priced, transient experts might be to upgrade the local staff, select a few "doable" projects, and labor diligently in the hope of accomplishing something more durable than just one more unread report.

The problems encompassed by the Community Renewal Program will be with us for a long time; everyone should be skeptical of expert advisers who offer to solve them with the promise of a "quick-fix" computer model at the conclusion of a two-year contract.

PART IV

MEETING THE CHALLENGE

14

Expanding the Focus of
Attention: Some
Recommendations

> *There remains something in all of us of the*
> *childish belief that there is a world of grownups*
> *who know. There must be—because we, evi-*
> *dently don't know. It is very shocking then to*
> *suspect that the knowers do not exist at all.*
> *Everyone is groping around in the dark, just as*
> *we are.*
>
> Peter Berger
> *The Precarious Vision*[1]

Perhaps we should admit that we "don't know" very much about the
complexity of urban decision. We don't. That admission, earnestly
made, might facilitate some honest and possibly productive "groping
around."

The Premise Is Experimental

In principle, models are worth the concerted, continuous expenditure
of time, talent, and resources they require. However, results from real
contexts to date have been so checkered that even the eventual realization of the mythical policy-assisting model is in doubt.

This appraisal of two prominent models reveals them to be frail and
only marginally satisfactory devices. The reader may object, as others
have, that it is "unfair" to judge so harshly these ambitious "pioneering" attempts. As long as the stated purpose of these projects is
public policy-making, appraisal cannot be harsh or comprehensive
enough. The reader may object, as others have, that the best result

possible was accomplished, considering the data and resources at hand. Granting this specific point, it is still problematic how much difference added resources or data would have made. Even in those few instances where the cry of data deficiency is not a viable subterfuge, and where the processes are thought to be understood, e.g. transportation studies, the models produced have not been particularly useful nor have they been used by policy-makers.[2] Clearly the difficulties are more fundamental.

Public officials may be led to expect too much, from social science research in general and from simulation activities in particular, in the way of answers to a class of difficult questions that are not scientific in the commonly accepted sense. Unfortunately, these are political questions, such as, "What should the goals of the city be?" "What should politicians do about them?" "To whom should it be done?" In the absence of information on the limits and the possibilities of present-day social science, expectations become inflated. Prediction is expected even where the crudest understanding has not yet been reached. This particular misconception is widespread and not limited to any special group of individuals. Indeed, underestimation of the difficulty of integrating computers into the urban decision context is a basic theme in the collective lament.

Let's redefine a common premise and trace out some possible implications.

Elaborate research documents and operational computer models are relatively unimportant by-products of the more valuable problem-solving process. One respondent's invective about "going in to do one endless study,"[3] contains a key to the problem. At present, the tendency is to hold out hope that a specific project, a particular computer model, or a given demonstration project run under a particular contract will provide *the* much-desired *answer*. A more productive strategy might be to devise questions, techniques, and procedures that shift the focus of attention away from particular solutions and over to the difficulty of the problem itself. The need and desirability of many complementary efforts, which together approximate an "endless study," is thereby clarified. Redefining innovation efforts as *experiments*—what our two cases turned out to be according to significant numbers of respondents—removes the onus of having to produce *the* answer, and frees us to focus attention on appraisal of the current experiment. A distinction between *trapped* and *experimental* administrators drawn by Donald Campbell illustrates the point. The former "have so committed themselves in advance to the efficacy of the reform that they cannot afford honest evaluation," and the latter "have justified the reform on the basis of the importance of the problem, not the certainty of their answer, and are committed to going on to other potential solutions if the one just tried fails."[4]

Once the experimental premise is taken, objectives are to keep open a wide range of problem-solving options and to increase overall analytic flexibility. Theories and models are no longer seen as final and immutable; rather they are undertaken provisionally and are subject to revision as new problems or policies generate new questions and compel the collection of new contextual measurements.[5]

Models

Several categories of models are suggested by this inquiry. None is better than any other; their value depends on the intended use and the analytic question. However, the adoption of a perspective of organized complexity and the acceptance of an experimental premise frees one to consider several potentially useful possibilities.

Protocols. Protocols are precise summaries of personal behavior. Writing protocols—codes that represent an order of precedence or procedure—has three discernible purposes: theory generation, reality checking, and education.[6]

Policy-makers are visceral theorists. The images they routinely employ are important because they are to some degree successful. A most difficult phase in building a model is deciding what should be included in the formalized state vector. Policy-makers repeatedly make that decision with respect to a wide range of contingencies for specific analytic contexts. We must learn how to observe and then exploit in systematic ways the "operating codes" of both successful *and* unsuccessful policy-makers. Besides learning about the effective processes, there is an added opportunity for the policy-maker to be made self-conscious and hopefully self-correcting of his own orders of precedence and procedure.

Functional Models. We are already reasonably adept with special kinds of functional models. Economists, demographers, and, at another level, psychologists, have fairly well developed tool kits. The unresolved issue is how and when to reconcile these typically narrow, partial perspectives with a policy-maker's broader requirements. At the moment, explanatory exigencies seem too often to override manipulative requirements. The thrust of our arguments will likely have little impact on those specialists whose intellectual capital is already heavily invested; i.e. the form and content of this category of models appears to be relatively fixed. What is needed is increased and better understanding of the strenuous limitations of partial, functional models and of the appropriate situations into which they may be fruitfully introduced.

Spatial Models. Every city seems to have a few neighborhoods or sections that for one reason or another cause policy-makers extra concern. The greater the concern, the greater the opportunity for the research enterprise; for if nothing else, one can hold the policy-maker's attention. In these high-concern areas, expending scarce resources for serious, continuous survey and direct measurement may have considerable payoff. It is a strategy fraught with great risk, as the Pittsburgh experience attests. Prudence is recommended. Timing may be important; efforts to model contexts of fine spatial detail may be most productive if undertaken after protocol writing and functional modeling have given researchers a "sense" of the context.

Normative Models. Expanding the analytic time frame so confounds analysis that predictive power rapidly deteriorates. This problem, taken with the extreme difficulty of accounting ex ante for large, "lumpy" investment decisions, may in practice be turned to our advantage. Why not liberate imagination to search for creative alternatives?[7] Precise prediction of an expanded time frame is so speculative anyway, why not develop our capacities to specify desirable end states and alternative ways of attaining them? Politicians, as Dahl and Lindblom among others have noted,[8] cannot or choose not to elaborate end state conditions—goals. What politicians are eminently qualified to do is to choose from among a given set of end states those alternatives that seem "right" or "reasonable" to them:

The problem is to dream up plausible alternatives and to expose their structure [for] what these alternatives mean in terms of things that are of interest to those who are running the city and to those who are living in a city.[9]

The possibilities may be even greater and more basic:

A simulation model can potentially help to democratize the process of city decision-making by producing a number of explicit statements about alternative futures for evaluation by citizen committees. For such statements to possess any credibility, the simulation model itself must, at least in outline form, be understood by the layman. [And the politicians!] [10]

The academic task is to generate the collective, albeit disciplined, fantasy; the policy-maker's job is to figure out tactical ways to execute one among many of these fantasies.

A rare example of this category of model may help to make the key distinctions. When Hawaiian policy-makers began asking questions like, "What is the level of federal spending going to be in 1990?" and "How many tourists will there be, and how much will they spend?" Roland Artle turned the questions around and asked, "How much government spending do you want?" "How many tourists do you want?"[11] Once those questions are asked, and the normative model built, solving the continuous tactical problem is facilitated. "If you know where you are

236

aiming, it helps a lot tactically."[12] Artle's model may not have widespread applicability, but the principles involved most certainly do.

Hierarchical Models. Using macro, highly aggregated versions of the functional models, constrained by the operating preferences and procedures adduced from protocols, it may be possible to develop control totals for important elements in the context. Policy-makers, one suspects, are more likely to ask questions about total percent nonwhite, level of voter support, or total revenues available for distribution than questions about the number of blacks under forty-five in census tracts *x, y,* and *z,* the voting patterns of middle-class Italians in precincts 1, 2, and 3, or the amount of government revenue generated by various SIC types. Once the grossest detail and control totals are accounted for in terms salient to policy-makers, fuller explication of the links or transactions of more detailed configurations may be in order. That a policy-maker doesn't care *how* the population evolved into a present state does not mean that a detailed explanation is unimportant. It does imply that the shrewd researcher should not confuse the explanatory detail that interests him with the crude approximations that the policy-maker uses.

The recommended model-building strategy calls for fewer detailed observations on more distinct variables configured in empirically satisfying relationships. At the aggregate level simplification gains us an advantage in flexibility, the ease with which new variables and configurations may be brought to bear on a constantly changing context.

Documentation

The lack of documentation in the two cases is shocking. In large part documentation of the projects was ignored in the headlong rush to get an "operational" model. Progress is unnecessarily impeded by the lax or nonexistent accounting of the problem-solving process. How many times must we reinvent the wheel? Given our new experimental premise, several suggested changes in present practices are worth considering.

Staff Mobility. The market for skilled computer specialists is as volatile as its participants are mobile. Keeping skilled personnel appears to be a function of the amount of wages paid, the number of opportunities for technical education and for participation in creative, innovational activities, and the age and sophistication of the available hardware. Cities by and large pay less, demand more "ordinary" programs, and lag behind the current state of hardware technology. In other words, attracting and keeping skilled computer technicians in city jobs is, if anything, more difficult than in other contexts. This fact, taken with the eccentric nature of the creative programming process, is reason enough for city documentation to be thorough, perhaps even intentionally redundant.

Good Documentation Costs Money. For the sake of discussion, let's say that as much money should be spent on documentation as on the model itself; this is a rule of thumb that many computer software producers currently employ. If one concedes that the process of problem-solving is more important than any one product, doesn't it then follow that as many resources should be devoted to recording the process as to developing the product? Besides aiding communication between all participants, good documentation insures a user against the loss of technicians, allows program modifications and updates to be routinely made, and enhances appraisal efforts. The San Francisco model, for example, has been operated successfully by *one* person, the man who did the original programming. It is highly doubtful whether modifications could be made to the model, given its present state of unsatisfactory documentation.

In any future expenditure of public funds for computer-based research, at least one-half of the total expenditures should be earmarked for documentation.

Data

Differential orientations among participants must be taken into account in the development of information bases and systems needed to support problem-solving activities. With any public information system, the need of policy-makers for "data and informed opinions [already] selected and analyzed"[13] to fit their special, separate purposes must be set off against the need of researchers and analysts for greater quantities of timely, raw, detailed data. If the purpose of an information system is to serve policy-makers, as we think it should be, the separate needs of researchers and assorted levels of petty officials must be suppressed, to avoid compromising the biases and needs of those in truly authoritative centers of value allocation and control.

Past Problems. Data deficiencies have been detailed in our two cases; these, and experiences from other contexts where data collection and management purposes were even more central, indicate several fundamental unresolved problems:[14]

- Information systems that are meant to service research are ignored by policy-makers.

- Information systems tend to service clerical requirements and are irrelevant to policy-makers.
- Information produced by the system is so finely detailed and in formats so unfamiliar that it is rejected out of hand by the policy-makers.
- Attempts to aggregate research or clerical data up to some level thought to be useful for policy-making are dismissed because the created variables are not those normally used.
- More often than not, the information that is abstracted from the research data base reflects what lower-level personnel (research and operational) think the policy-maker ought to look at, instead of what the policy-maker does look at.

Obviously, the tension generated by the different orientations of active participants must be reduced in a "satisficing" way because there is no "best" solution.

Level of Detail. Three distinct categories and sources of data appear to be emerging.

Data definition and standardization are issues far from any satisfactory resolution; however, through census initiatives, population data seem at once reasonably standardized and of considerable general utility for use in any research enterprise. While social accounting schemes are still ill-defined and subject to considerable intellectual and pragmatic adjustment and accommodation, one must agree with Otis Dudley Duncan that "there is, to be sure, no reason to believe that any reasonable proposal for social accounts will result in discarding our well-developed system of demographic bookkeeping ... "[15] Current interest in building research-oriented clearinghouses for the anticipated 2,000 reels of Bureau of Census information augur well for more demographic information and hopefully better social research.

Another level of data detail is embodied in present-day activities to build Integrated Municipal Information Systems in several cities.[16] While similar activities have had only marginal success,[17] the potential payoffs in terms of cheap, operational, time series information are enormous.

Problems presented by both census and operational data are that models demand higher levels of accuracy[18] than one has come to expect from census data,[19] and that operational data are rarely collected in standard units, for comparable areas, at comparable times, etc., even within the same city, to say nothing of between cities.[20] This suggests the need for sample surveys, our third data level.

In the interests of upgrading the quality of census base lines, of insuring standardization, and of generating highly disaggregated time series in the one or a few politically salient spatial sectors of a city, we must survey. This is *expensive*; but for these requirements, the "only known technique for getting [these] data at a reasonable cost is a scientifically designed and executed sample survey."[21] Continuous sampling allows one the flexibility to adjust for initial measurement errors and, more important, for changing contexts; collective, institutional learning may be partially structured into ongoing procedures.

Our two cases have amply demonstrated the limitations of cross-sectional census and transportation study data for policy models. The renewed thrust to develop Integrated Municipal Information Systems has great potential for making routine operational data available for analytic purposes. However, our new experimental premise bears very much on these activities. One trusts that comprehensive appraisal is an integral part of that problem-solving process.

Data Base Management. It is not so much that data are not collected, it is more that "much of what is collected is in effect lost, because there has been no cheap way of putting questions to the data."[22] A threshold has just about been reached where reliable, tested, and relatively cheap data base management will be realized.[23] The process has been fitful, marked by false starts and plain error, and enormously more difficult than anyone could have initially imagined.[24] But throughout, one suspects, *the difficulty of the problem was given more attention than any approximate answer to the problem.*

The information glut from the 1970 census, coupled with better data-management procedures, is simultaneously encouraging and disturbing. It is encouraging because present conditions are abysmal and any improvement is welcome. It is disturbing because contextual, problem-oriented, and multimethod research demands so much more than census data alone can ever provide.

Procedures

The interaction and flow of the problem-solving process realized in our two cases is instructive. The addition of several new participants into the interaction may be a means to improve both the flow and preferred outcomes of the process.

Goal: An Amended Decision Sequence. Unless and until public officials are themselves technically qualified to appraise the merits of the research that they now routinely buy, it seems likely that the interests of the seller will be better served than are those of the buyer. Ritualized and piecemeal contracting for research, whatever particular benefits may accrue, seems to be generally inefficient, and up to now has been an unproductive way to expend *scarce* research resources.

Rather than "casting about" for problem solutions and having to settle for entrepreneurs, public decision-makers would be better served by an intermediary explicitly equipped to make technical judgments at all phases of the decision sequence, to separate "in principle" from "in practice," and to reduce the stifling effects of selling.

While there is no one institution expressly configured for this task, several exist that are specialized to aspects of it. Let us concentrate only on the appraisal phase because it is currently so neglected and because it seems to be a potential "leverage point" in the sequence, i.e. a place where a small change may produce an unexpectedly large impact.

Standards and Certification. If the long-term and difficult nature of the problems we have variously cited becomes commonly known, it may not be too much to hope that institutions like the Urban Institute, the Institute of Management Science, *or suitable surrogates,* will receive less niggardly, more wholehearted, and longer-term support from government at all levels.

A potential role as the setter of general standards by which research efforts may be appraised is clear. If, for example, a sizable portion of payment for a contract were to be withheld until documentation standards had been met, think what might happen: more, better, and more useful documentation; more carefully executed models; a written testimony of the problem-solving process in many locales; better communication and education; and in time, perhaps, models that can be understood and eventually put to use.

A potential role as a certifier of research personnel is equally clear. The present policy of incentives tends to relegate project execution to the "academic plebeians." Consider an analogy with the doctor, who is certified and must take responsibility for all events of consequence to his patients. A master-modeler qualification might be made to assume similar stature and symbolic meaning. At a minimum, attention would be redirected to the execution and appraisal phases of the sequence. There is something quite chilling about the present practice of allowing inexperienced or substantively unqualified persons to write the computer programs that ostensibly will help make public policy.

Increase Incentives. A more practical and direct intervention into the sequence would be to allocate a percentage of each contract for external appraisal. For instance, 10 percent of the total San Francisco project was $101,965; for Pittsburgh, it was $114,888. If our premise is experimental and our purpose is problem-solving, diverting 10 percent for appraisal to learn what a current experiment has contributed to the understanding and management of the greater problem seems a not unreasonable action.

Increase Capacity. External appraisal could proceed in several fashions; however, consider this recommendation.

Evenly divide the appraisal tithe. One share is offered to qualified bidders, including but not limited to consulting firms, research corporations, and "policy analysis" centers. The other share is made available to an institution of higher learning, e.g. a university, college, or institute situated near the major project site. In the first instance, we hope to stimulate continuing interest in appraisal as a valued and valuable private enterprise. In the second, we hope to stimulate enlightenment institutions to participate constructively without demanding the mobilization of large numbers of people. Both shares should serve our experimental premise and problem-solving purpose.

Increased Awareness. With the establishment of adequate general standards and improved procedures for personnel certification, *comprehensiveness, competence,* and *reliability* of appraisal may move nearer realization. With the innovation of a tithe, divided between two distinct types of appraisal institutions, *independence, promptitude,* and *economy,* the remaining three of our preferred outcomes, may also be more nearly approximated.

However, we must remember that these proposed recommendations are experiments. If they provide some insight into the complexity of urban decision, or if they aid in integrating the computer into that process, then rejoice, take and use them. But if the experiments fail, as well they might, then the creative burden of devising ways to meet the "challenge of complexity" falls back on us all.

APPENDICES AND NOTES

APPENDIX A

Questionnaire

Biographical Survey of
Simulation Project Participants

A. PERSONAL
   1. _____
      Name

   2. _____
      Date and Place of Birth

B. JOB EXPERIENCES AND PROFESSIONAL CAREER

   1. Beginning with present position first, please list in reverse order all professional positions held during the past ten years.

		Average Annual Compensation		
	1 $10K	2 10-15	3 15-20	4 20K
a. _____	1	2	3	4
b. _____	1	2	3	4
c. _____	1	2	3	4
d. _____	1	2	3	4
e. _____	1	2	3	4
f. _____	1	2	3	4

   2. What were you doing just prior to the CRP simulation project?
      _____
      _____
      _____

   3. Who recruited you (or, How did you come to work on the project)? _____
      _____

   4. What was your exact function during the project? (E.g. give a short "job description") _____
      _____
      _____

   5. What are you striving for as an ultimate professional goal (or, What would you like to be doing in 5-10 years)? _____
      _____
      _____

C.   EDUCATIONAL EXPERIENCES
1.   Post-secondary institutions attended (include all professional institutes, etc.)
    a.   Name of Institution: _____
       Location: _____
       Field or Major: _____
       Degree and Date: _____
    b.   Name of Institution: _____
       Location: _____
       Field or Major: _____
       Degree and Date: _____
    c.   Name of Institution: _____
       Location: _____
       Field or Major: _____
       Degree and Date: _____
2.   Do you have any professional publications? _____
3.   If "Yes" to #2, please list those that you consider most significant. Please list no more than 3. _____

_____

4.   Are you presently skilled and/or have you received training in any of the following areas?

                    Level of Skill
    a.   Computer Languages: 1 = poor;   2 = OK;   3 = excellent
       (List, e.g. FORTRAN,
       etc.)

    b.   Mathematics:
       (List, e.g. calculus, etc.)

5.   Could you, at this moment, write a computer program—beginning with flow charts, proceeding with coding, and including debugging and running—of some social process? _____

6.   To what professional societies or groups do you belong?

_____

7.   Would you list the periodicals or books that you regularly read and/or use: _____

_____

8.   If you were given a year or two off from your present responsibilities (assume a foundation grant or some special fellowship) for some graduate work of your own choosing, where would you go and what kind of a program would you follow? What difference would this training make on your career? _____

_____

_____

_____

D.   PROJECT PURPOSES

1.   Could you succinctly state what the fundamental purpose(s) was for the construction of the CRP simulation model? _____

_____

_____

2.   What do you think the project (model) should have been able to do (accomplish)? _____

_____

_____

_____

3.   Did the model have outputs that had any impact on the operations of the City? If "Yes," please describe: _____

_____

_____

_____

4.   What do you think the City got from the project? _____

_____

_____

5.   Would you rank in order (1, 2, 3, etc.) the degree to which the model seemed to be used for the following purposes:

- _____   Development of social science theory
- _____   Experimentation
- _____   Operational tool
- _____   Educational tool/instructional aid
- _____   Data management device
- _____   Projective device
- _____   Other—specify _____
- _____   Other _____

6.   Do you think any "political" benefits derived from this project? If "Yes," what kind and for whom? _____

_____

E.   PROBLEMS

1.   What, in your opinion, are the greatest problems that have to be overcome before computer models are to become useful and

used tools for planning and government decision-making?

_____
_____
_____
_____
_____
_____
_____
_____

2. What were (are) some of the impediments that you experienced in executing the project? Please describe and attempt to rank them from *greatest* problem to *least.*

_____
_____
_____
_____
_____
_____
_____
_____

Do you want a copy of the final report?   _____
_____   — Mailing Address
_____
_____

_____

Thank you very much for your cooperation and indulgence.

APPENDIX B

Code Book

General Class	Variable Name	Definition	Attributes	Column
Employment	AGE	Present Age	0— 30-40 1— 41-50 2— 51-60+	1
	WAGE1	Wage at the time project	0— 10K 1— 10-15K 2— 15-20K 3— 20K+	2
	WAGE2	Present wage	Same as above	3
	DWAGE	Difference in wage, then and now	0— −2 categories 1— −1 category 2— no change 3— +1 4— +2 5— +3	4
	ASPIRE	What position would you like to have in 5-10 years?	0— Academic sector 1— Private sector 3— Other	5
Education	DEGREE	Level of academic achievement	0— B.A. 1— Masters 2— Ph.D. 3— Other	6
	DISCPL	General area of discipline preparation	0— Humanities 1— Professional 2— Social science 3— Natural sciences	7
	PUBLSH	Any professional publications?	0— None 1— Few (2 or less) 2— Several (more than 2)	8

General Class	Variable Name	Definition	Attributes	Column
	COMLNG	How many computer languages do you have skill in?	0— None 1— 1 2— 2 3— $\geq$ 3	9
	COMSKL	What is your level of proficiency with your best computer language?	0— None 1— Poor 2— OK 3— Excellent	10
	MATH	How many and what math have you had in college?	0— None 1— 1 2— 2 3— $\geq$ 3	11
	MTHSKL	What is your level of proficiency with your best math subject?	0— None 1— Poor 2— OK 3— Excellent	12
	COMRIT	Can you write a computer program from start to end?	0— No 1— Yes	13
	EDASPR	If you had the chance, what kind of extra academic work do you want?	0— None 1— Humanities 2— Social science 3— Natural science	14
Purpose	PRPSI1	What was the initial purpose of the project? First purpose?	0— None/other 1— Education 2— Data management 3— Theory development 4— Experimentation 5— Projection 6— Operations/Policy making	15
	PRPSI2	Second Purpose?	Same as above	16
	PRPSI3	Third Purpose?	Same as above	17
	PRPSF1	What purpose did the project finally serve? First Purpose?	Same as above	18
	PRPSF2	Second Purpose?	Same as above	19

General Class	Variable Name	Definition	Attributes	Column
	PRPSF3	Third Purpose?	Same as above	20
	OPSIMP	Did the project have any operational impact on the city?	0— None 1— Very little 2— Some 3— Great deal	21
	CITGOT	What do you think the city got out of it?	Same as above	22
	POLBEN	Were there any political benefits for anyone as a result of the project?	Same as above	23
Problems	PRBS*	What are the root causes for difficulty in project?	0— Education 1— Bad theory 2— Orientations/Personal 3— Data/Technical	24
	IMPDTS*	How would you class the impediments to doing this work?	0— Technical 1— Political 2— Theoretical 3— Personal 4— Incentives	25
	PRBSCL	Based on answers to #2 21, 22, 23, all max=none; all min=fatal.	0— None 1— Minimum 2— Moderate/Low 3— Moderate/High 4— Fatal	26
Verbals	VALMAX	Of the values used in interview, which was predominant?	0— Power 1— Enlightenment 2— Wealth 3— Skill	27
	WRDPOW	Percentage of attention to power/others.	0— 25% 1— 26-50% 2— 51-75% 3— 76-100%	28
	WRDENL	Percentage of attention to enlightenment.	Same as above	29
	WRDWLT	Percentage of attention to wealth	Same as above	30

*Not used in Scales

APPENDICES AND NOTES

General Class	Variable Name	Definition	Attributes	Column
	WRDSKL	Percentage of attention to skill	Same as above	31
City	CITY	Which of the two places?	0— San Francisco 1— Pittsburgh	59
Discipline Profession	XDISC	Alphanumeric label of profession or discipline.		60-71
Name	XNAME	Alphanumeric label with last name		72-80

APPENDIX C

Multidimensional Scaling: Some Methodological Comments

Multidimensional scaling, a technique more widely known to psychologists than to political scientists,[1] offers some interesting possibilities.[2] Generally, the technique is directed to the problem of finding "n points whose interpoint distances match in some sense the experimental dissimilarities of n objects."[3] The major breakthrough, with respect to multidimensional scaling of ordinal data, occurred when Roger Shepard demonstrated that a monotonic relationship between experimental dissimilarities or similarities (d_{ij} or $k - d_{ij}$) and the interpoint distances in a configuration was itself satisfactory, without resort to considerations of variability in one's data, to

obtain very tightly constrained solutions and [to] recover simultaneously the form of the assumed but unspecified monotonic relationship. In other words, he showed that the rank order of the dissimilarities is itself enough to determine the solution. . . . Thus his technique avoids all the strong distributional assumptions which are necessary in variability-dependent techniques . . .[4]

The problem is to take given measurements of dissimilarity and then to calculate a configuration whose interpoint distances best fit the dissimilarities. A statistic labeled "stress," the degree to which configuration and data fit, has been developed. In general, "stress" values of 10 percent are "fair," 5 percent are "good," and 2.5 percent are "excellent."[5]

The variables measured in the present analysis were with two exceptions coded ordinally. For example, *COMSKL* (variable #10 in Appendix B) was either "none," "poor," "OK," or "excellent," in that order. Project purpose variables (*PRPSI1-3* and *PRPSF1-3*) were ordered according to stringency of demands on the model with respect to stated purposive application: "none," "education," "data management," "theory development," "experimentation," "projection," "operations or policy making," in that order, according to our discussion in chapter 6, "Pragmatic Appraisal."[6] Discipline and occupational variables were ordered according to assumed levels of technical (mathematical and computer-oriented) training. For example, variable *DISCPL*, the general area of disciplinary preparation, was respectively coded as "humanities," "professional," "social science," and "natural science."

An intersubject distance matrix was computed using all variables except *PRBS* and *IMPDTS* (# 24 and 25 in the Code Book [see Appendix B]. They were classificatory variables, and did not measure degrees of a single characteristic, and were therefore not used.)[6] To illustrate the procedure used in this preprocessing, consider the simple illustration in three-space in Figure C-1. All variables were transformed

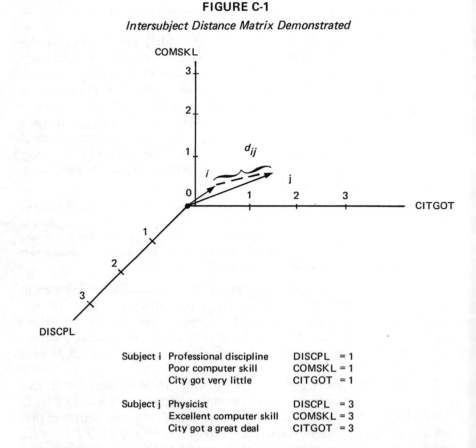

FIGURE C-1

Intersubject Distance Matrix Demonstrated

Subject i	Professional discipline	DISCPL = 1
	Poor computer skill	COMSKL = 1
	City got very little	CITGOT = 1
Subject j	Physicist	DISCPL = 3
	Excellent computer skill	COMSKL = 3
	City got a great deal	CITGOT = 3

into unit normal form and the simple Euclidean geometric distance d_{ij} was calculated over n variables for all respondent pairs. The smaller

$$d_{ij} = \sqrt{\sum_{n=1}^{n} (X_{in} - X_{jn})^2}$$

d_{ij}, the more similar the pairs were judged to be (and the converse). This distance matrix then becomes input for J. B. Kruskal and Robert F. Ling's MDSCL package, which runs at the Yale Computer Center.

To determine how many dimensions are recoverable from these data is a matter of purpose and judgment, although certain guidelines exist. A plot of "Stress versus Dimension," in Figure C-2, is helpful. Achieving some level of stress where additional dimensions contribute little to

FIGURE C-2

Stress versus Dimension—Full Sample of Thirty-six Respondents: Dissimilar

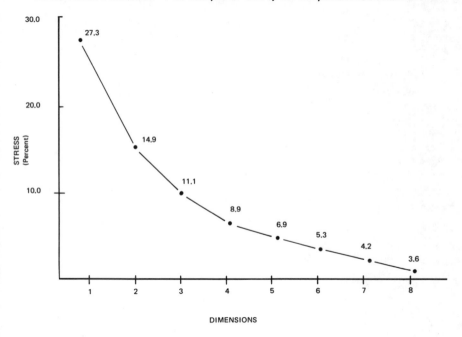

further stress reduction may indicate a recoverable number of dimensions. Another guideline is more pragmatic. If the "t-dimensional solution provides a satisfying interpretation, but the $(t + 1)$-dimensional solution reveals no further structure, it may be well to use only the t-dimensional solution."[7]

In our case, six dimensions satisfy the first criterion: 5.3 percent of stress is quite "good," and improvements thereafter are not large. What six dimensions may be operating is extremely difficult to say. Interpretation of structure beyond three dimensions pressed the limits of time, patience, and imagination; however, three- and two-dimensional configurations presented relatively straightforward interpretive tasks.

NOTES

PART I

Introduction

1. Harold D. Lasswell, "Technique of Decision Seminars," *Midwest Journal of Political Science* 4 (August 1960): 222.

2. Frederick E. Balderston and Austin C. Hoggatt, *Simulation of Market Processes* (Berkeley: IBER; Special Publication #1, 1962), p. 1.

3. Strict disciplinary undertakings frequently suffer from oversimplification so severe that the work is rendered useless for direct application to real settings. See Ragnar Frisch, "On the Notion of Equilibrium and Disequilibrium" *Review of Economic Studies* 3 (1936): 100-105, for a concise and respected view on these matters. More recently, Herbert A. Simon and Arthur Ando in their "Aggregation of Variables in Dynamic Systems," *Econometrica* 29 (April 1961): 111-38, helped clarify the problem.

4. These integrative shortcomings have long been recognized and are fundamental to this and virtually any other social scientific enterprise. See Olaf Helmer, "On the Epistemology of the Inexact Sciences," *Management Science* 6 (October 1959): 25-52.

5. Cohen and Cyert, "Computer Models in Dynamic Systems," *Quarterly Journal of Economics* 75 (February 1961): 127.

6. Hayward R. Alker, Jr., has made this point in the context of the applicability of simulation to theory building: "The synthetic power of simulation studies is . . . truly enormous." See his "Computer Simulations as Political Theories" (Paper read at Annual Meeting of International Political Science Association, Brussels, September 18-23, 1967), p. 14.

7. John Rader Platt, "Strong Inference," *The Step to Man* (New York: John Wiley, 1966), p. 28 (citing T. C. Chamberlin).

8. Jay Forrester, among others, has speculated on this difficult, judgmental question. Comments, in Martin Greenberger, ed., *Computers and the World of the Future* (Cambridge: MIT Press, 1962), pp. 88 ff.

9. MATHEMATICA, "Final Report: Review of TEMPER Model" (Washington, D.C.: Defense Communication Agency—Contract #DCA 100-66-C-0083, September 30, 1966), pp. 16-17.

10. See Morten Gorden, "Burdens for the Designer of a Computer Simulation of International Relations: The Case of TEMPER," in Davis Bobrow and Judah Schwarz, eds., *Computers and the Policy-Making Community* (Englewood Cliffs: Prentice-Hall, 1968), pp. 222-45.

11. John G. Kemeny and J. Laurie Snell, *Mathematical Models in the Social Sciences* (New York: Ginn & Co., 1962), pp. 4,8. The question of what constitutes a "well-defined field," and hence the applicability of mathematics, is raised and never resolved in their thesis. It is a matter of fundamental importance.

12. Herbert A. Simon in Paul Lazarsfeld, ed., *Mathematical Thinking in the Social Sciences* (Glencoe: Free Press, 1954), p. 388.

13. Martin Shubik, "Microeconomic Analysis, Course Notes" (Administrative Sciences Department, Yale University, 1967 rev. ed.), pp. 7,10.

14. Mortimer Taube, *Computers and Common Sense: The Myth of Thinking Machines* (New York: Columbia University Press, 1961), pp. 94-95. "If a machine is to simulate the behavior of a human brain, the designer of the machine must have a good notion of the behavior which is being simulated. That is to say, it is an initial requirement that any such enterprise specify as exactly and as completely as possible those activities or functions of the brain which are to be simulated, imitated, or even surpassed. . . . It is necessary to begin with some concept of the brain's activities or some definition of its functions. Such a definition can then provide an empirical measurement of the degree to which any machine simulation of the brain is successful." *Ibid.*, p. 69.

15. James M. Beshers, "Substantive Issues in Models of Large-Scale Social Systems," in James M. Beshers, ed., *Computer Methods in the Analysis of Large-Scale Social Systems* (Cambridge: JCUS; MIT-Harvard, 1965), p. 86. See also James M. Beshers, "Models and Theory Construction," *American Sociological Review* 22 (1957).

16. "Revolutionary Technological Advances." See Ralph E. Lapp, *The New Priesthood* (New York: Harper and Row, 1965), pp. 63-70.

17. I have been enormously stimulated on these points by the work and conversation of Ida R. Hoos. (Personal interview, Berkeley, California, July 1969). See also Ida R. Hoos, "A Critical Review of Systems Analysis: The California Experience" (Berkeley: Space Sciences Laboratory Working Paper #89, December 1968).

18. See John K. Galbraith, *The New Industrial State* (Boston: Houghton Mifflin, 1967) and Jacques Ellul, *The Technological Society* (New York: Random House, 1964).

19. Fritz Machlup, *The Production and Distribution of Knowledge in the United States* (Princeton: Princeton University Press, 1962). Knowledge is an interesting commodity characterized by its unlimited quantities of inputs and increased qualitative advantage acquired through use.

20. John Gilmore, et al., *Defense Systems Research in the Civil Sector* (Washington: Arms Control and Disarmament Agency, 1967).

1. An Overview of the Task

1. Harold D. Lasswell, "Strategies of Inquiry: The Rational Use of Observation," in Daniel Lerner, ed., *The Human Meaning of the Social Sciences* (New York: Meridian Books, 1959), p. 101. "It is of continuing significance to discover by what modes of organization and operation it will be feasible to hold antidemocratic tendencies in check . . . the prospects of popular government depend upon the vitality of the system of unofficial controls."

2. *Ibid.*, p. 104.

3. Harold D. Lasswell, "Towards Continuing Appraisal of the Impact of Law on Society," *Rutgers Law Review* 21, no. 4 (Summer 1967): 645.

4. National Academy of Sciences, *Technology: Processes of Assessment and Choice* (Washington: Government Printing Office, July 1969), pp. 26, 27-28. (italics deleted)

5. Alexander L. George, "Bridging the 'Gap' between Scholarly Research and Policy-Makers: The Problem of Theory and Action" (Paper read at Inter-University Faculty Seminar, University of Denver, May 3, 1968).

6. Max F. Millikan, "Inquiry and Policy: The Relation of Knowledge to Action," in Lerner, *Human Meaning of Social Sciences*, p. 161.

7. Kathleen Archibald, "Possible Criteria for a Theoretical Approach Useful to Policy" (Unpublished paper; The RAND Corporation, March 1966), p. 2.

8. Robert P. Bush and Frederick Mosteller, "A Comparison of Eight Models," in Paul Lazarsfeld and Neil W. Henry, eds., *Readings in Mathematical Social Science* (Chicago: Science Research Associates, 1966), p. 335.

9. Harold D. Lasswell, "The Political Science of Science," *American Political Science Review* 50, no. 4 (December 1956): 978.

10. Harold D. Lasswell, "The Public Interest: Proposing Principles of Content and Procedure," in Carl J. Friedrich, ed., *NOMOS V—The Public Interest* (New York: Atherton Press, 1967), p. 66.

11. Jack D. Douglas, "Freedom and Tyranny in a Technological Society" (La Jolla, Calif.: University of California, San Diego, Dept. of Sociology, MS, 1969), p. 39. "This *conspiratorial silence of experts* can literally go on for decades before men not captured by the expert category reopen the whole issue and point out what should have been obvious."

12. See James Gustafson, "Context versus Principles: The Misplaced Debate," *Harvard Theological Review* (April 1965).

13. Gibson Winter, *Elements for a Social Ethic: Scientific Perspectives on Social Process* (New York: Macmillan, 1966), p. 215. Winter has considerably shaped my thinking with his prose and his conversation. Hopefully, his work is the harbinger of a more vital, policy-specific social ethics.

14. Abraham Kaplan, *American Ethics and Public Policy* (New York: Oxford Press, 1963), p. 94.

15. Robert A. Dahl and Charles E. Lindblom, *Politics, Economics and Welfare* (New York: Harper, 1953), pp. 77-78.

16. Winter, *Elements for a Social Ethic,* pp. 254-85.

17. C. West Churchman, *Challenge to Reason* (New York: McGraw-Hill, 1968), p. 163.

18. Harold D. Lasswell, "Impact of Law," p. 676.

2. Views of the World

1. *King Henry IV* has special meaning for this work. William Aldis Wright, ed., *The Complete Works of William Shakespeare* (Garden City: Doubleday, 1936, Cambridge Edition text), p. 484. I am indebted to my colleague and friend Ronald D. Brunner for many stimulating discussions on the matters in this chapter.

2. Harold D. Lasswell, "The Transition to More Sophisticated Procedures," in Davis B. Bobrow and Judah L. Schwartz, eds., *Computers and the Policy-Making Community* (Englewood Cliffs: Prentice-Hall, 1968), pp. 307-14.

3. See Paul A. Lazarsfeld and Robert K. Merton, "Friendship and Social Process," in Berger, et al., eds., *Freedom and Control in Modern Society* (New York: The Free Press, 1954), p. 62, for a note of caution developed in terms of avoiding "premature and misplaced concreteness," where "one has failed to acknowledge what is being left out of the analysis and assumes that conclusions apply to the complex situation as it really is rather than to the relations of the few elements in it . . . "

4. Stuart Bruchey, *The Roots of American Economic Growth, 1607-1861: An Essay in Social Causation* (New York: Harper Torchbooks, 1968 edition), p. 10.

5. Harold D. Lasswell, "The Future of the Comparative Method," *Comparative Politics* 1 (October 1968): 13.

6. Harold D. Lasswell, "The World Revolution of Our Time," in *World Revolutionary Elites,* Harold D. Lasswell and Daniel Lerner, eds. (Cambridge: MIT Press, 1966 paperback edition), p. 77.

7. Lee Benson, "Research Problems in American Political Historiography," in Mirra Komarovsky, ed., *Common Frontiers of the Social Sciences* (Glencoe: The Free Press and Falcon's Wing Press, 1957), p. 116 (italics deleted).

8. Bruchey, *American Economic Growth,* p.11.

9. Indeed, a most famous cycle in the sociology of historical knowledge—that of Frederick Jackson Turner's "frontier thesis," which was supplanted by Arthur Schlesinger's "urban thesis," and further modified by the "class" or "interest-group thesis" of Charles A. Beard, points out the tentativeness of any single pronouncement of trend. Frederick Jackson Turner, *The Frontier in American History* (New York: Holt, Rinehart & Winston, 1962 edition), pp. 1-38; Arthur M. Schlesinger, Sr., *The Rise of the City* (New York: Macmillan, 1933), pp. 302-303; and Bernard C. Borning, *The Political and Social Thought of Charles Beard* (Seattle: University of Washington Press, 1962), pp. 64-138.

10. Hayward R. Alker, Jr., "The Long Road to International Relations Theory: Problems of Statistical Nonadditivity," *World Politics* 18 (July 1966): 623-55.

11. Bush and Mosteller, "Eight Models."

12. Harold D. Lasswell, "World Revolution," p. 74.

13. Natural science has in many instances been manipulatively useful because it does have certain predictive power. Why it does is a separate matter. See Helmer, "Epistemology of Inexact Sciences."

14. "The resulting tension between the desire of the researcher to satisfy his scientific conscience and the desire of the management to get the job done sometimes border on the tragic, or the comic." Britton Harris, "The Uses of Theory in the Simulation of Urban Phenomena," *Journal of the American Institute of Planners* 32 (September 1966): 272.

15. Allen Newell has discussed this principle of bringing multiple, shifting purposes to bear on a well-defined problem in "Some Problems of Basic Organization in Problem-Solving Programs," in M. C. Yovits, et al., eds., *Self-Organizing Systems, 1962* (Washington: Spartan Books, 1962).

16. See Abraham Edel, *Method in Ethical Theory* (Indianapolis: Bobbs-Merrill, 1963) for a well-respected, balanced, perceptive survey of this general area.

17. Robert A. Dahl and Charles E. Lindblom, *Politics, Economics, and Welfare,* p. 25.

18. *Ibid.*, pp. 25-54.

19. Bernard Berelson, et al., *Voting* (Chicago: University of Chicago Press, 1954), chapter 14.

20. Lasswell and Lerner, *World Revolutionary Elites*, pp. 35-36.

21. Marvin Minsky, "Steps Toward Artificial Intelligence," *Proceedings of the IRE* 49 (1961): 8, 29.

22. Robert A. Dahl, *A Preface to Democratic Theory* (Chicago: University of Chicago Press, 1956), pp. 48-50.

23. Ill-definition may have systemic benefits: stating vague goals, a politician or any other institutional entity may be able to maintain certain flexibility through time. It is reasonable behavior, but it makes analysis very difficult.

24. See Geoffrey Vickers, *Value Systems and Social Process* (New York: Basic Books, 1968), pp. 112-32.

25. Dahl and Lindblom, *Politics, Economics, and Welfare*, pp. 81 f. on changing goals.

26. J. Roland Pennock, "Political Development, Political Systems, and Political Goods," *World Politics* 18 (April 1966): 433.

27. Yehezkel Dror, *Public Policy-Making Reexamined* (San Francisco: Chandler, 1968), p. 135.

28. See Philip Morse, ed., *Operations Research for Public Systems* (Cambridge: MIT Press, 1967); and J. R. Lawrence, ed., *Operational Research and the Social Sciences* (New York and London: Tavistock Publications, 1966) for recent examples of the range of social problems treated by operations researchers.

29. See the famous "Arrow Paradox" in Kenneth Arrow, *Social Choice and Individual Values* (New York: John Wiley, 1951), pp. 51-59, 75-81. The problem has recently been articulated by Dahl: "The language of political values is perhaps most easily translated into the language of qualitative data: but it stubbornly resists accurate and satisfying translations into the language of quantitative data." "The Evaluation of Political Systems," in Ithiel de Sola Pool, ed., *Contemporary Political Science: Toward Empirical Theory* (New York: McGraw-Hill, 1967), p. 174.

30. W. Arthur Lewis, "Planning Public Expenditures," in Max F. Millikan, ed., *National Economic Planning* (New York: National Bureau of Economic Research, 1967), p. 207.

31. See Melvin Webber, "The Validity and Variety of Planned Interventions," in *Planning in an Environment of Change* (Berkeley: Center for Planning and Development Research, Reprint #44, 1969).

32. As cited in Lawrence Frank, "The Nature and Limitations for Forecasting," *Daedalus* 96 (Summer 1967): 941.

33. Martin Shubik, as cited in Frank, "Forecasting," p. 945.

34. *Ibid.*

35. Churchman, *Challenge to Reason*, p. 165, verbalizes these distinctions in summary fashion: "The model-building rationalizer [Explanatory Mode] sees the world to be a world he can adequately and precisely describe mathematically. The practical philosopher [Manipulative Mode] sees the world to be the world of action—of compromise and doing. The intuitive [Reflective Mode] sees the world to be one of his own making—made out of his genius."

36. "To be any good, . . . a scientist has to think of one thing, deeply and obsessively, for a long time. An administrator has to think of a great many things, widely, in their inter-connections, for a short time. There is a sharp difference in the intellectual and moral temperaments." C. P. Snow, *Science and Government* (New York: Mentor Books, 1962), pp. 64-65.

37. The easy alternative to offering policy-makers analytical assistance is to ignore their requirements. J. V. Krutilla, for one, argues that the latter choice is untenable as long as analysis affords even a marginally better prospect of producing results more satisfying than would be expected otherwise. "Welfare Aspects of Benefit-Cost Analysis," *Journal of Political Economy* 69 (1961): 226-35.

38. Willis W. Harman, "Contemporary Social Forces and Alternative Futures" (Paper read at Airlie House Conference on Educational Research, June 16-17, 1969).

3. *Theoretical Appraisal*

1. Lewis Carroll, *Alice's Adventures in Wonderland* and *Through the Looking Glass*, and *What Alice Found There* (New York: Macmillan, 1892), p. 124.

2. Many lists surely exist. Agnew and Pyke, for example, single out *simplicity, testability, novelty, goodness of fit, internal consistency,* and *predictability* as general categories for theory evaluation. Our purposes are more specific and will require narrower concepts. Neil McK. Agnew and Sandra Pyke, *The Science Game* (Englewood Cliffs: Prentice-Hall, 1969), pp. 162-68.

3. Fred Massarik, "Magic, Model, Man and the Cultures of Mathematics," in Fred Massarik and Philburn Ratoosh, eds., *Mathematical Exploration in Behavioral Science* (Homewood: Dorsey, 1965), p. 12.

4. This reproduces and summarizes a similar definitional exercise in Ronald D. Brunner and Garry D. Brewer, *Organized Complexity: Empirical Theories of Political Development* (New York: The Free Press, 1971), pp. 5-18. The points are fundamental enough to warrant their reproduction here.

5. Richard Bellman and Robert Kalaba, *Dynamic Programming and Modern Control Theory* (New York: Academic Press, 1965), p. 2.

6. Totem: "in animistic religion, an object, usually animal, which a man regards with unusual respect, and to which he considers himself intimately related, as by kinship or descent. Clan totem, to which all members of clan consider themselves related in same way, is most common form. Member of clan totem bears totem name; must marry outside totem group (exogamy); believes himself to be descended from totem; and must not kill, eat, or touch totem animal, or call it by its true name. Totemism exists largely in Australia, Melanesia, and North America. No generally acceptable theory for origin of totemism exists." William Bridgwater, ed., *The Columbia Viking Desk Encyclopedia* (New York: Viking, 1953), 1:1276.

7. Abraham Kaplan, *The Conduct of Inquiry* (San Francisco: Chandler, 1964), pp. 276, 279.

8. Ira G. Wilson and Marthann Wilson, *Information, Computers, and System Design* (New York: Wiley, 1965), p. 243.

9. Stanley Hoffman, "Long Road to Theory," in Stanley Hoffman, ed., *Contemporary Theory in International Relations* (Englewood Cliffs: Prentice-Hall, 1960), p. 45. A similar argument is developed in a sizzling critique by Albert O. Hirschman entitled, "The Search for Paradigms as a Hindrance to Understanding," *World Politics* 22 (April 1970).

10. See Earl B. Hunt, "The Evaluation of Somewhat Parallel Models," in Massarik and Ratoosh, *Mathematical Exploration*, pp. 37-39.

11. Paul A. Samuelson, *Foundations of Economic Analysis* (New York: Atheneum, 1965), pp. 311-17.

12. Samuel Goldberg, *Introduction to Difference Equations* (New York: Wiley Science Editions, 1961), chapter 1, especially section 1.7, "Analogies between the Difference and Differential Calculus."

13. Colin B. Clark, *The Economics of 1960* (London: Macmillan, 1942), critized in K. C. Kogiku, "The Economics of 1960 Revisited," *Review of Economics and Statistics* 4 (November 1960). "The main difficulty seems to be that Clark's model is static; its structural equations do not contain time, and theoretically his model is to hold at any point in time as well as in 1960 . . . His static model does not accommodate . . . the dynamics of growth."

14. The original forecast is contained in Harold D. Lasswell, "Sino-Japanese Crisis: The Garrison State versus the Civilian State," *China Quarterly* 3 (Fall 1937): 643-49. An appraisal of the forecast is in Lasswell, "The Garrison State Hypothesis Today," in Samuel P. Huntington, ed., *Changing Patterns of Military Politics* (New York: The Free Press, 1962).

15. W. Ross Ashby, *An Introduction to Cybernetics* (London: Chapman and Hall, 1961), pp. 241-43. See William J. Baumol, *Economic Dynamics* (New York: Macmillan, 1959 edition), pp. 213-17, 301-303, for concepts of stability and equilibrium.

16. One is commended to read Robert Lekachman's "The Non-Economic Assumptions of John Maynard Keynes," in Mirra Komarovsky, ed., *Common Frontiers of the Social Sciences* (Glencoe: The Free Press and Falcon's Wing Press, 1957), pp. 338-57.

Some economists concluded that [Keynes's theoretical] relationships were stable enough to assume that a repetition of any historically observed national income would carry with it the same level of consumption within a small margin of error. In other words, *these investigators generalized Keynes' short run theoretical consumption function into a longer run historical relationship* and imputed to income a truly dominating actual as well as theoretical role in the determination of consumption. . . .

. . . Most of these forecasts [for post-World War II] relied on Keynesian methods and in most cases they predicted for the spring of 1946 much lower income and much higher unemployment than actually ensued. Although there are many reasons why these forecasts went wrong, one is especially relevant: forecasters assumed stability in consumer's tastes. *Ibid.*, pp. 344-45.

17. For example, Walter Isard, *Location and Space-Economy* (Cambridge: Technology Press, 1956); Ralph H. Brown, *Historical Geography of the United States* (New York: Harcourt, Brace, and World, 1948); Ellen Churchill Semple, *American History and Its Geographic Condition* (New York: Houghton Mifflin, 1903); and Brian J. L. Berry and Duane F. Marble, eds., *Spatial Analysis: A Reader in Statistical Geography* (Englewood Cliffs: Prentice-Hall, 1968).

18. Everett M. Rogers, *Diffusion of Innovations* (New York: The Free Press, 1962); Torsten Hägerstrand, *The Propagation of Innovational Waves* (Lund, Sweden: Royal University, 1952); and William Bunge, *Theoretical Geography* (Lund: Gleerup, 1962).

19. Jane Jacobs, *The Economy of Cities* (New York: 1969), pp. 161-62. Cf. William T. Fay, "The Geography of the 1970 Census: A Cooperative Effort," *Planning 1966* (September 1966), pp. 99-106.

20. Karl W. Deutsch, "On Theories, Taxonomies, and Models as Communication Codes for Organizing Information," *Behavioral Science* 11 (January 1966): 3.

21. Ira S. Lowry, "A Short Course in Model Design," *Journal of the American Institute of Planners* 31 (May 1965): 160.

22. Kaplan, *Conduct of Inquiry*, p. 205.

23. I am deeply indebted to Peter A. Busch for assistance on these points. See his, "An Assessment of Mathematical Models of Arms Races," mimeographed (Yale University Department of Political Science, 1969). For example, Paul Smoker apparently found especial beauty in a symbolic formulation that produces harmonic motion. His application of this form to an empirical context was not quite as esthetic, for as Peter Busch comments: "The real issue is that an oscillating function has been chosen but no meaningful political oscillations have been demonstrated." *Ibid.*, p. 13. See Paul Smoker, "The Arms Race: A Wave Model," *Papers of the Peace Research Society* 14 (1966): 151-92 for the referenced article.

24. I. M. D. Little, *A Critique of Welfare Economics* (Oxford: Clarendon Press, 1957 edition), p. 3.

25. Monroe C. Beardsley, *Thinking Straight* (Englewood Cliffs: Prentice-Hall, 1961 edition), p. 66.

26. Bush and Mosteller, "Eight Models," p. 335.

27. Albert Ando, Franklin M. Fisher, and Herbert A. Simon, *Essays on the Structure of Social Science Models* (Cambridge: MIT Press, 1963), pp. 4, 11, 61, 67-70, 80, 85-88, 92-106, 113-68.

28. Computer models of social contexts generally have so many degrees of freedom and operate with such horrible data that extreme precision is out of reach. For anal personality types this fact often causes extreme discomfiture.

29. MATHEMATICA, pp. 17-18.

4. Technical Appraisal

1. Wright, *Works of Shakespeare*, p. 523.

2. These are learned, in most cases, by doing. In this instance, keen insights and continuous stimulation were derived from Martin Shubik's seminar-workshop on "Gaming and Simulation," which is held in the Administrative Sciences Department at Yale University. Much of what follows evolved out of the experiences learned there and subsequently learned in the production of several small models for *Organized Complexity*, a joint effort with Ronald D. Brunner. Special indebtedness is owed J. S. Fitch III for his conversation and clear thinking. See his, "A Simulation Model of Political Change in Latin America" (dissertation prospectus, Department of Political Science, Yale University, November 1968). Needless to say, all who participate in Martin Shubik's seminar are in his intellectual debt.

3. Ira S. Lowry, "A Short Course in Model Design," *Journal of the American Institute of Planners* 31 (May 1965): 159. Also, recall James Besher's point on this matter, above.

4. Herbert L. Costner and Robert K. Leik, "Deductions from Axiomatic Theory," *American Sociological Review* 29 (December 1964): 819-35.

5. Wilson and Wilson, *Information, Computers, and System Design*, p. 245.

6. Howard S. Krasnow and Reino Merikallio, "The Past, Present, and Future of General Simulation Languages," *Management Science* 11 (November 1964): 236-68.

7. "... many adjustments and, indeed, fresh starts are required as the several segments of the model are debugged, tested, and finally validated. It is precisely during this critical period of program testing and evaluating that the traditional channels of communication between analyst and programmer are likely to break down. ...

"A solution to this dilemma is to eliminate the problem of communication by combining the functions of analyst and programmer into a single person." Maynard M. Hufschmidt and Myron B. Fiering, *Simulation Techniques for Design of Water Resource Systems* (Cambridge: Harvard University Press, 1966), p. 194.

8. John Meyer, "Regional Economics—A Survey," *American Economic Review* (March 1963): 32 for discussion of coefficient stability assumption.

9. See C. P. Bonini, *Simulation of Information and Decision Systems in the Firm* (Englewood Cliffs: Prentice-Hall, 1963) for such an example.

10. MATHEMATICA, p. 122.

11. Thomas H. Naylor and J. M. Finger, "Verification of Computer Simulation Models," *Management Science* 14, no. 2 (October 1967): B-92.

12. Tjalling C. Koopmans, *Three Essays on the State of Economic Science* (New York: McGraw-Hill, 1957), p. 136.

13. See Brunner and Brewer, *Organized Complexity*, pp. 33-59 for one treatment of the problem. See J. Johnston, *Econometric Methods* (New York: McGraw-Hill, 1963), pp. 5-6.

14. The literature on parameter estimation techniques is voluminous. Consideration of the issues is outside the purpose of this research. The interested reader may peruse any standard econometric textbook, J. Johnston, *Econometric Methods* (New York: McGraw-Hill, 1963), for example.

15. Most models depend upon statistics to a great extent in the estimation of their parameters. No model will ever fit the reality data in any more than a "satisficing" way. The best one can do, given data and model errors, is to close in on some goodness-of-fit between real and generated series.

16. Robert P. Abelson, for one, has used this term in discussing psychological models.

17. Cohen and Cyert, "Computer Models in Dynamic Economics," *Quarterly Journal of Economics* 75 (February 1961): 127.

18. Henri Theil, *Applied Economic Forecasting* (Chicago: Rand McNally, 1966), p. 28.

19. Richard M. Cyert, "A Description and Evaluation of Some Firm Simulations," *Proceedings of the IBM Scientific Symposium on Simulation Models and Gaming* (White Plains, N.Y.: IBM, 1966).

5. Ethical Appraisal

1. Scientism, with its reductionist premises, has been seriously considered by R. L. Means, *The Ethical Imperative* (New York: Doubleday, 1969). Citations are from Winter, *Elements for a Social Ethic*, p. 266.

2. Harold D. Lasswell and Abraham Kaplan, *Power and Society* (New Haven: Yale University Press, 1950), p. 83.

3. Kaplan, *American Ethics and Public Policy*, p. 6.

4. Personal Interview with Professor Gibson Winter, Divinity School, University of Chicago, October 27, 1969.

5. Kaplan, *American Ethics and Public Policy*, p. 6.

6. Paul Ramsay and Gene H. Outka, *Norm and Context in Christian Ethics* (New York: Scribner, 1968).

7. Nicholas M. Smith, Jr., "A Calculus for Ethics: A Theory of the Structure of Value," *Behavioral Science* 1 (April 1956): 112.

8. Gibson Winter, "Toward a Comprehensive Science of Policy" (Houghton Lecture, Harvard University, November 1969), p. 7.

9. J. Roland Pennock, "Political Philosophy and Political Science," in Oliver Garceau, ed., *Political Research and Political Theory* (Cambridge: Harvard University Press, 1968), p. 55.

10. Kenneth E. Boulding, *The Image* (Ann Arbor: Ann Arbor Paperbacks, 1961 edition), pp. 25-26.

11. Wilson and Wilson, *Information, Computers, and System Design*, p. 236.

12. S. Watanabe, "Prediction and Retrodiction," *Review of Modern Physics* 27 (1955): 179-86.

13. Charles E. Lindblom, *The Policy-Making Process* (Englewood Cliffs: Prentice-Hall, 1968), pp. 26-27.

14. William Alonso, "The Quality of Data and the Choice and Design of Predictive Models," in Highway Research Board, *Urban Development Models* (Washington: HRB and the National Academy of Sciences, Special Report #97, 1968), around pp. 188-89.

15. Harman, "Contemporary Social Forces and Alternative Futures," and Bertrand de Jouvenal, *The Art of Conjecture* (New York: Basic Books, 1967).

16. Personal Interview with Ira S. Lowry, Management Sciences Department, The RAND Corporation, Santa Monica, California, July 10, 1969. "It seems to me that the strategy for planning models . . . is not trying to forecast what will happen. But trying to decide what the city ought to want to have happen and then leave it to executive maneuverings . . . to push it in those directions." And later, "the problem is to dream up plausible alternatives and to expose their structure . . . what these alternatives mean in terms of things that are of interest to those who are running the city and to those who are living there."

17. Abraham Maslow, *The Psychology of Science* (New York: Harper and Row, 1966).

18. Archibald MacLeish has termed this need for a fuller, more hopeful image "The Great American Frustration," *Saturday Review* (July 13, 1968), pp. 13-16.

19. Anthropologists have been doing this sort of analysis for years, and their activities serve as a useful emulative paradigm. "The ultimate aim in describing social change is twofold: first, to plot the course of change: second, to describe the process through which individuals discard a relationship which belongs to one structure and take on a relationship which belongs to a different structure." Frederick G. Bailey, "Political Change in the Kondmals," *Eastern Anthropologist* 11, no. 2 (1957): 104; and S. N. Eisenstadt. "Religious Organizations and Political Process in Centralized Empires," *Journal of Asian Studies* 21, no. 3 (May 1962): 271-94.

20. Winter, *Elements for a Social Ethic*, p. 282.

21. Social accounting schemes are still ill-defined and subject to considerable intellectual and pragmatic adjustment and accommodation before they begin to be realized. See *The Public Interest* 15 (Spring 1969) for a survey of the project.

22. The PPBS debate, thankfully outside the scope of the present inquiry, has brought this issue into focus. Aaron Wildavsky, among others, has adopted the skeptical point of view in these matters: "The Political Economy of Efficiency," *The Public Interest* 8 (Summer 1967): 30-48.

23. See J. S. Mill, "Utilitarianism," in *Britannica Great Books* (Chicago: Encyclopaedia Britannica, 1952 edition), 43:445-76.

24. Dahl and Lindblom, *Politics, Economics and Welfare*, p. 74.

25. *Ibid.*, pp. 75-76 (emphasis added).

26. A well-known tragic example is recited in Herbert Gans, *The Urban Villagers* (New York: Free Press, 1962), where mobility and "newer, better housing" were valued, i.e. preferred, by the urban renewal policy-makers and, "inexplicably," the ungrateful Italians had other preferences, which only after the fact became salient. See also William Michelson, "Most People Don't Want What Architects Want," *Trans-action* (July-August 1968), pp. 37-43; and Wilson and Wilson, *Information, Computers, and System Design*, p. 23: "To 'pin down' qualitative decision rules for a computer program is not a trivial job. To select the qualities to be rated and to assign ratings may not be easy, but a human designer must (or should have) such information before he makes a choice."

27. "For a particular problem, the decision rules may all be compatible. However, if two rules give contradictory answers, one must override. Human intervention might resolve such contradictions." Wilson and Wilson, *Information, Computers, and System Design*, p. 234.

28. Winter Interview.

29. Philip H. Abelson, "Social Responsibilities of Scientists," *Science* 167 (January 16, 1970: 1 (editorial).

30. "From one point of view, the man who programs the computer really designs the system. But it does not follow that he can always choose the best design from many possibilities." Wilson and Wilson, *Information, Computers, and System Design*, p. 236.

31. Winter, "Science of Policy," p. 20.

32. See American Anthropological Association, *Fellow Newsletter*, 8, no. 1 (January 1967), for a comprehensive map prepared by one group of specialists to navigate these troubled waters.

33. Kaplan, *American Ethics and Public Policy*, p. 103.

6. Pragmatic Appraisal

1. Edmund N. Bacon, "American Houses and Neighborhoods, City and Country," *Annals of the American Academy of Political and Social Science* (July 1968): 117-29.

2. MATHEMATICA, pp. 23-24 (emphasis in original).

3. Werner Z. Hirsch, "An Application of Area Input-Output Analysis," *Papers and Proceedings of the Regional Science Association* 5 (1959), 79-92; and Wassily Leontief, *Input-Output Economics* (New York: Oxford University Press, 1966).

4. Martin Shubik, "Simulation of Socio-Economic Systems" (New Haven: Cowles Foundation Discussion Paper #203, March 1, 1966), p. 12.

5. See Lowdon Wingo, Jr., *Transportation and Urban Land* (Washington: Resources for the Future, 1961) and Pittsburgh Area Transportation Study, *Final Report* 1 & 2 (Pittsburgh, 1961-62).

6. Ithiel de Sola Pool, Robert P. Abelson, and Samuel Popkin, *Candidates, Issues and Strategies* (Cambridge: MIT Press, 1962).

7. Kalman J. Cohen, *Computer Models of the Shoe, Leather and Hide Sequence* (Englewood Cliffs: Prentice-Hall, 1960).

8. Lawrence Klein, et al., *The Brookings Quarterly Econometric Model of the United States* (Chicago: Rand McNally, 1965).

9. George S. Fishman and P. J. Kiviat, "The Analysis of Simulation-Generated Time Series," *Management Science* 13 (March 1967): 525-57.

10. Lewis S. Feuer, "Causality in the Social Sciences," *Journal of Philosophy* 51 (November 1954): 683-84.

11. Millikan, "Inquiry and Policy," p. 172.

12. Guy H. Orcutt, Martin Greenberger, John Korbel, and Alice M. Rivlin, *Microanalysis of Socioeconomic Systems: A Simulation Study* (New York: Harper Brothers, 1961).

13. Geoffrey P. S. Clarkson, *Portfolio Selection: A Simulation of Investment Trust* (Englewood Cliffs: Prentice-Hall, 1962).

14. John P. Crecine, *Government Problem Solving* (Chicago: Rand McNally, 1969).

15. Brunner and Brewer, *Organized Complexity*.

16. Richard D. Duke and Barton Burkhalter, *The Application of Heuristic Gaming to Urban Problems* (East Lansing: Institute for Community Development, Tech. Paper #B-52, Michigan State University, January 1966).

17. Alan G. Feldt, "Operational Gaming in Planning Education," *Journal of the American Institute of Planners* 32, no. 1 (June 1966): 17-23, and Feldt, *The Cornell Land-Use Game* (Ithaca: Cornell University, October 1966).

18. Feldt, "Operational Gaming," p. 22.

19. The alert reader may recognize this as only a modern-day extension of the older and more familiar "stall-by-referral-to-commission" ploy.

20. Robert K. Merton, "The Role of Applied Social Science in the Formation of Policy: A Research Memorandum," *Philosophy of Science* 16 (July 1949): 161-81.

21. The following are examples of models that have some demonstrated policy applications. Others might be noted, but, as compared with the amount of promotional activity that exists, true policy applications are few. See the following: Balderston and Hoggatt, *Simulation of Market Processes*, and Shubik's simulation of Ecuador's socioeconomic context, "Simulation of Socio-Economic Systems," for two examples of models with potential policy applications; Henri Theil, *Economic Forecasts and Policy* (Amsterdam: Elsevier, 1961); idem, *Applied Economic Forecasting*; H. O. Stekler, "Forecasting with Econometric Models: An Evaluation," *Econometrica* 36 (1968): 437-63; and Daniel Suits, "Forecasting and Analysis with an Econometric Model," *American Economic Review* 52 (March 1962): 104-32. The Brookings Model, in one guise, has also been used in this fashion: G. Fromm and P. Taubman, *Policy Simulations with an Econometric Model* (Washington: Brookings, 1968); Norman Jennings and Justin Dickens, "Computer Simulation of Peak Hour Operations in a Bus Terminal," *Management Science* 5

(October 1958): 106-20, is a near classic application of operations research cum simulation techniques for policy purposes. A more diffuse "model" from the planning context is provided by Thomas Reiner, *The Place of the Ideal Community in Urban Planning* (Philadelphia: University of Pennsylvania Press, 1963); Edward Suchman, *Evaluative Research: Principles and Practices in Public Service and Social Action Programs* (New York: Russell Sage Foundation, 1967); and finally, Murray Geisler, "Appraisal of Laboratory Simulation Experiences," *Management Science* 8 (April 1962): 239-45.

22. Millikan, "Inquiry and Policy," pp. 172-73.

23. Merton, "Social Science in the Formation of Policy," p. 171.

24. Catherine Bauer, "Social Questions in Housing and Community Planning," *Journal of Social Issues* 7 (1951): 7.

25. Martin Shubik and Garry D. Brewer, *Questionnaire: Models, Computer Machine Simulations, Games and Studies* (Santa Monica: The RAND Corporation, P-4672, July 1971), pp. 1-3, and idem, *Models, Simulations, and Games—A Survey* (Santa Monica: The RAND Corporation, R-1060-ARPA/RC, June 1972).

PART 2

Introduction

1. New York: Doubleday Dolphin Books (1961), pp. 74-75.

2. David Easton, "An Approach to the Analysis of Political Systems," *World Politics* 9 (1957): 383.

3. "The Architecture of Complexity," in Ludwig von Bertalanffy and Anatol Rapoport, eds., *General Systems: The Yearbook of the Society for General Systems Research*, 15 vols. (New York: Braziller, 1967), 10: 63-76.

4. *Dynamic Programming and Modern Control Theory* (New York: Academic Press, 1965), p. 5.

5. George Miller, *The Psychology of Communication: Seven Essays* (New York: Basic Books, 1967), p. 42.

6. *Ibid.*, p. 49.

7. "Science and Complexity," *American Scientist* 36 (1948): 539 (emphasis in original).

8. "Planning under the Dynamic Influences of Complex Social Systems," (Paper prepared for OECD Working Symposium on Long-Range Forecasting and Planning, October 27-November 2, 1968, Bellagio, Italy), pp. 1, 5.

9. Simon, "Architecture of Complexity," p. 69.

10. *Architectural Forum* 122, Parts I & II (April and May 1965): 58-62 and 58-61.

7. On Size and Organized Complexity: Some Theoretical Considerations

1. *Great Books*, 35:107.

2. Miller, *Psychology of Communication*, p. 50.

3. *Ibid.*, pp. 49-50. See also D. B. Yntema and G. E. Mueser, "Remembering the Present States of a Number of Variables," *Journal of Experimental Psychology* 60 (1960): 18-22.

4. Jean Rostand, *Error and Deception in Science* (New York: Basic Books, 1960), p. 174.

5. John von Neumann, *The Computer and the Brain* (New Haven: Yale University Press, 1957), p. 51.

6. *Ibid.*, pp. 79-80. Other related points von Neumann discusses include these: (1) Neural stimulations on a given cell appear to be distributed across time, and neural networks appear to be redundant and randomly distributed (pp. 53-55). (2) There is not much certainty about the location, organization, or fundamental composition of human memory. Its existence is postulated upon the observable complexity of the human nervous system (p. 61).

7. L. Uhr, et al., "Pattern Recognition over Distortions by Human Subjects and a Computer Model of Human Form Perception," *Journal of Experimental Psychology* 63 (1962): 227-34.

8. George Miller, *Psychology of Communication*, p. 32. See also W. R. Garner, "An Information Analysis of Absolute Judgments of Loudness," *Journal of Experimental Psychology* 42 (1951): 538-66.

9. Miller, *Psychology of Communication*, p. 37. See also Allen Newell, J. C. Shaw, and H. A. Simon, "Chess-Playing Programs and the Problem of Complexity," *IBM Journal of Research and Development* 2 (October 1958): 321. "There is a close and reciprocal relation between complexity and communication. On the one hand, the complexity of the systems we can specify depends on the language in which we must specify them. Being human, we have only limited capacities for processing information. Given a more powerful language, we can specify greater complexity with limited processing powers."

10. Francis Bacon, *Novum Organum*, Book I, *Great Books*, 35:10

11. Weaver, "Science and Complexity," p. 536.

12. *Ibid.*, p. 538.

13. *Ibid.*, p. 539.

14. M. G. Kendall, *Journal of the Royal Statistical Society* 124A (1961): 1-16, esp. 13-14. "If a pattern is reproducible we can use it both for the control of the social organization and for prediction of the future, just as we can use Boyle's Law as a macro-phenomenon . . . However, we clearly cannot be satisfied with the mere eliciting of pattern . . . In one sense we have to aggregate to some extent to get a pattern at all. We must clearly take care not to aggregate too much. But how we know what is 'too much' is a question I cannot answer."

15. Weaver, "Science and Complexity," p. 540 (emphasis added).

16. Forrester, *"Dynamic Influences of Complex Social Systems,"* p. 3.

17. Bruchey, *American Economic Growth*, pp. 13-14.

18. Brunner and Brewer, *Organized Complexity*, Table I.1 and pp. 9-10.

19. Gabriel Almond, "Political Theory and Political Science," in Ithiel de Sola Pool, ed., *Contemporary Political Science: Toward Empirical Theory* (New York: McGraw-Hill, 1967), pp. 13-14.

20. Herbert A. Simon and Albert Ando, "Aggregation of Variables in Dynamic Systems," in Albert Ando, Franklin Fisher, and Herbert A. Simon, *Essays on the Structure of Social Science Models* (Cambridge: MIT Press, 1963), p. 85.

21. Simon, "Architecture of Complexity," p. 69.

22. On the use of matrix notation to denote structure, see Morris F. Fridell, "Organizations as Semi-lattices," *American Sociological Review* 32 (February 1967): 46-54; Ian C. Ross and Frank Harary, "Identification of Liaison Persons of an Organization Using the Structure Matrix," *Management Science* 1 (April-July 1955): 251-58; and Maynard Shelley, "The Mathematical Representation of Individuals in Models," in Cooper, et al., *New Perspectives in Organization Research* (New York: Wiley, 1962).

23. This program (and others used in the research) are available from the author. See James S. Coleman, *Introduction to Mathematical Sociology* (New York: Free Press, 1964), pp. 444-47, for a discussion of the technique.

24. Reiner, *Ideal Community in Urban Planning*.

25. Alexander, "A City Is Not a Tree," *Architectural Forum*, 122, Part II (May 1965): 60.

26. I am profoundly indebted to Todd LaPorte for discussing several of these issues and for allowing me to read and contribute to his unpublished collection, "Social Complexity: Challenge to Politics and Policy" (Berkeley: Department of Political Science, December 1969). Much of the argument that follows relies heavily on the contribution of H. Wilson, "Complexity and the Problem of Conceptual Reevaluation," to LaPorte's collection.

27. C. Walsh, *From Utopia to Nightmare* (New York: Harper and Row, 1962), p. 63, as cited in Wilson, "Complexity and Conceptual Reevaluation," p. 20.

28. Ernest Barker, ed., *The Politics of Aristotle* (Oxford University Press, 1948), pp. 50-60.

29. Robert A. Dahl, *Modern Political Analysis* (Englewood Cliffs: Prentice-Hall, 1963), p. 22.

30. R. Dahrendorf, "Out of Utopia: Toward a Reorientation of Sociological Analysis," *American Journal of Sociology* 54 (1958): 116-27.

31. Wilson, "Complexity and Conceptual Reevaluation," p. 21.

32. See Cynthia Eagle Russett, *The Concept of Equilibrium in American Social Thought* (New Haven: Yale University Press, 1966), esp. chapter 10.

33. Joan Robinson, *Economic Philosophy* (Chicago: Aldine, 1963), p. 81.

34. Robert Boguslaw, *The New Utopians: A Study of System Design and Social Change* (Englewood Cliffs: Prentice-Hall, 1965), p. 5.

35. *Ibid.*, p. 202.

36. Plato, *Laws 5*, Benjamin Jowett (trans.), in Hutchins, ed., *Great Books* 7:692.

37. The literature is fairly extensive. See Charles Tiebout, "Economies of Scale and Metropolitan Governments," *Review of Economics and Statistics* 42 (November 1960): 442-443.

38. *Introduction to Cybernetics*, p. 61.

39. Goldberg, *Introduction to Difference Equations*, p. 60, remarks: ". . .for the class of linear difference equations we can always find at least one solution and, under certain conditions, only one solution. . . . [However] some difference equations have infinitely many solutions whereas others have no solutions at all . . . "

40. See above, chapter 3.

41. Mario Bunge, "The Weight of Simplicity in the Construction and Assaying of Scientific Theories," *Philosophy of Science* 28 (April 1961): 127.

42. *Ibid.*, p. 128.

43. Ashby, *An Introduction to Cybernetics*, pp. 61-62.

44. The system is never totally connected because *Y, C, I,* and *G* never produce outputs in *N*.

45. Ashby, *An Introduction to Cybernetics*, pp. 67-68.

46. Johnston, *Econometric Methods*, pp. 5-6.

47. Robert A. Dahl and Edward R. Tufte, *Size and Democracy* (Department of Political Science, Yale University, July 1967).

48. De Jouvenal's image, *The Act of Conjecture* (New York, Basic Books, 1967).

8. On Size and Organized Complexity: Some Operational Considerations

1. De Jouvenal, *The Art of Conjecture*, p. 271.

2. See A. L. Samuel, "Some Studies in Machine Learning Using the Game of Checkers," in E. A. Feigenbaum and J. Feldman, eds., *Computers and Thought* (New York: McGraw-Hill, 1963).

3. This label was suggested by Martin Shubik. It is appropriate. Many of the insights and doubtless quite a few of the words and ideas are Shubik's as well . . . these are the costs and benefits of working closely with a colleague for intense and prolonged periods of time.

9. Disentangling the Problem-Solving Process

1. Charles E. Merriam, *New Aspects of Politics* (Chicago: University of Chicago Press, 1925), pp. 124-25.

2. Hubert M. Blalock, *Causal Inferences in Non-experimental Research* (Chapel Hill: University of North Carolina Press, 1964), p. 8.

3. David R. Seidman, *The Construction of an Urban Growth Model* (Philadelphia: Delaware River Valley Planning Commission, Plan Report #1, n.d.), pp. 54-64. This describes the famous Penn-Jersey Transportation Study efforts to model a large social system.

4. Irma Adelman and Cynthia Taft Morris, "An Econometric Model of Change in Underdeveloped Countries," *American Economic Review* (December 1968): 1184-1218.

5. Association for Computing Machinery, "President's Letter," *ACM* 13, no. 12 (December 1970): 173.

PART 3

Introduction

1. Harold D. Lasswell, "Toward a Continuing Appraisal of the Impact of Law on Society," *Rutgers Law Review* 21 (Summer 1967): 648.

2. *Ibid.*, p. 671.

3. Interview Document, October 10, 1969, p. 23.

10. The Community Renewal Program

1. *Through the Looking Glass*, p. 75.

2. William Alonso, "Cities and City Planners," *Daedalus* (Fall 1963): 824-39.

3. *Ibid.*, p. 827.

4. The interested reader is directed to this selected list:

The *public sector* thread is represented in these sources: Section 103(d), Housing Act of 1949, S.1070, 81st Congress, 1st Session [63 Stat. 414, 42 U.S.C.]; Section 405 (3), Housing Act of 1959 [73 Stat. 672, 42 U.S.C.A.]; Philadelphia Housing Association, *Ends and Means of Urban Renewal* (Report of a Series of Discussions, 1959 and 1960); Robert Weaver, "The Urban Complex," reprinted in Jewell Bellusch and M. Hausknect, eds., *Urban Renewal: People, Politics, and Planning* (Garden City: Doubleday Anchor edition, 1967), pp. 90-101; William L. Slayton, "The Operation and Achievements of the Urban Renewal Program," reprinted in James Q. Wilson, ed., *Urban Renewal: The Record and the Controversy* (Cambridge: MIT Press, 1967 edition), pp. 189-229; Jerome L. Kaufman, "The Community Renewal Program: The First Years" (Chicago: American Society of Planning Officials, Report #159, April 1962); Walter Gaby, "The Evolution of an Idea," *Planning 1966* (Chicago: Proceedings of 1966 ASPO), pp. 20-26; S. Leigh Curry, Jr., "The Community Renewal Program," *Federal Bar Journal* 21 (Summer 1961); Urban Renewal Administration, Local Planning Agency (LPA) *Letter No. 276* (Washington: August 1963); *LPA Letter No. 227* (Washington: October 1961); David A. Grossman, "The Community Renewal Program," *JAIP* 29 (November 1963): 259-69; and Hilda M. James, "History of Congressional and Related Activities Concerned with the Establishment of a Department of Urban Affairs," mimeographed (Washington: Library of Congress, 1963).

The *technical* thread is evidenced in these sources: Miles L. Colean, *Renewing Our Cities* (New York: Twentieth Century Fund, 1953); Martin Meyerson, "Building the Middle-Range Bridge for Comprehensive Planning," *JAIP* 22 (Spring 1956): 58-64; Robert Mitchell, "A New Frontier in Metropolitan Planning," *JAIP* 27 (August 1961); Herbert A. Gans, "Urban Poverty and Social Planning," in Paul Lazarsfeld, et al., eds., *The Uses of Sociology* (New York: Basic Books, 1967), pp. 437-76; C. F. Stover, "Technology for Cities," *National Civic Review* 53 (June 1964), pp. 297-300; and Harvey S. Perloff, *A National Program of Research in Housing and Urban Development* (Washington: Resources for the Future, 1961).

5. See Slayton, "Operation and Achievements," pp. 198-99.

6. Ashley A. Foard and Hilbert Fefferman, "Urban Renewal: Part I," *Law and Contemporary Problems* 25, no. 4 (Autumn 1960): around 659-62.

7. Weaver, "Urban Complex," p. 100.

8. Slayton, "Operation and Achievements," p. 198.

9. *Ibid.*, p. 199.

10. Martin Anderson's polemic, *The Federal Bulldozer* (New York: McGraw-Hill, 1967 p.b. edition), was begun in 1960 and used data up to and including 1961. His reportage captures the restive sentiments, pp. xxi-xxii.

11. Norman Beckman, "Federal Long-Range Planning: The Heritage of the National Resources Planning Board," *JAIP* 26 (1960): 89-97.

12. Philip M. Morse and C. E. Kimball, *Methods of Operations Research* (New York: Wiley, 1951).

13. Alan B. Vorhees, ed., "Land Use and Traffic Models," *JAIP* 25 (May 1959).

14. Herbert J. Gans, "Planning, Social: II. Regional and Urban Planning," in International *Encyclopedia of the Social Sciences* (New York: Free Press, 1968), 12:129-37. (Reprinted in Gans, *People and Plans*, p. 71.)

15. Philip M. Morse, ed., *Operations Research for Public Systems* (Cambridge: MIT Press, 1967), p. v.

16. A fourth and emerging strand that bears close attention is the conscience-driven natural scientist whose impeccable academic credentials provide entrée into the problem-solving, social process. That these incursions do not concern us directly is not to say that they are not potentially important.

17. Meyerson, "Building the Middle-Range Bridge."

18. Gans, "Urban Poverty and Social Planning," pp. 438-39.

19. Gaby, "Evolution of an Idea," p. 22. The total magnitude of expenditure exceeded $36 million as of February 1967.

20. Ira M. Robinson, "Beyond the Middle-Range Planning Bridge," *JAIP* 31 (November 1965): 305. Robinson was the project leader at Arthur D. Little for the San Francisco case.

21. Factual information is abstracted from several Department of City Planning memos and fact sheets and from a personal interview with the federal program manager on July 10, 1969.

22. Interview Document, July 16, 1969.

23. *Ibid.*, p. 2. The city, incidentally, elected to build its EDP facility with in-house personnel.

24. Interview Document, July 17, 1969.

25. They evidently had known one another at the University of Pennsylvania.

26. Interview Document, July 16, 1969.

27. *Ibid.*

28. Arthur D. Little, Inc., "Purpose, Scope, and Methodology," p. 6. There are few copies of this document in existence.

29. *Ibid.*, p. 11.

30. *Ibid.*, p. 12.

31. *Ibid.*, p. 13.

32. *Ibid.*

33. *Ibid.*

34. *Ibid.*, pp. 13-14.

35. *Ibid.*, p. 21.

36. *Ibid.*, pp. 45-46.

37. *Ibid.*, p. 24.

38. Factual information is taken from City of Pittsburgh, Department of City Planning, "Community Renewal Program, Amended Application," October 1962; and from the Covering Letter, Mayor Joseph M. Barr to the Housing and Home Finance Agency, dated October 5, 1962.

39. Interview Document, October 29, 1969, p. 1.

40. Interview Document, July 9, 1969, p. 8.

41. Interview Document, September 29, 1969, p. 1.

42. Interview Document, October 29, 1969.

43. *Ibid.*, p. 2. Evidence of the role that federal money played is contained in City of Pittsburgh, "Council Presentation: Simulation Model and Budget," September 26, 1962. The clinching argument for the council was fiscal: "Item #6. Costs: None to City—Feds all excited—will pay," p. 3.

44. Barr to HHFA, October 5, 1962.

45. "Amended Application," p. CR-121-21.

46. Memo, Professor Benjamin Chinitz (CRES) to Mr. Russell Jalbert, "Background Information for Meeting on March 25, 1963: THE CONTRACT."

47. Interview Document, November 3, 1969.

48. Chinitz to Jalbert, p. 3 (emphasis in original).

49. "Amended Application," p. CR-121-1.

50. *Ibid.*, p. 6.

51. *Ibid.*, p. 4.

52. *Ibid.*, p. 7

53. *Ibid.*, pp. CR-121-14 and 15.

54. See for example Neiland J. Douglas, Jr., "Data Input for Simulation" (Pittsburgh: DCP, November 10, 1964), p. 1. "The periods covered in the program will be 1960-1964, 1965-1969, 1970-1974, 1975-1980."

55. *Ibid.*, pp. CR-121-13 and 14.

56. *Ibid.*, p. CR-121-39.

57. *Ibid.*, p. CR-121-40.

58. *Ibid.*, pp. CR-121-41 through 44.

59. *Ibid.*, pp. CR-121-45 and 46.

60. Interview Document, July 24, 1969 (San Francisco).

11. San Francisco

1. ADL. CRP Brochure used as a "mailer" and "handout" for public relations.

2. Interview Document, December 11, 1969, p. 3.

3. *Ibid.*, pp. 2-3.

4. Interview Document, July 24, 1969, p. 2

5. Interview Document, July 23, 1969, p. 15

6. Interview Document, December 11, 1969, p. 1.

7. Interview Document, July 16, 1969, p. 5. Another participant's assessment of the selling skill is insightful: "He is a very effective talker particularly in terms of new concepts in planning and economics. He doesn't know the technical details, but he is quite good at not only talking but getting some excitement about it. They had a lot of confidence in him and said in effect that they would be willing to go along with this provided he was involved. He could talk the balls off a brass monkey. These guys had personal empathy with him." Interview Document, October 6, 1969, p. 12.

8. Interview Document, December 11, 1969, p. 1.

9. Interview Document, December 18, 1969, pp. 1-2.

10. Interview Document, August 12, 1969, p. 8. The prime conceptualizer "had other administrative duties," and therefore was able "to come out here [San Francisco] . . . I don't know, you could document this I suppose, every six months, maybe." Interview Document, December 18, 1969, p. 2.

11. Interview Document, December 18, 1969, p. 1.

12. Interview Document, July 23, 1969, p. 9.

13. Interview Document, October 6, 1969, p. 1.

14. Arthur D. Little, Inc., "Technical Paper #8, San Francisco Community Renewal Program," January 1966 (hereafter cited as "T.P. #8").

15. Besides the "official" accounting of the model by ADL in "T.P. #8," the interested reader is directed to the following sources of information, which are noteworthy mostly for their recitation of the points made in "T.P. #8": Arthur D. Little, *Community Renewal Programming: A San Francisco Case Study* (New York: Frederick A. Praeger, 1966), esp. chapter 8, "The Community Renewal Program Model"; Ira M. Robinson, Harry B. Wolfe, and Robert L. Barringer, "A Simulation Model for Renewal Programming," *JAIP* 31 (May 1965): 126-34; Cyril Hermann, "Using Research Experimentation to Improve the Urban Environment"(Paper presented to Symposium on Science, Engineering and the City; National Academy of Sciences, April 27, 1967) [Available from ADL, 500 Sansome Street, San Francisco, California, 9—111] ; Cyril Hermann, "Systems Approach to City Planning," *Harvard Business Review* (September-October 1966); Harry B. Wolfe and Martin L. Ernst, "Simulation Models and Urban Planning," in Philip M. Morse, ed., *Operations Research for Public Systems* (Cambridge: MIT Press, 1967), pp. 49-81; John P. Crecine, "Computer Simulation in Urban Research," *Public Administration Review* 28 (January-February 1968): 72-73; Ira S. Lowry, "Seven Models of Urban Development: A Structural Comparison," in Highway Research Board, *Urban Development Models* (Washington: HRB, National Academy of Sciences, HRB Special Report #97, 1968), pp. 141-46; Robert P. O'Block, "The San Francisco Housing Simulation Model" (Cambridge: Harvard Graduate School of Business, Case Study Materials, Spring 1968); Maurice D. Kilbridge, Robert P. O'Block, and Paul Teplitz, "A Conceptual Framework for Urban Planning Models" (Cambridge: Harvard Graduate School of Business, Case Study Materials, Spring 1968); John W. Dyckman, "The Scientific World of City Planners," *American Behavioral Scientist* 6 (February 1963); Martin L. Ernst, "Use of Simulation Models for Urban Planning—An Application to the City of San Francisco" (Paper read at OECD Symposium on "The Contribution of Operational Research to Urban and Regional Planning," Rome, December 5-7, 1966) [Available from ADL, Acorn Park, Cambridge, Massachusetts, 02140] ; Harry B. Wolfe, "Model of San Francisco Housing Market," *Socio-Economic Planning Sciences* 1 (September 1967): 71-95; and Wolfe, "Models for Condition Aging of Residential Structure, *JAIP* 33 (May 1967): 192-95.

I am deeply indebted to Mr. Maurice F. Groat of San Francisco's City Planning Department for several extended conversations and open access to his meticulously kept files, and for his report, *Status of the San Francisco Simulation Model* (San Francisco: Department of City Planning, 1968).

16. ADL, "Purpose, Scope and Methodology."

17. O'Block, "San Francisco Housing Simulation Model," pp. 11-12; and, Interview Document, July 17, 1969, p. 3.

18. Internal Memo, IMR-12-4, February 1964 (ADL memo).

19. Internal Memo, HBW to CRP Team, May 7, 1965, "Status of the CRP Model" (ADL memo).

20. See above, chapter 10.

21. "The conceptual lineage of this model [ADL/SF] is close to the household distributing model presented by Professors Herbert and Stevens in their work for the Penn-Jersey Transportation Study." "T.P. #8," p. 10. [Reference to John D. Herbert and Benjamin H. Stevens, "A

Model for the Distribution of Residential Activity in Urban Areas," *Journal of Regional Science* 2 (Fall 1960): 21-36.] Familial resemblance is not obvious to the casual observer.

22. "T.P. #8," p. 25. An interesting footnote on the sociology of knowledge is the proliferation of this citational error in other learned discussions and evaluations of the model.

23. David M. Blank and Louis Winnick, "The Structure of the Housing Market," *Quarterly Journal of Economics* 67 (May 1953): 181.

24. Internal Memo, IMR-19-3, September 18, 1964. Subject: "Working Memo 4: CRP Outputs (Part II)," p. 10.

25. "T.P. #8," pp. 5-6.

26. October 1964 (hereafter cited as "T.P. #1").

27. Interview Document, July 17, 1969, p. 23.

28. Department of City Planning, Internal Memo, April 16, 1965, "The Status of the Development of the Model for Residential Market Simulation as of April 16, 1965," p. 1.

29. ADL, "Final Report to the City Planning Commission, City and County of San Francisco, California," October 1965.

30. Groat, *San Francisco Simulation Model.*

31. "T.P. #8," p. 27. For example, income class 1—"Blacks"—is defined as $0-2000/year. Class 1—"Whites" and "Others"—ranges from $0-4000/year. Other incomparabilities exist. I presume that intragroup differentiation was judged to be more important than the establishment of bases for intergroup comparison.

32. "T.P. #8," pp. 28-29. It appears that several paragraphs have been shuffled out of sequence in ADL's account of the preference list.

33. An enumeration district is the working, practical unit assigned to a census enumerator. It represents more the expected information-collection capacity of a single person than any particular geographic or social characteristic.

34. Interview Document, July 23, 1969, p. 1.

35. ADL, "Technical Paper #3," May 1965.

36. See *ibid.,* pp. 11-13 for a full discussion. Christopher Alexander bears intellectual responsibility for these differentiations.

37. "[City Planner] I developed the original L categorization. They [ADL] had been working on that over a year trying to fit together all of the various things that they could think of that would define an L category, but when it came down to the last two weeks before the model became operational, they said, 'What are we going to do?' Given the information available, I worked out an L system that we could use." Interview Document, July 23, 1969, p. 4.

38. "T.P. #8," p. 15 (emphasis added).

39. *Ibid.*

40. *Ibid.,* p. 31.

41. ADL, "Models for Condition Aging of Residential Structures," "Technical Paper #2," November 1964, p. 2 (hereafter cited as "T.P. #2").

42. "T.P. #8," p. 20.

43. *Ibid.,* p. 24.

44. *Ibid.,* p. 23.

45. Program Listing, MOD II, run 12, January 29, 1965. See "T.P. #8," p. 24, for discussion.

46. Clarence E. Bennett, *Physics* (New York: Barnes and Noble, 1952 edition), pp. 96-101.

47. "T.P. #8," pp. 25, 27.

48. Sources for population estimation procedures are ADL, "Final Report," and "San Francisco Housing Simulation Model."

49. ADL, "Final Report," p. 5.

50. Interview Document, December 18, 1969, p. 2.

51. In a more competently executed piece of work, the 1960 population level was projected to continue its postwar decline until reaching a low of 703,712, after which time the changing age and racial composition would cause gradual increases to 710,050 by 1980. Department of City Planning, *Population Projection for San Francisco 1960-1990* (San Francisco: DCP, April 1968), p. 11. While one may debate the details of these forecasts, one does not have cause to reject them out of hand as absurd.

52. Internal Memo, #C-65400-9, January 17, 1964. Subject: "The Distribution of Rent Paying Abilities Within One User Group" (ADL memo).

53. "T.P. #2," and "Models for Condition Aging of Residential Structure."

54. Francis H. Hendricks, "The Measurement of Housing Quality for Urban Renewal" (Master's Thesis, Department of City and Regional Planning, University of California, Berkeley, 1958). In an interview Hendricks remarked: "The survey was done during the Depression at a cost of about 50 cents a unit. Today it would cost millions and it wouldn't be done as thoroughly or competently as they did; then they had all the time in the world." Interview Document, July 24, 1969, p. 9.

On the general quality of census data for use in models, see Bureau of the Census, "Working Paper #25: On the Quality of Housing Statistics" (Washington: U.S. Department of Commerce, 1967): "There does not appear to be any feasible method of improving the quality of enumerator ratings in a decennial census. This is a consequence of the ambiguities, nonoperational elements, and complexities of the rating process itself, as well as the biasing factors in the environment in which ratings have to be made." ("Working Paper #25" has had wide distribution.)

For a thorough empirical study on house decay, see John Quigley and Walter Hanson, "Residential Blight in St. Louis, Missouri" (Study prepared for the U.S. Bureau of the Budget, 1968). The 1970 census omits race questions.

55. Interview Document, July 24, 1969, p. 9.

56. Department of City Planning, *Population Projection*, pp. 5, 11.

57. See Hayward R. Alker, Jr., *Mathematics and Politics* (New York: Macmillan, 1965), pp. 104-105, on the "Contextual Fallacy."

58. "T.P. #2," p. 3. See Kaplan, *Conduct of Inquiry*, p. 28: " . . . it comes as no surprise . . . that a scientist formulates problems in a way which requires for their solution just those techniques in which he himself is especially skilled." The author of "T.P. #2" received his Ph.D. in physics.

59. "T.P. #2," p. 10.

60. Richard F. Muth, *Cities and Housing: The Spatial Pattern of Urban Residential Land Use* (Chicago: University of Chicago Press, 1969), pp. 130-35; "Implications of Slum Housing for the Spatial Pattern of Land Use," p. 130.

61. Leo Grebler, *Housing Market Behavior in a Declining Area: Long-Term Changes in Inventory and Utilization of Housing on New York's Lower East Side* (New York: Columbia University Press, 1952), pp. 14-15, 17.

62. See above, pp. 38-40.

63. See A. E. Fitzgerald and David E. Higginbotham, *Basic Electrical Engineering* (New York: McGraw-Hill, 1957 edition), pp. 172-75.

64. I have deliberately cited theoretical works that were available at the time of the project, i.e. work that could have been utilized. Sherman J. Maisel, "A Theory of Fluctuations in Residential Construction Starts" *American Economic Review* 53 (June 1963): 359-83.

65. Chester Rapkin, Louis Winnick, and David Blank, *Housing Market Analysis, A Study of Theory and Methods* (Washington: HHFA, Division of Housing Research, December 1953), pp. 22-23.

66. Luigi Laurenti, *Property Values and Race* (Berkeley: University of California Press, 1960).

67. Richard F. Muth, "The Demand for Non-Farm Housing," in A. C. Harberger, ed., *The Demand for Durable Goods* (Chicago: University of Chicago Press, 1960).

68. Wallace F. Smith, *Aspects of Housing Demand—Absorption, Demolition, and Differentiation* (Berkeley: Center for Real Estate and Urban Economics, 1966), pp. 52, 48-49).

69. There is every indication that the choice between rehabilitation and new construction is far more political than economic in character. Harold Kaplan, *Urban Renewal Politics: Slum Clearance in Newark* (New York: Columbia University Press, 1963), pp. 23-38; and James Q. Wilson, "Planning and Politics: Citizen Participation in Urban Renewal," *JAIP* 29 (November 1963): 242-49. The model, of course, overlooks any of this.

70. Jack Guttentag, "The Short Cycle in Residential Construction, 1946-1959," *American Economic Review* 51 (June 1961): 291.

71. Arthur F. Burns, "Long Cycles in Residential Construction," in *Essays in Honor of Wesley C. Mitchell* (New York: Columbia University Press, 1935), pp. 65-104. See also, J. B. Dirksen, "Long Cycles in Residential Building: An Explanation," *Econometrica* 8 (1940); W. H. Newman, "The Building Industry and Business Cycles," *Journal of Business* (University of Chicago, 1935); and Clarence Long, *Business Cycles and the Theory of Investment* (Princeton: Princeton University Press, 1940).

72. Rapkin, et al., *Housing Market Analysis*, p. 27.

73. Internal Memo, JWM-15-1, May 7, 1964. Subject: "Construction and Rent" (ADL memo). In another interesting memo bearing on increased property valuation and rehabilitation costs, it was determined that "the ratio of changes in assessment to the estimated cost of work done under a building permit varied from a high of +1600% to a low of .9% with most census tracts showing a range in this ratio in excess of 100%." Internal Memo, DB-22-1, December 11, 1964. Subject: "Valuation of Property." Data, in other words, were terrible.

74. Interview Document, July 24, 1969, p. 3.

75. Personal Letter, City Planning Department, June 15, 1970.

76. Internal Memo, DB-16-1, June 3, 1964. Subject: "Conclusions Re. Yield" (ADL memo).

77. See above, "Theoretical Appraisal: Processing. Step Five."

78. Model Data, Input Listing, p. 51.

79. Internal Memo, CG-26-1, April 9, 1965. Subject: "Limitations and Alterations in the Existing Model," p. 2, para. C (ADL memo).

80. Internal Memo, HBW to CRP Team, June 15, 1965. Subject: "Modifications for MOD III." This same point turned up in many of the interviews, exemplified in the following informed observations: "The data were not accurate. Some of the data were changed almost orders of magnitude several different times. That will show you how accurate it was. . . . If the data are lousy anyway, there is no point in going on . . . it's hopeless. If the data don't mean anything [pause] the model is only as good as the data." Interview Document, July 18, 1969, p. 9.

81. ADL, "Technical Paper #4: Estimated Costs for New Construction and Rehabilitation of Existing Residential Structures," June 1965.

82. Letter from Mark W. Eudey to James R. McCarthy, Director of City Planning, July 22, 1965, p. 1, Appendix p. 2.

83. See above, Part 1.

84. Interview Document, August 12, 1969, p. 4.

85. *Ibid.*

86. Interview Document, December 18, 1969, p. 3.

87. Interview Document, December 11, 1969, p. 7.

88. *Ibid.*, p. 8.

89. Interview Document, July 23, 1969, p. 2.

90. Interview Document, August 12, 1969, p. 7.

91. Interview Document, August 18, 1969, p. 2.

92. Interview Document, October 6, 1969, pp. 13-14.

93. Interview Document, December 5, 1969, p. 11.

94. Interview Document, July 18, 1969, p. 7.

95. *Ibid.*, pp. 9-10. "I had to call a halt to ADL's structural modifications in order to proceed with the programming. They kept bugging me to the point where I was spending a great deal of time just reprogramming around their changes."

96. In response to a question on computer skill, only six of the eighteen principal San Francisco respondents would claim ability to " . . . write a computer program—beginning with flow charts, proceeding with coding, and including debugging and running—of some social process." Out of these six, only three claimed to have "excellent" command of *any* computer language. As one respondent stated in extolling the programmer's skill virtue: "It is interesting with all of the people who were involved with the project, how very few knew what the model was all about. He did." Interview Document, July 17, 1969, p. 8. Citation is from Interview Document, October 6, 1969, p. 17.

97. Interview Document, July 17, 1969, pp. 10-11.

98. *Ibid.*, p. 23.

99. ADL, *Community Renewal Programming*, pp. 196-97. In a later version it was stated: "The model was therefore calibrated to the construction activity in San Francisco during the period 1960-1964 by an extensive series of tuning runs." Harry B. Wolfe and Martin L. Ernst, "Simulation Models and Urban Planning," in Morse, ed., *Operations Research for Public Systems*, p. 58.

100. ADL Staff Memo from Cyril Hermann to CRP Staff, June 4, 1965.

101. Model Listing, version 12, p. 126. "Dangling Vector," p. 86. One waggish participant suggested that it might be "a loose thread depending [hanging] from the worn sharkskin suit of

your typical bureaucrat." At least that is an explanation with an empirical referent. ADL fails to mention it.

102. See relationships (11.2) and (11.3), above.

103. Internal Memo, CG-26-1, April 9, 1965 (ADL memo).

104. *Ibid.*

105. *San Francisco Simulation Model*, p. 27.

106. Interview Document, December 5, 1969, pp. 2-3.

107. "T.P. #8," pp. 36-43.

108. *Ibid.*, p. 40.

109. Interview Document, December 5, 1969, p. 7.

110. Eudey to McCarthy, July 22, 1965.

111. This phenomenon has been documented in a report by David Bradwell Associates of Berkeley, California, for the Department of City Planning on the "Housing Stock of San Francisco, 1969." The house market of San Francisco is very much related to migrational patterns and is highly interrelated with the housing stock and market of the contiguous region. My thanks to David Bradwell for this point.

112. The CRP, constricted by federal guidelines, encourages this separation and isolation of a recipient city from its inclusive environment.

113. See Wolfe and Ernst, in Morse, ed., *Operations Research for Public Systems*, p. 57.

114. "T.P. #1," p. 14.

115. *Ibid.*

116. Wallace F. Smith notes that race may be an important source of market imperfection to the extent that mortgage-lenders practice discrimination. The model ignores this. See Smith, *Aspects of Housing Demand*, p. 49.

117. On investment decision-making in construction see Long, *Business Cycles and the Theory of Investment.*

118. One of the many striking innovations contained in the work of Frederick E. Balderston and Austin C. Hoggatt, *Simulation of Market Processes*, is their explicit consideration of the information problem in terms of bid-ask message interactions. This work was done at Berkeley, was well-known as early as 1962, and would have provided invaluable insights for the management of this deficiency. ADL, however, did not incorporate it.

119. Interview Document, July 24, 1969, p. 2.

120. Interview Document, July 23, 1969, p. 5.

121. Interview Document, December 18, 1969, p. 7.

122. Interview Document, December 5, 1969, p. 11.

123. *Ibid.* p. 6.

124. Interview Document, December 18, 1969, p. 3.

125. Interview Document, October 6, 1969, p. 9.

126. Interview Document, July 24, 1969, p. 10.

127. Interview Document, December 5, 1969, p. 8.

128. Interview Document, December 11, 1969, p. 4.

129. *Ibid.*

130. Internal Memo, Department of City Planning, "The Status of the Development of the Model for Residential Market Simulation as of April 16, 1965," p. 3.

131. Interview Document, December 11, 1969, p. 11.

132. Interview Document, July 24, 1969, p. 2.

133. *Ibid.*

134. The "trained group of specialists" turns out to be the *one* junior planner, whose technical competency differs considerably from that advertised by ADL. In his own words: "It is true that I know more about the model than anyone except those involved in its formulation and execution. But that is a far step from having knowledge sufficient to operate, modify, and generally administer this model. . . . I never claimed the competence [ADL] has attributed to me." "Status of Development of Model," p. 3.

135. Letter from Dr. Claude Gruen, urban economist, Arthur D. Little, to George M. Belknap, Department of Housing and Urban Development, dated April 7, 1966.

136. *Ibid.*

137. Letter from Warren H. Deem, Arthur D. Little, to Charles M. Haar, Assistant Secretary for Metropolitan Development, Department of Housing and Urban Development, dated July 29, 1966, p. 1 (paras. 2-4), p. 2 (para. 2), p. 5.

138. Interview Document, July 24, 1969, p. 8. People change, too. Two key backers of a research component in the CRP were out of the picture. "At that point [1963] they didn't have any R&D money, and they were using the CRP in an R&D way. But there was no possibility that we could follow through once they ran out of funds. They didn't happen to pick a very conducive atmosphere [San Francisco] to try out their R&D." Interview Document, December 18, 1969, p. 4.

139. Interview Document, December 18, 1969, p. 5.

140. See Ronald D. Brunner, "Some Comments on Simulating Theories of Political Development," in William Coplin, ed., *Simulations of Decision Makers' Environments* (Chicago: Markham, 1968).

141. Interview Document, July 17, 1969, pp. 3,8.

142. Interview Document, December 5, 1969, p. 1.

143. Interview Document, December 18, 1969, p. 2.

144. Interview Document, October 6, 1969, pp. 14-15.

145. Interview Document, July 17, 1969, p. 21.

146. Interview Document, July 22, 1969, p. 6.

147. Interview Document, December 18, 1969, p. 6.

148. Interview Document, December 5, 1969, pp. 1,5.

149. Interview Document, December 18, 1969, p. 9.

150. Interview Document, July 17, 1969, p. 17.

151. Interview Document, July 22, 1969, p. 4.

152. See above, Part 1.

153. As an aside, it is worth noting that in the course of my doing the field research for this inquiry, Planning Director Allan Jacobs invited me to undertake this task. However, after reading my description of the project and assessment of the model, he curtly withdrew his invitation. It is a pity because the model is still undocumented satisfactorily.

154. Television Station KQED, San Francisco, "Profile Bay Area," television program, June, 1965.

155. Interview Document, December 18, 1969, p. 8.

156. Interview Document, December 11, 1969, pp. 9-10.

157. Interview Document, December 18, 1969, p. 8.

158. *Ibid.*

12. Pittsburgh

1. Interview Document, October 23, 1969, p. 3.

2. *Ibid.*, pp. 3-4.

3. Interview Document, October 21, 1969, p. 2 (emphasis added).

4. Interview Document, October 23, 1969, p. 5.

5. *Ibid.* "The selling point was that it wasn't going to cost us anything. The Federal Government was underwriting it. They were very enthusiastic about the idea."

6. "I didn't have any experience, but I did need the money [$7,000 per year]. So I applied for the job and got it." Interview Document, September 29, 1969, p. 2.

7. *Ibid.*

8. Interview Document, July 9, 1969, p. 1.

9. *Ibid.*, p. 2.

10. Interview Document, January 29, 1970, p. 5.

11. Interview Document, October 29, 1969, pp. 3-4.

12. Cf. above, chapter 10.

13. By November, 1963, the Pittsburgh and San Francisco paradigms were already being extolled—publicly in David A. Grossman, "The Community Renewal Program: Policy Development, Progress and Problems," *JAIP* 29 (November 1963): 259-69, esp. 264-65, 268; and administratively in Urban Renewal Administration, *LPA Letter No. 276* (August 19, 1963), "Revised Policies for Community Renewal Programs."

14. Interview Document, October 29, 1969, p. 4.

15. *Ibid.*, p. 3.

16. Interview Document, November 18, 1969, p. 4.

17. Only two of CONSAD's eight members were full-time employees at CONSAD, Steger and Snoyer. The others retained jobs with other firms, awaiting expansion of CONSAD's

activities. The following summarizes, according to the CONSAD of California Corp., *Plans and Programs of the CONSAD Corporation: Capabilities, Organization, Scientific Composition, Experience, and R & D Effort* (Santa Monica: CONSAD CTR 62-1, n.d.), the work being done by CONSAD personnel just prior to Pittsburgh. R. S. Snoyer: "Active in weapon and space logistics studies, financial advice to business community and investment organizations. Also specializes in Government contract and procurement practices. Participates in advance planning activities for contemplated major weapon and space programs" (p. 99). Stanley Deutsch: "Active in the fields of systems and missions analysis, mission profiling, engineering psychology, man-machine interaction, . . . active in the identification and technical description of manned space system for both outer space and inner space systems" (p. 102). Wilbur Steger: "Application of computer and manned simulation techniques to research problems in areas of logistics, weapon system analysis; tax policies and planning for emerging nations; general business application of simulation techniques; *urban renewal planning and techniques*; reliability and cost analyses for complex systems; the creative aspects of management systems; long-range oceanographic planning and operations" (p. 110; emphasis added).

18. Interview Document, October 30, 1969, p. 5.

19. *Ibid.*, p. 6.

20. Interview Document, September 29, 1969, p. 5.

21. Interview Document, November 18, 1969, p. 4.

22. Wilbur A. Steger, "A Proposed Use of Simulation Experimentation Techniques in the Pittsburgh Urban Renewal Planning Process" (Santa Monica: CONSAD TP 62-110, May 1962).

23. *Ibid.*, p. 4.

24. Interview Document, July 9, 1969, p. 4.

25. See above, chapter 10, note 43.

26. Wilbur A. Steger, "Review of Analytic Techniques for the CRP," *JAIP* 31 (May 1965): 166-72; idem, "The Pittsburgh Urban Renewal Simulation Model," *JAIP* 31 (May 1965): 144-50; idem, "Analytic Techniques to Determine the Needs and Resources for Urban Renewal Action," *Proceedings of the IBM Scientific Computing Symposium on Simulation Models and Gaming* (Yorktown Heights, N.Y.: IBM, December 1964), pp. 79-95; idem, "Urban Simulation: Taking Stock of the Recent Past," (Lawrence, Kansas: Center for Regional Studies, University of Kansas, December 1967); John P. Crecine, "Spatial Location Decisions and Urban Structure: A Time-Oriented Model" (Ann Arbor: Institute of Public Policy Studies, Discussion Paper No. 4, March 1969); Charles L. Leven and Bruce E. Newling, "Employment, Income, and Population Submodels," *CRP Progress Report #4* (Pittsburgh: CRES, January 1964); Stephen H. Putnam, "Industrial Location Model (INIMP)," *CRP Technical Bulletin No. 5* (Pittsburgh: CONSAD, December 1963); idem, "Intra-Urban Industrial Location Model Design and Implementation," *Papers and Proceedings of the Regional Science Association* 19 (1967): 199-214; Bruce E. Newling, "Population Projections for Pittsburgh to 1980," *CRP Technical Bulletin No. 8* (Pittsburgh: CRES, September 1964); and Wilbur A. Steger and Neiland J. Douglas, Jr., "Simulation Model," *CRP Progress Report No. 5* (Pittsburgh: CONSAD & Department of City Planning, January 1964).

27. Steger, works cited in note 26 above.

28. *CRP Progress Report Number 15*, pp. 8-9, and opposite p. 1.

29. Interview Document, November 18, 1969, p. 5.

30. Interview Document, July 9, 1969, p. 7.

31. Interview Document, November 18, 1969, p. 9.

32. Interview Document, April 14, 1969, p. 1. "I did nearly *all* the simulation modeling in that project. . . . I feel *very* strongly about the highly dysfunctional nature of expediency." Personal Correspondence, February 13, 1969.

33. Interview Document, October 22, 1969, p. 2.

34. Interview Document, November 18, 1969, p. 37.

35. Steger, "Proposed Use of Simulation Experimentation Techniques," pp. 8-9.

36. Steger and Douglas, "Simulation Model," p. 4.

37. Steger, "Pittsburgh Urban Renewal Simulation Model," p. 144.

38. Steger, "Analytic Techniques for the CRP," p. 167.

39. "The strongest reason for using this [regional] area is the large amount of material which has been collected for it . . . " C. L. Leven, *CRP Progress Report No. 4*, p. 2. See Leven, "Regional Income and Product Accounts: Construction and Applications," in Werner Hoch-

wald, ed., *Design of Regional Accounts* (Baltimore: Johns Hopkins, 1961), pp. 148-95 for a discussion of the relative advantages of each approach.

40. *CRP Progress Report No. 4*, p. 5.

41. *Ibid.*, p. 6.

42. *Ibid.*, p. 4.

43. Telephone conversation with Professor Edgar Hoover, October 16, 1969. Hoover, a distinguished economist of the highest reputation, did not participate, although his reputation and name were liberally used by his subordinates, according to several respondents. My impression is that Hoover would just as soon forget that the CRP ever existed. He declined to be interviewed.

44. *CRP Progress Report No. 4*, p. 5.

45. Interview Document, November 18, 1969, pp. 11-12.

46. Interview Document, October 23, 1969, pp. 35-36.

47. *Ibid.*, p. 36.

48. INIMP was originally reported in *CRP Technical Bulletin No. 5*, (December 1963). A far more comprehensive treatment is offered in Putman, "Intra-Urban Industrial Location Model." Special thanks are due Mr. Putman for providing a listing of INIMP and for yielding to a thoughtful, detailed interview.

49. Putman, "Intra-Urban Industrial Location Model," p. 8 (manuscript version).

50. *Ibid.*, p. 9.

51. *Ibid.*, p. 11.

52. The literature comes from business administration and decision-making. Benjamin Chinitz and Raymond Vernon, "Changing Forces in Industrial Location," *Harvard Business Review* (January-February 1960); C. R. Wasson, *The Economics of Managerial Decisions: Profit Opportunity Analysis* (New York: McGraw-Hill, 1965); M. H. Spencer and L. Siegelman, *Managerial Economics: Decision Making and Forward Planning* (Homewood: Richard D. Irwin, 1964); Delbert J. Duncan and Charles Phillips, *Retailing: Principles and Methods* (Homewood: Irwin, 1967 edition), chap. 4, "Site Location"; Kevin Lynch, *Site Planning* (Cambridge: MIT Press, 1965); and Beryl Robichaud, *Selecting, Planning, and Managing Office Space* (New York: McGraw-Hill, 1958).

53. John F. Kain and John R. Meyer, "Computer Simulations, Physio-Economic Systems, and Intra-Regional Models" (Harvard: Program on Regional and Urban Economics, Discussion Paper #25, December 1967), p. 13. This is not to say that there has been *no* attention given the problems. Quite the contrary, there is a body of theoretical literature explaining patterns of industrial location. As with the decision-making literature, the work on patterns tends to be abstract, to deal with highly aggregated concepts, and to be unsuitable for use in a small-area forecasting model like INIMP. In other words, the model demands more theoretical rigor by virtue of the number, scale, and configuration of its incorporated variables than extant theory is able to supply. See Edgar M. Hoover, *Location of Economic Activity* (New York: McGraw-Hill, 1948); Walter Isard, *Location and Space Economy* (Cambridge: MIT Press, 1956); and August Lösch (Wolfgang Stolper, trans.), *The Economics of Location* (New Haven: Yale University Press, 1954).

54. Interview Document, October 22, 1969, p. 6.

55. In about one week of work a modified version of the model was made to run on Yale's 7040/7094 Direct Couple System. Running times, using 5 SIC types, five years, twenty-five tracts, and hypothetical data were consistently under two minutes.

56. I had neither Pittsburgh data inputs nor sufficient computer time to do otherwise. Given the known poor quality of the Pittsburgh data, it is probably an "adequate" compromise.

57. Putman, "Intra-Urban Industrial Location Model," p. 28.

58. This static bias may be modified slightly by manipulating site attribute weights and by adjusting ranges of criterion values or thresholds. The assessment nonetheless holds.

59. Morton Grodzins, *The Metropolitan Area as a Racial Problem* (Pittsburgh: University of Pittsburgh Press, 1958); and Karl E. Taeuber and Alma F. Taeuber, *Negroes in Cities* (Chicago: Aldine, 1965).

60. See above. The author, now a research associate in city and regional planning at the University of Pennsylvania, intends to use INIMP in this fashion.

61. Steger, "Pittsburgh Urban Renewal Simulation Model," p. 144.

62. Interview Document, October 22, 1969, p. 6.

63. Interview Document, October 23, 1969, p. 15.

64. Interview Document, October 21, 1969, p. 6. In fairness, one can hardly expect more when the city was then willing to pay only *$7,000 per year.*

65. Interview Document, October 22, 1969, p. 1.

66. See above, chapter 12, note 4.

67. Interview Document, November 18, 1969, p. 11.

68. Interview Document, October 21, 1969, p. 7.

69. Interview Document, September 29, 1969, p. 8.

70. Ira S. Lowry, *A Model of Metropolis* (Santa Monica: The RAND Corporation, RM-4035-PR, August 1964). Reported at an earlier stage of development as Ira S. Lowry, *Design for an Intra-Regional Locational Model* (Pittsburgh: Pittsburgh Regional Planning Association, September, 1960); and, to cite its earliest intellectual antecedent, Ira S. Lowry, "Residential Location in Urban Areas" (Ph.D. diss., Department of Economics, University of California, Berkeley, 1959).

71. Lowry departed for The RAND Corporation in January, 1963, and did not participate in the Pittsburgh CRP, although "with my consent but with no direct involvement [Steger] took over my model as one component of the much larger structure that he was building. I had nothing to do with what he did and what his people did thereafter. I don't even recall being called in as a critic after that." Interview Document, July 10, 1969, p. 1.

72. Indeed, much of the TOMM write-up and most of the modeled variables are the same. *CRP Technical Bulletin No. 6.*

73. Lowry, *Model of Metropolis*, p. 128. Lowry's self-assessment of the limitations of his work is worthy of praise and emulation.

74. Gerald A. P. Carrothers, "An Historical Review of the Gravity Potential Concepts of Human Interaction," *JAIP* 22 (May 1956): 94.

75. Relationships are from Lowry, *Model of Metropolis*, pp. 10-19. Notation for TOMM differs only insignificantly.

76. Interview Document, July 10, 1969, p. 1.

77. Carrothers, "Gravity Potential Concepts of Human Interaction."

78. John Q. Stewart, "Empirical Mathematical Rules Concerning the Distribution and Equilibrium of Population," *Geographical Review* 37 (1947): 464-85; and Stewart, "Demographic Gravitation: Evidence and Applications," *Sociometry* 11 (February 1948): 31-58.

79. Morton Schneider, "Gravity Models and Trip-Distribution Theory," *Papers and Proceedings of the Regional Science Association* 5 (1959): 51-56; and William L. Garrison, "Estimates of the Parameters of Spatial Interaction," *Papers and Proceedings of the Regional Science Association* 2 (1956): 280-90.

80. David L. Huff, "The Use of Gravity Models in Social Research," in Massarik and Ratoosh, *Mathematical Exploration*, p. 317.

81. Lowry, *Model of Metropolis*, p. 131. And on data (p. 132): "The original design of the Pittsburgh Model was tailored directly to the data-bank of the Pittsburgh Area Transportation Study [regional] which offered as much small-area detail (particularly about employment) as was available anywhere in the nation. Even so, I was forced to assume an implausible level of reliability for small-area samples . . . "

82. Information is derived primarily from *CRP Technical Bulletin No. 6.*

83. See Wilbur R. Thompson, *A Preface to Urban Economics* (Baltimore: Johns Hopkins University Press, 1965), pp. 27-31, for some comments on demand analysis.

84. *CRP Technical Bulletin No. 6*, p. 10. For unknown reasons, TOMM changed Lowry's (T_{ij}) to (Y_{ij}). For clarity's sake, the original is retained to indicate the distribution index of accessibility.

85. *Ibid.*, pp. 12, 17.

86. *Ibid.*, pp. 12, 16.

87. *Ibid.*, p. 12. What is apparently being simulated is the idea that large collections of households will tend to attract more of their own type than small collections. If so, then some means of comparison between tracts and some maximum of households/type/tract are called for.

88. Pittsburgh has 189 census tracts. The model operated with three retail and six household types. That is to say, $(189)(188)(3)(6) = 639,576$, or 532,980 more bits than if there were no household disaggregation.

89. Charles M. Tiebout, "The Urban Economic Base Reconsidered," and "The Community Income Multiplier: A Case Study," in Ralph Pfouts, ed., *The Techniques of Urban Economic Analysis* (West Trenton, N.J.: Chandler-Davis, 1960), pp. 279-89, 341-58.

90. I am indebted to Ira S. Lowry for calling my attention to this point.

91. Management and Economic Research Inc., for Office of Regional Development Planning, *Industrial Location as a Factor in Regional Economic Development* (Washington: U.S. Department of Commerce, 1967).

92. Emphasis added. Michael A. Stegman, "Accessibility Models and Residential Location," *JAIP* 35 (January 1969): 24-25. Stegman's zeal to reject accessibility obscures the importance of the idea in other contexts. See above, chapter 11, "Ethical Appraisal." Accessibility is one of many images, but should not be solely depended upon.

93. Karl W. Deutsch, *The Nerves of Government: Models of Political Communication and Control* (New York: The Free Press, 1966 paperback edition), p. 150; idem, *Nationalism and Social Communication* (Cambridge: MIT Press, 1953), pp. 70-74; and Richard Meier, *A Communications Theory of Urban Growth* (Cambridge: MIT Press, 1962).

94. F. Stuart Chapin, Jr., "Activity Systems and Urban Structure: A Working Scheme," *JAIP* 34 (January 1968): 11-12.

95. Walter F. Martin reports that of 832 households interviewed, the major reasons for choosing a particular residential site were: "best buy at the time (24.4 percent), "only place available" (18.1 percent), "liked the neighborhood" (12.5 percent), "close to work" (7.5 percent), and "liked the house" (6.2 percent). *The Rural-Urban Fringe: A Study of Adjustment to Residential Location* (Eugene: University of Oregon Press, 1953), passim.

96. "Report on Summer Work—June to September, 1966" (Pittsburgh: Douglass B. Lee, Jr., Department of City Planning, 1966).

97. *Ibid.*, p. 5.

98. Interview Document, October 21, 1969, p. 10. "Q: What about documentation of the models here? I mean a listing of the model, a manual on how to run ... A: Not a chance. We never got to that point. We never even got close." (City planning technician charged with models and data management.)

99. Lowry, *Model of Metropolis*, p. 129.

100. Reported in CONSAD Research Corp., "Impact on Allegheny County Due to the Relocation of Residential and Commercial Activity in the East Street Valley" (Pittsburgh: Department of City Planning, March 8, 1967).

101. Letter, March 17, 1967.

102. CONSAD, "Impact on Allegheny County," p. 5.

103. *Ibid.*, p. 9.

104. Steger, "Urban Simulation," p. 12. Steger went on to list five "applications" of the models. Given the poor to nonexistent nature of the data base, the limited theoretical content, and the dubious technical quality of the models, it could be disastrous if anyone in fact *were* acting on the results.

105. Stegman, "Accessibility Models and Residential Location," p. 25.

106. Lowry, *Model of Metropolis*, p. 124. "Broadly speaking, the model generates a more symmetrical metropolis than actually exists."

107. Carroll, *Through the Looking Glass*, p. 100.

108. We may be moving full circle in this regard. The early efforts of Wesley C. Mitchell and the National Bureau of Economic Research and the highly productive work of C. E. Merriam at Chicago in political science had as a common characteristic a deep concern for system *change through time*. Social science, one must agree, flowered under these men and did so without benefit of electronic computers. Perhaps statistical analysis has been diversionary, causing us to formulate research in forms more amenable to techniques—to the detriment of the analytical issues.

109. Interview Document, October 22, 1969, p. 10.

110. Interview Document, April 14, 1969, p. 1.

111. Duke, his game, most of his staff, his Lansing, Michigan, data base, and his computer moved from Michigan State University to the University of Michigan. The mating of TOMM and METRO at Ann Arbor is reported in Duke and Paul Ray, "The Environment of Decision Makers in Urban Simulations," in William Coplin, ed., *Simulations of Decision Maker's Environments* (Chicago: Markham, 1969).

112. John P. Crecine, "Spatial Location Decisions and Urban Structure."

113. Interview Document, October 23, 1969, pp. 21-22.

114. Interview Document, October 22, 1969, pp. 4-5.

115. *Ibid.*, pp. 10-11.

116. Interview Document, July 10, 1969, p. 8.
117. Lowry, *Model of Metropolis*, p. 134.
118. Interview Document, October 22, 1969, pp. 5-6.
119. *Ibid.*, p. 2.
120. Interview Document, January 29, 1970, p. 7.
121. Interview Document, July 9, 1969, p. 12.
122. Interview Document, October 21, 1969, p. 6.
123. Interview Document, September 29, 1969, p. 9.
124. Interview Document, October 23, 1969, p. 33.
125. Interview Document, October 22, 1969, p. 7.
126. Interview Document, October 21, 1969, pp. 4-5.
127. See above, chapter 10, "Pittsburgh's CRP, Technics: Methods and Promises."
128. Interview Document, November 13, 1969, p. 1.
129. Interview Document, November 18, 1969, p. 6.
130. *Ibid.*
131. Interview Document, October 30, 1969, p. 8.
132. *Ibid.*
133. Interview Document, October 21, 1969, p. 9.
134. Interview Document, January 29, 1970, pp. 15-16.
135. Interview Document, October 27, 1969, p. 18.
136. Interview Document, November 18, 1969, p. 7.
137. Interview Document, July 9, 1969, p. 5.
138. See above, chapter 3.
139. Interview Document, October 27, 1969, p. 9.
140. Interview Document, October 30, 1969, p. 7.
141. Interview Document, October 22, 1969, p. 10.
142. Interview Document, July 9, 1969, p. 5.
143. *Ibid.* p. 6.
144. Interview Document, October 21, 1969, pp. 5-6.
145. *Ibid.*, p. 6.
146. Interview Document, October 23, 1969, pp. 26-27.
147. Interview Document, July 9, 1969, p. 8 (emphasis added).
148. Interview Document, January 29, 1970, p. 13.
149. Interview Document, September 29, 1969, p. 5.
150. Interview Document, January 29, 1970, p. 7.
151. *Ibid.* p. 5.
152. Interview Document, September 29, 1969, p. 1.
153. Interview Document, April 14, 1969, p. 2.
154. Interview Document, January 29, 1970, p. 9.
155. Interview Document, October 22, 1969, pp. 1, 3.
156. Interview Document, October 29, 1969, p. 10.
157. *Ibid.*, p. 12.
158. Interview Document, July 9, 1969, p. 8.
159. *Ibid.*, p. 5.
160. Interview Document, October 29, 1969, p. 6.
161. Interview Document, October 30, 1969, p. 10.
162. Interview Document, October 22, 1969, p. 18.
163. See above, "INIMP, Pragmatic Appraisal."
164. Interview Document, October 22, 1969, p. 9.
165. *Ibid.*, p. 2. This attitude is stated publicly by the new director in his ironically titled, "Social Change in Pittsburgh," *Planning 1968* (May 4-9, 1968), pp. 59-67. " . . . Pittsburgh, and many other cities, with the help of well-intentioned experts and professionals, have been examining their social navels for years" (p. 59).

13. The Problem-Solving Process

1. Kenneth E. Boulding, *The Image: Knowledge in Life and Society* (Ann Arbor: University of Michigan Press, 1956) p. 107.

2. The general range of interview questions is suggested in Appendix B.

3. Thomas Brewer, et al., "The Lasswell Value Dictionary," mimeographed and cards (New Haven: Yale University, Political Science Research Library, 1967 edition).

4. Harold D. Lasswell, "The Study of Political Elites," in Lasswell and Lerner, *World Revolutionary Elites*, pp. 88-89.

5. These are four of Harold Lasswell's notorious value categories. See Lasswell and Kaplan, *Power and Society*, and Brewer, "Lasswell Value Dictionary."

6. A fuller technical description and literature summary is contained in Appendix C.

7. See above, chapter 6.

8. The label was used in a related descriptive exercise by Morton Lustig, "Thorns in the Rosebush," *Planning 1966* (April 17-21, 1966), p. 28.

9. R. P. Abelson and John Tukey, "Efficient Conversion of Nonmetric Information into Metric Information," *Proceedings American Statistical Association Meetings (Social Statistics Section), 1959*, pp. 229-30.

10. George Herbert Mead, *The Philosophy of the Act* (Chicago: University of Chicago Press, 1938). Several variables were not quite appropriate; suitable "estimates" were made in those two or three instances.

11. The major adjustment was a further reduction in average interrespondent distance in the southeast quadrant.

12. See Yehezkel Dror, "Teaching of Policy Sciences: Design for a Doctorate University Program" (Santa Monica: The RAND Corporation, P-4128-1, November 1969); and idem, *Public Policymaking Reexamined* (San Francisco: Chandler, 1968), pp. 163-96.

13. Interview Document, October 20, 1969, pp. 3-6 passim.

14. Lasswell, "World Revolution of Our Time," p. 77.

15. *Ibid.*, p. 91.

16. Interview Document, July 22, 1969, p. 5.

17. Wilson and Wilson, *Information, Computers, and System Design*, pp. 134, 136.

18. Edward E. Furash, "The Problem of Technology Transfer," in Raymond A. Bauer and Kenneth J. Gergen, eds., *The Study of Policy Formation* (New York: The Free Press, 1968), pp. 322-24.

19. A comment made by a local official; see above, chapter 12, note 97.

20. See above, chapter 1, note 3.

14. Expanding the Focus of Attention: Some Recommendations

1. Berger, *The Precarious Vision* (Garden City: Doubleday, 1961), p. 83.

2. Richard M. Zettel and Richard R. Carll, *Summary Review of Major Metropolitan Area Transportation Studies in the United States* (Berkeley: Institute of Transportation and Traffic Engineering, November, 1962). The report, unfortunately, is out of print.

3. Interview Document, October 22, 1969, pp. 4-5.

4. This argument has been made most convincingly by Donald T. Campbell, "Reforms as Experiments," *American Psychologist* 24 (April 1969): 428.

5. See above, chapter 3.

6. Geoffrey P. S. Clarkson, *Portfolio Selection: A Simulation of Investment Trust*, offers an excellent, clear paradigm for these activities. We do not mean to imply that these protocols need be programmed and run as formal models. Some may, but the bulk of the activity will never progress, nor will we want it to progress, that far.

7. I am indebted to Ira S. Lowry of The RAND Corporation, himself a careful innovator, for a detailing of this possibility.

8. Dahl and Lindblom *Politics, Economics, and Welfare*, pp. 74-76.

9. Ira S. Lowry, Interview Document, July 10, 1969, p. 3.

10. I am indebted to David Bradwell, of David Bradwell Associates, Berkeley, California, for suggesting several of these points. Personal correspondence, December 7, 1969.

11. Roland Artle, "Planning and Growth—A Simple Model of an Island Economy: Honolulu, Hawaii," *Papers and Proceedings of the Regional Science Association* 15 (1965): 29-44.

12. Again, I acknowledge my debt to Lowry. Interview Document, July 10, 1969, pp. 3-5.

13. Seyom Brown, Paul Y. Hammond, William Jones, and Robert L. Patrick, "An Informa-

tion System for the National Security Community" (Santa Monica: The RAND Corporation, RM-6054, August 1969), p. 3.

14. The literature is diffuse and rapidly growing, but the interested reader is directed to the following illustrative sources: Robert A. Clark, "LOGIC: The Santa Clara County Government Information System and its Relationship to the Planning Department," *Planning 1967* (May 12, 1967); A. M. Hair, Jr., "EDP Offers Key to Information in City Hall," *Public Management* (April 1965); L. S. Jay, "Data Collection Systems for Metropolitan Planning," *Papers and Proceedings of the Regional Science Association* 16 (1966): 77-92; Michael B. Teitz, "Land Use Data Collection Systems: Some Problems of Unification," *Papers and Proceedings of the Regional Science Association 16 (1966): 179-94;* and Peter R. Gould, "Structuring Information in Spacio-Temporal Preferences," *Journal of Regional Science* 7 (Winter 1967): 259-74. For a more complete listing of these matters, see Garry D. Brewer, "A Selected Reading and Reference List on Urban Information Systems" (Santa Monica: The RAND Corporation, December 17, 1969).

15. Otis Dudley Duncan, "Social Forecasting—The State of the Art," *The Public Interest* 17 (Fall 1969): 111.

16. Department of Housing and Urban Development, "HUD RFP H-2-70 of July 31, 1969," mimeographed.

17. Metropolitan Data Center Project (Tulsa), *Final Report* (Washington: HUD, 1966).

18. William Alonso, "The Quality of Data in the Choice and Design of Predictive Models," in *Urban Development Models* (Washington: Highway Research Board Report #97, 1968), pp. 178-92. "The point being made is that the choice of a model depends in part upon the quality of the data. The more complex the model, . . . the more measurement errors cumulate as the data churn through their arithmetic. The gains in correctness of specification in a more complex model may be offset by the compounding of measurement errors" (p. 183).

19. Arthur F. Young and Joseph M. Selove, "Housing Quality in the 1970 Census" (Paper read at 1968 Annual Meetings of the American Institute of Planners, October 14, 1968). With respect to the 1960 census it was concluded, "There does not appear to be any feasible method of improving the quality of ennumerator ratings in a decennial census" (p. 3).

20. See Robert A. Clark, "LOGIC."

21. Guy Orcutt, et al., *Microanalysis of Socioeconomic Systems* (New York: Harper, 1961), p. 8.

22. W. J. M. Mackenzie, *Politics and Social Science* (Baltimore: Penguin, 1967), pp. 70-71.

23. Foremost in the field is Vladimir V. Almendinger and his SPAN (Statistical Processing and Analysis) collection of software. Originally built in the early 1960s to manage the Penn-Jersey Transportation Study, SPAN has grown and improved, based on experiences with several practical applications, including the Bay Area Transportation Study Commission (BATSC) and New Haven's Special Census efforts in 1967. A third-generation version is available. See System Development Corporation, TM(L) 4269/000/00 of April 10, 1969; TM 1563/010/02 of December 1, 1965; TM 1563/014/03 of July 29, 1966; TM 1563/021/02 of December 1, 1965; SP-2652 of November 9, 1966; and, TM 4073/000/00 of August 27, 1968. All are publicly available from the System Development Corporation, Santa Monica, California.

24. Interview Document, November 26, 1969. I am indebted to Almendinger for his generous and insightful discussions, over the last two years, of these and related matters.

Appendix C: Multidimensional Scaling: Some Methodological Comments

1. See Herbert F. Weisberger and J. G. Rusk, "Dimensions of Candidate Evaluation," *American Political Science Review* 64 (December 1970): 1167-85, for a well-executed, recent application of the method.

2. The literature is fairly well surveyed by these works: James S. Coleman, "Multidimensional Scale Analysis," *American Journal of Sociology* 63 (November 1957): 253-63; Robert P. Abelson, "A Technique and a Model for Multidimensional Attitude Scaling," *Public Opinion Quarterly* 18 (1954): 405-18; Robert P. Abelson and John W. Tukey, "Efficient Conversion of Nonmetric Information into Metric Information," *Proceedings American Statistical Association*

APPENDICES AND NOTES

Meetings (Social Statistics Section), 1959: 226-30; C. H. Coombs, "Psychological Scaling without a Unit of Measurement," *Psychological Review* 57 (1950): 145-58: C. H. Coombs and R. C. Kao, "On a Connection between Factor Analysis and Multidimensional Unfolding," *Psychometrica* 25 (1960): 219-31; and W. S. Torgerson, "Multidimensional Scaling: I. Theory and Method," *Psychometrica* 17 (1952): 401-19.

Three particularly useful articles, however, are most noteworthy: Roger N. Shepard, "The Analysis of Proximities: Multidimensional Scaling with an Unknown Distance Function," Part I, *Psychometrica* 27 (June 1962): 125-40; Part II, *ibid.* (September 1962): 219-46; and J. B. Kruskal, "Multidimensional Scaling by Optimizing Goodness of Fit to a Nonmetric Hypothesis," *Psychometrica* 29 (March 1964): 1-27.

3. Kruskal, "Multidimensional Scaling," p. 1.

4. Roger N. Shepard, "Stimulus and Response Generalization: A Stochastic Model Relating Generalization to Distance in Psychological Space," *Psychometrica* 32 (1957): 333-34; Kruskal, "Multidimensional Scaling," p. 2; and Coombs and Kao, "Factor Analysis and Multidimensional Unfolding."

I am deeply indebted to Donald Berry of the Department of Statistics at the University of Minnesota for his instructive comments on MDSCL routines at the Yale Computer Center.

5. Kruskal, "Multidimensional Scaling," p. 3.

6. See above, chapter 6.

7. Kruskal, "Multidimensional Scaling," p. 16.

INDEX

Abelson, Robert P., 222
Academic context, problem-solving and, 84, 90-91, 208-212
Accessibility:
  in SF/CRP MOD II,* 157
  in TOMM, 198-200, 202
ADL (Arthur D. Little Corp.)
  City Planning Dept. and, 104-105, 116
  initial model design and, 117
  management problems of, 116
  motives of, 116
  prospectus from, 105-107, 118
  sales promotion of, 159-162
  staff of, 107-108
  See also San Francisco CRP
Aggregations:
  levels of, 30-32
  in MOD II, 122-125
  necessity for, 72, 267n
  in TOMM, 197-199
Alexander, Christopher, 68, 76
Allegheny Conference on Community Development, 170
Almond, Gabriel, 73
American Institute of Planners, 104
Analogies, problems of, 29-30
Ando, Albert, 73
Applications of models:
  data manipulation, 55
  educational, 57-58
  measurement, 55-56
  policy-making, 58-62
  selectivity of, 26
  theoretical, 56-57
Appraisal, 6
  ethical, 13-14, 48-53
    of INIMP, 187-188
    of IOIIM, 182
    of MOD II, 153-162
    of TOMM, 202
  importance of, 14
  incentives for, 241-242
  pragmatic, 14, 54-62
    of INIMP, 188-190
    of IOIIM, 182

  of MOD II, 162-168
  of TOMM, 202-205
  technical, 13, 34-47
    of INIMP, 187
    of IOIIM, 181-182
    of MOD II, 143-152
    of TOMM, 200-202
  theoretical, 12-13, 23-33
    of INIMP, 186
    of IOIIM, 181
    of MOD II, 134-143
    of TOMM, 197-200
Arthur D. Little Corp. (San Francisco, Calif.).
    See ADL
Artle, Roland, 236-237
Ashby, W. Ross, 77, 81
Assumptions
  ad hoc, 30
  formalization and, 41-42

Bacon, Edmund, 54
Bacon, Francis, 71, 72
Barr, Joseph, 100, 213
Bauer, Catherine, 60
Bay Area Rapid Transit (BART), 153
Belknap, George, 161
Bellman, Richard, 24, 67
Bentham, Jeremy, 51
Beshers, James, 5
Biases:
  academic, 210-212
  individual, 51-52
  observational, 26
  static, 181, 187, 202
  systemic, 144-145
  temporal, 76
  utopian, 187-188
  See also Selectivity
Blank, David M., 119, 141, 142
Boulding, Kenneth, 49-50
Boundaries
  INIMP and, 187-188
  MOD II and, 153
  TOMM and, 202
  in urban planning, 76

*Hereinafter, "MOD II."

285

INDEX

Brain, functions of, 71, 226n
Brookings Institution, 56
Bruchey, Stuart, 16, 73, 75
Bunge, Mario, 78
Burns, Arthur F., 142
Bush, Robert, 12, 30

California Municipal Statistics, Inc., 145-146
Campbell, Donald, 234
Candidates, Issues and Strategies
(Pool, et al.), 55
Census data:
accuracy of, 239
use of, 273n
in MOD II, 118, 122, 144, 240
in TOMM, 200, 240
Center for Regional Economic Studies.
See CRES
Chapin, F. Stuart, Jr., 199-200
Chartists, 20
Chinitz, Benjamin, 169, 172-173
Clark, Colin, 27, 261n
Clarkson, Geoffrey, 57
Cohen, Kalman, 3, 45, 56
Colautti, Aldo, 169
Coldwell-Banker (real estate brokers), 144
Comfort test, 45
Community Renewal Program. *See* CRP
Complexity, 4
communication and, 267n
disorganized, 72
organized, 68, 71-73
systemic, 67
Computer simulation models. *See* INIMP;
IOIIM; MOD II; Models; TOMM
Conflict, interparticipant, 20, 69, 86
in Pittsburgh CRP, 208-215
in San Francisco CRP, 146-148
See also Orientations
Connectedness, structural and model
size, 81-81
CONSAD Research Corp., 172
credentials of, 173
CRES and, 110, 210
motives of, 173-174
staff of, 112
See also Pittsburgh CRP
Consistency checking, 37-38
of variables, 55
Contagion phenomenon of housing, 139
Correlations, problems with, 29-30
Coulomb's law of magnetics, 140
Crecine, John P., 57, 169

CRES (Center for Regional Economic
Studies):
City Planning Dept. and, 110
CONSAD and, 110, 210
credentials of, 172, 173
evaluation of, 208-212
motives of, 172-173
staff of, 112
technical proposals of, 111
See also Pittsburgh CRP
Critical path analysis, 19
CRP (Community Renewal Program):
assessment of, 229-230
expectations for, 111-112
functions of, 101-102
history of, 101
political aspect of, 102-103
technical aspect of, 103-104
See also Pittsburgh CRP, San Francisco CRP
Cyert, Richard, 3, 45, 47

Dahl, Robert A., 13, 18, 236
Data:
deficiencies in, 228, 239
in INIMP, 187
in IOIIM, 181-182
in MOD II, 144-146
in TOMM, 202
level of detail of, 239-240
in measurement models, 56
sample surveys as, 239-240
standardization of, 239
See also Census data
Data manipulation model 14, 55
INIMP as, 189
IOIIM as, 182
MOD II as, 162-163, 166
Debugging of programs:
importance of, 43
in MOD II, 150
Decomposability of systems, 68, 73-75
Deutsch, Karl W., 199
Dimensionality checking, 36-37
Documentation:
importance of, 43, 87-88, 237-238
of MOD II, 149-150, 163, 166
of TOMM, 200
Douglas, Neil, 169
Dror, Yehezkel, 19, 223
Duke, Richard, 57, 203
Duncan, Otis Dudley, 239

Educational model, 14, 57-58

INIMP as, 188
MOD II as, 163
TOMM as, 203
Empiricism and formalization, 5
Entrepreneurs and problem-solving, 84-85,
    90, 224-225
Equilibrium, static:
MOD II and, 153
as temporal bias, 76
Ethical appraisal, 13-14, 48-53
of INIMP, 187-188
of IOIIM, 182
of MOD II, 153-162
of TOMM, 202
Explanatory mode of orientation:
characteristics of, 17-18, 21
Lowry model and, 195-196
measurement models and, 55
MOD II and, 146-147
theoretical models and, 56

Face validity of output, 29
Factor analysis, 45
Feldt, Alan, 57
Fisher, Franklin, 73
Fishman, George, 56
Flow charts, 35-36
of INIMP, 184
of Lowry model, 193
of MOD II, 126, 166
for overall Pittsburgh model, 175, 177
Ford Foundation, 110
Forecasting. See Predictive value
Formalization of theory, 25, 28-30, 34-41
assumptions in, 41-42
empiricism and, 5
information loss in, 5, 28
Forrester, Jay, 68, 73
FORTRAN (computer language), 38, 42, 200
Fract (analysis unit), 123-124, 139 , 165
Fudge factors, 30
in MOD II, 158-159
Fundamentalists, 20
Futurizing, 49-50

Garrison State hypothesis, 27
General Neighborhood Renewal Program
    (GNRP), 103
GPSS (computer language), 38, 42
Gravity models, 192, 196
Guttentag, Jack, 142

Haar, Charles, 161

Hamilton, Calvin, 169, 171, 210, 212-214
hiring of, 109, 170
objectives of, 174
speeches of, 207
Harman, Willis, 22
"Hendricks-Barringer Aspiration Index," 122-
    123, 136
Herbert-Stevens model, 119
HHFA. See Housing and Home Finance
    Agency
Hoffman, Stanley, 26
Hoover, Edgar, 171, 181, 278n
Housing, MOD II and, 121-127
evaluation of, 137-142
Housing Act of 1949, 101, 102, 104
Housing and Home Finance Agency (HHFA),
    101, 104, 109-110
Housing-market theory, 119
Hysteresis effect in MOD II, 130-132, 140

Industrial Spatial Allocation Model. See
    INIMP
Infinite regression, 73, 75
INIMP (Industrial Spatial Allocation Model),
    178, 179, 182, 215
ethical appraisal of, 187-188
flow chart of, 184
pragmatic appraisal of, 188-190
processes of, 183-186
technical appraisal of, 187
theoretical appraisal of, 186
Input/Output Inter-Industry Model. See
    IOIIM
Institute of Management Science, 241
Integrated Municipal Information Systems,
    239, 240
Intended vacancy concept, 141
IOIIM (Input/Output Inter-Industry Model),
    178, 179
ethical appraisal of, 182
pragmatic appraisal of, 182
processes of, 180-181
technical appraisal of, 181-182
theoretical appraisal of, 181

Jacobs, Jane, 28
Journal of the American Institute of Planners,
    179, 208

Kain, John, 186
Kalaba, Robert, 24, 67
Kaplan, Abraham, 29, 48
Kemeny, John, 4-5

INDEX

Kendall, M. G., 72
Keynes, John Maynard, 261n

Languages, computer, 38
Lasswell Value Dictionary, 217
Leontieff, Wassily, 20, 55
Leven, Charles, 169
Limitations, human, 67-68, 70-71, 76, 267n
Lindblom, Charles E., 13, 18, 236
Lowry, Ira S., 30, 169, 204
    metropolitan model of, 190-192, 199
        appraisal of, 195-196
        processes of, 192-195

McCarthy, James R., 115
McGee, Ed, 213
MAD (computer language), 38
Maisel, Sherman, 141
Managers and problem-solving, 85-86, 90-91,
    224-228
Manipulative mode of orientation:
    characteristics of, 18-19
    MOD II and, 146, 147
Markov processes:
    assumptions of, 138
    in MOD II, 126-127, 138-139
Massarik, Fred, 23-24
Master modelers, 89, 146, 147-148
Mathematics:
    formalization and, 36-38
    organized complexity and, 78
    social science and, 4-5, 24
Matrix notation, 74-75
Mauro, John, 169
Measurement error in models, 81-82
Measurement model, 14, 55-56
    INIMP as, 189
    MOD II as, 163
    TOMM as, 202
Meier, Richard, 199
Merton, Robert K., 59
METRO game-simulation, 57, 203
Meyer, John, 186
Meyerson, Martin, 104
Miller, George, 67-68, 70, 94
Millikan, Max, 12, 56
MOD I, 120
MOD II, 120-121
    characteristics of, 121-122
    documentation of, 149-150, 163, 166
    ethical appraisal of, 153-162
    housing aging procedures in, 125-127
        evaluation of, 137-140

    output from, 133, 154-156, 163
    policy-making and, 163-167
    population estimates in, 127, 157
        evaluation of, 134-135
    pragmatic appraisal of, 162-168
    preference lists in, 122-123, 128-129, 157
        evaluation of, 135-137
    processes of, 125-133
    promotion of, 159-162
    purposes of, 119-120
    rent pressure function in, 129-133
        evaluation of, 140-143
    technical appraisal of, 143-152
    theoretical appraisal of, 134-143
MOD III, 121, 151
    evaluation of, 152
Model of Metropolis (Lowry), 190-192, 199,
    204
Models:
    applications of, 55-62
    selectivity of, 26
    data manipulation applications of, 55
    educational applications of, 57-58
    error indications in, 46-47
    ethical appraisal of, 13-14, 48-53
    expectations for, 234
    as experiments, 234-235
    functional, 94, 235
    gravity, 192, 196
    hierarchical, 237
    measurement applications of, 55-56
    normative, 50, 236-237, 264n
    policy-making applications of, 58-62
    pragmatic appraisal of, 14, 54-62
    principle of, 3-4
    problems with, 5, 86-88
    promotion of, 86-87, 205, 207-208
    protocol, 94, 235, 282n
    size of, 77, 78-82, 93-94
    spatial, 94, 236
    standards for, 85, 241
    static, 26
    technical appraisal of, 13, 34-47
    testing of, 42-47
    theoretical applications of, 56-57
    theoretical appraisal of, 12-13, 23-33
    transfer of, 89-90
    See also INIMP; IOIIM; MOD II;
        TOMM
Monte Carlo techniques, 186, 189
Morse, Philip, 103-104
Mosteller, Frederick, 12, 30
Multidimensional scaling, 221, 253-256

Multiple working hypotheses, 4
Muth, Richard, 141

National Academy of Sciences, 11
National Resources Planning Board, 103
"Natural Law in the Social Sciences"
    (Kendall), 72
Neumann, John von, 71

Operations research and urban planning,
    103-104
Optner, Stanford, 105
Orcutt, Guy, 57
Order in urban planning, 76
Orientations, intellectual:
    differential, 77-78
        analysis of, 220-223
        data and, 238
        policy-making models and, 59
    explanatory mode of, 17-18
    interrelatedness of, 15
    manipulative mode of, 18-19
    reflective mode of, 16-17
    summary of, 21, 260n
    See also Conflict

Parameters:
    definition of, 24
    estimation of, 42, 44, 45
    free, 12, 30
    in MOD II, 135
    in measurement models, 56
    model size and, 79
    time and, 27
Pease, Robert, 207
Pennock, J. Roland, 49
Performance levels, determination of, 45
Pittsburgh Area Transportation Study, 199,
    200, 279n
Pittsburgh CRP:
    application for, 110-111
    assessment of, 218-220
    choice of, 99-100
    City Council and, 170, 171
    City Planning Dept. and, 110, 170, 214
    conclusions about, 215
    CRES and, 208-212
    data availability for, 170-171, 178
    decision to model in, 169-174
    expectations for, 179, 207-208, 218
    financing of, 108, 109-110
    model flow charts for, 175-177
    models for, 179-180

    See also INIMP; IOIIM; TOMM
    participants in, 112, 208-215, 217-218
        See also CONSAD; CRES
    politics and, 212-215
    promotion of, 205, 207-208
    purposes of, 110-111, 178-179
    scope of, 174, 176, 178
    Technical Advisory Council for, 112
Pittsburgh Regional Economic Study, 172,
    178, 180
Pittsburgh Regional Planning Association,
    110, 191
Platt, John Rader, 4
Policy-makers as theorists, 94, 235
Policy-making models, 235-237
    criteria for, 59-62
    INIMP as, 189-190, 191
    MOD II as, 163-167
    reasons for, 87
    TOMM as, 203-205, 206
    uses of, 58-59
    utility of, 14, 54
Population estimates, 137, 272n
    in IOIIM, 182
    in MOD II, 127, 157
        evaluation of, 134-135
Pragmatic appraisal, 14, 54-62
    of INIMP, 188-190
    of IOIIM, 182
    of MOD II, 162-168
    of TOMM, 202-205
Predictive value, 18
    of INIMP, 188, 190
    of MOD II, 164
    of theoretical models, 57
    of TOMM, 204
Preference scales:
    as ethical problem, 51-52
    in MOD II, 122-123, 128-129, 157
        evaluation of, 135-137
Principle of minimum devotion, 26
Principle of selectivity, 26, 28
"Problems of simplicity," 71-72
Problem-solving:
    academics and, 84, 90-91, 208-212
    CRP and, 102
    fragmentation in, 69, 83-86, 90-91, 94-95
    institutional complexity and, 83-86
    operational considerations of, 92, 94-95
    operations research and, 104
    participants in, 216-224, 227
    policy-makers and, 59, 77-78, 90-91
    procedures in, 224-228

INDEX

Problem-solving: (cont'd.)
    products and, 228-229
    salesmen and, 84-85, 90, 224-225
    scientists and, 59, 77-78
    theoretical considerations of, 92, 93-94
Programming:
    documentation of, 43, 87-88, 237-238
    formalization and, 38-41
    of MOD II, 148-149
    as theory translation, 25, 28-30, 38-42
    of TOMM, 200
Proposal writing, importance of, 88
Protocols and theory-building, 94, 235
Putman, Steve, 169, 190

Quantification as ethical problem, 51
Questions, analytical:
    formulation of, 59-60
    importance of, 89, 228
    INIMP and, 190
    MOD II and, 164-165
    TOMM and, 204-205

Rapkin, Chester, 141, 142
Rationality in urban planning, 76
Reality, dismemberment of, 26, 28
Referents, empirical, determination of, 30-31
Reflective mode of orientation, characteristics
    of, 16-17, 21
Regression analysis, 45
Reiner, Thomas, 76
Relevance, policy vs. discipline, 52, 56, 210-
    212
Rent pressure function in MOD II, 129-133
    evaluation of, 140-143
Research context, 90-91
Rostand, Jean, 70-71
Royal Statistical Society, 72

Salesmen and problem-solving, 84-85, 90,
    224-225
Sample surveys, 239-240
Samuelson, Paul, 26, 27
San Francisco CRP:
    ADL and, 105, 107-108
    assessment of, 218-220
    choice of, 99-100
    City Planning Dept. and, 104-105, 115-
        116, 165
    conclusions about, 168
    data availability for, 118
    decision to model in, 105, 115-118
    expectations for, 107, 218

    financing of, 104-105, 115
    master modeler of, 146, 147-148
    models for, 120-121
        See also MOD II
    participants in, 107-108, 146-148, 217-218
        See also ADL
    promotion of, 159-162
    prospectus for, 105-107
    purposes of, 106
    report on, 167-168
    scope of, 118-119
    Technical Advisory Committee for, 107,
        108
Scientists and problem-solving, 12, 59, 77-78
Scott-Morton, Michael, 169
Sectors, disaggregated, 79-80
Selectivity:
    of application, 26
    spatial, 27-28
    system description and, 25-28
    temporal, 26-27
    See also Biases
Sensitivity analysis of models, 45-47
SF/CRP. See San Francisco CRP
Shepard, Roger, 253
Shubik, Martin, 20
SIC (Standard Industrial Classification), 183-
    185
Simon, Herbert, 5, 24, 67, 68, 73, 171
Simplification:
    advantages of, 237
    as ethical problem, 51
    operational necessity for, 68-69, 83-91
    theoretical necessity for, 67-68, 70-82
    verification and, 78
SIMSCRIPT (computer language), 38
Simulation models. See INIMP; IOIIM;
        MOD II; Models; TOMM
Slayton, William, 102-103, 109
Slumlords, MOD II and, 145, 158
Smith, Wallace F., 141-142
Snell, Laurie, 4-5
Snoyer, R. S., 172, 173
Social change, goals of, 50, 264n
Social ethics, 48-49
Social problems and technology, 6
Social science and mathematics, 4-5, 24
Space, selectivity of, 27-28
Specification error, 81
Standard Industrial Classification (SIC),
    183-185
State vector, definition of, 24
Steger, Wilbur, 169, 172-173, 178, 210, 211

Stegman, Michael A., 202
Stochastic processes, 42, 81
Stone, Don, 171
"Stress" statistic, 221, 253
Symmetry in urban planning, 76
Systems:
  behavior of, 24-25
  complexity of, 67
  decomposability of, 68, 73-75
  definition of, 24
  description of, 25-28
  dynamic, 73-74
  size of, 77, 78-82
  structure of, 24
  time frame of, 50

Technical appraisal, 13, 34-47
  of INIMP, 187
  of IOIIM, 181-182
  of MOD II, 143-152
  of TOMM, 200-202
Theil, Henri, 45
Theil inequality coefficient, 45
Theoretical appraisal, 12-13, 23-33
  of INIMP, 186
  of IOIIM, 181
  of MOD II, 134-143
  of TOMM, 197-200
Theoretical model, 14, 56-57
  INIMP as, 188
  MOD II as, 163
  TOMM as, 203
Theory, formalization of, 25, 28-30, 34-42
Theory-building:
  goal of, 25
  models and, 56-57
  protocols and, 94, 235
  science and, 12, 17
Thresholds and model size, 81
Time:
  assumptions about, 42
  model size and, 79
  as variable, 26-27
TOMM (Time-Oriented Metropolitan Model),
  178, 179, 190-192

documentation of, 200
ethical appraisal of, 202
output of, 200-202
pragmatic appraisal of, 202-205
processes of, 196-197
technical appraisal of, 200-202
theoretical appraisal of, 197-200
Totem, 25, 261n
  MOD II as, 164
Transportation studies, 55, 103, 199, 200,
  279n
Tukey, John, 222
Turing test, 47

Uncertainty and model size, 81
"Unique historical events," 16
University of Chicago, 103
University of Pittsburgh, 110
Urban Institute, 241
Urban planning:
  assumptions of, 76-77
  complexity of, 212-215
  coordination of, 102-103
  information requirements for, 102
  manipulative bias of, 146
  operations research and, 103-104
Utopias, 76-77

Values:
  adequacy of, 52-53, 264n
  contextual nature of, 49
Variables:
  consistency checking of, 55
  definition of, 24
  in measurement models, 56
  model size and, 79
  testing of, 43

Weaver, Robert, 102
Weaver, Warren, 68, 71, 72
Winnick, Louis, 119, 141, 142
Winter, Gibson, 13, 49, 50-51
WPA survey data, 273n
  in MOD II, 127, 137